# Mastering Spring AI

## The Java Developer's Guide for Large Language Models and Generative AI

**Banu Parasuraman**

Apress®

*Mastering Spring AI: The Java Developer's Guide for Large Language Models and Generative AI*

Banu Parasuraman
Frisco, TX, USA

ISBN-13 (pbk): 979-8-8688-1000-8               ISBN-13 (electronic): 979-8-8688-1001-5
https://doi.org/10.1007/979-8-8688-1001-5

Managing Director, Apress Media LLC: Welmoed Spahr
Acquisitions Editor: Melissa Duffy
Development Editor: Laura Berendson
Coordinating Editor: Gryffin Winkler

Cover designed by eStudioCalamar

Cover image by chandlervid85 on Freepik (freepik.com)

Distributed to the book trade worldwide by Apress Media, LLC, 1 New York Plaza, New York, NY 10004, U.S.A. Phone 1-800-SPRINGER, fax (201) 348-4505, e-mail orders-ny@springer-sbm.com, or visit www.springeronline.com. Apress Media, LLC is a California LLC and the sole member (owner) is Springer Science + Business Media Finance Inc (SSBM Finance Inc). SSBM Finance Inc is a **Delaware** corporation.

For information on translations, please e-mail booktranslations@springernature.com; for reprint, paperback, or audio rights, please e-mail bookpermissions@springernature.com.

Apress titles may be purchased in bulk for academic, corporate, or promotional use. eBook versions and licenses are also available for most titles. For more information, reference our Print and eBook Bulk Sales web page at http://www.apress.com/bulk-sales.

Any source code or other supplementary material referenced by the author in this book is available to readers on GitHub (https://github.com/Apress). For more detailed information, please visit https://www.apress.com/gp/services/source-code.

If disposing of this product, please recycle the paper

*To my beloved wife, Vijaya Anirudhran, whose unwavering support and love have been my anchor through every journey. And to my wonderful children, Pooja Anirudhran and Deepika Anirudhran, who inspire me every day with their curiosity, resilience, and boundless potential. This book is a testament to the love and strength of our family.*

# Table of Contents

# About the Author

 **Banu Parasuraman** is a seasoned technologist with over 30 years of experience in the IT industry, currently focusing on the transformative fields of AI and automation. Throughout his distinguished career, Banu has provided invaluable advisory services to clients across a multitude of industries, guiding them in leveraging AI-driven solutions and automation technologies to enhance their operations and achieve digital transformation. His expertise has been sought by over 25 leading companies spanning sectors like retail, healthcare, logistics, banking, manufacturing, automotive, oil and gas, pharmaceuticals, media, and entertainment across the United States, Europe, and Asia.

A passionate advocate for AI and automation, Banu has been at the forefront of encouraging organizations to adopt these technologies early, helping them to streamline operations, improve decision-making, and maintain a competitive edge. His deep knowledge extends across all major AI and automation platforms, including advanced cloud services and tools that integrate seamlessly into enterprise environments.

Banu is a respected speaker, having participated in numerous external engagements such as VMworld, SpringOne, Spring Days, and Spring Developer Forum Meetups, where he shared his insights with CXOs and engineers alike. His internal engagements include leading workshops on AI-driven solutions and automation strategies, where he has been instrumental in enabling sales plays and strategies focused on these cutting-edge technologies.

Beyond speaking engagements, Banu is an active thought leader in the industry, contributing to the wider adoption of AI and automation through his blogs on Medium and LinkedIn, where he shares his knowledge and promotes best practices in AI and automation development. He is also the author of the book *Practical Spring Cloud Function: Developing Cloud-Native Functions for Multi-Cloud and Hybrid-Cloud Environments*, available on Amazon. Banu's work continues to shape the future of technology, inspiring organizations to innovate and embrace the power of AI and automation.

# About the Technical Reviewers

 **Andres Sacco** has been a professional developer since 2007, working with various languages, including Java, Scala, PHP, Node.js, and Kotlin. His background is mainly in Java and its associated libraries or frameworks, like Spring, JSF, iBATIS, Hibernate, and Spring Data. He is focused on researching new technologies to improve the performance, stability, and quality of the applications he develops.

In 2017, he started to find new ways to optimize data transference between applications to reduce the cost of infrastructure. He suggested some actions, some applicable to all the microservices and others to just a few of them; as a result, the cost was reduced by 55%. Some of these actions are connected directly with the bad use of the databases.

He recently published some books with Apress about the last version of Scala and Spring Data. He also published a set of theoretical-practical projects on uncommon testing methods, such as architecture tests and chaos engineering.

**Debasish Banerjee**, Ph.D., is a seasoned thought leader, hands-on architect, and practitioner of cutting-edge technologies. He has a proven track record spanning more than a decade of advising and closely working with Fortune 500 and other customers in the United States, Europe, and Asia. He recently joined Guild Systems Inc (`www.guildsystems.com`) as the ITOps and FinOps lead. Until September 2024, he was a principal Customer Success Manager at IBM. Debasish's work successfully established several advanced IBM technologies in the field and has generated several hundred million USD in revenue for IBM.

Debasish's present areas of interest are superior observability to reduce the mean time to recovery, automatic application resource management, FinOps, and the use of AI to enhance these technologies. Debasish obtained his Ph.D. in combinator-based functional programming languages. He is the father of two brilliant software engineer daughters, Cheenar and Neehar, who are his pride and joy.

# Acknowledgments

I would like to express my deepest gratitude to the individuals who played a crucial role in bringing this book to life.

First and foremost, I extend my sincere thanks to **Melissa Duffy**, Editor at Apress, for reaching out to me and giving me the opportunity to write this book. Her belief in my vision and guidance throughout this journey were invaluable.

A special thanks to **Shonmirin P. A.**, Production Editor, whose meticulous attention to detail ensured that every aspect of this book was polished and perfected. Your dedication and hard work made this process smooth and successful.

I am also deeply grateful to **Andres Sacco** and **Debasish Banerjee** from IBM, who served as the technical reviewers for this book. Their expert insights and thorough reviews were instrumental in ensuring the technical accuracy and quality of the content. Their feedback was critical in refining the ideas presented in this book.

Finally, I would like to acknowledge the entire **Apress staff** who contributed to the creation of this book. Your professionalism, support, and collaborative efforts were essential in bringing this project to fruition. Thank you for your hard work and commitment to excellence.

This book is a result of the collective efforts of all these remarkable individuals, and I am truly thankful for their contributions.

# CHAPTER 1

# Introduction to Generative AI and Large Language Models (LLMs)

In the constantly evolving realm of artificial intelligence (AI) and machine learning (ML), few advancements have been as revolutionary in recent years as the ascent of Generative AI and Large Language Models (LLMs). These cutting-edge models have redefined our comprehension of AI systems, unleashing a wave of unprecedented opportunities and applications spanning diverse fields. In this chapter, we will embark on an enlightening exploration of the underpinnings, evolution, and profound impact of Generative AI and Large Language Models. Moreover, we will examine how Spring AI seamlessly integrates into this dynamic landscape, shaping the future of AI-driven solutions.

© Banu Parasuraman 2024
B. Parasuraman, *Mastering Spring AI*, https://doi.org/10.1007/979-8-8688-1001-5_1

# 1.1 Understanding the Basics of Artificial Intelligence

**Definition and Historical Perspective of AI**

Artificial intelligence, often abbreviated as AI, is a multidisciplinary field of computer science that aims to create systems and machines capable of performing tasks that typically require human intelligence. These tasks encompass a wide range of activities, from problem-solving and decision-making to natural language understanding and perception.

The concept of AI has been a part of human imagination for centuries, with early myths and stories featuring mechanical beings capable of human-like thought. However, it wasn't until the mid-20th century that AI as we know it today began to take shape.

The term "artificial intelligence" was coined by John McCarthy in 1956 during the Dartmouth Workshop, which marked the birth of AI as a formal academic discipline. Over the decades, AI has undergone several waves of enthusiasm and disappointment, known as AI winters, where the expectations often exceeded the capabilities of the technology at the time.

Today, AI has become an integral part of our lives, powering intelligent virtual assistants, recommendation systems, autonomous vehicles, and much more. Its historical journey from myth to reality highlights the persistence and determination of researchers and engineers to create machines that can mimic human intelligence. See Figure 1-1.

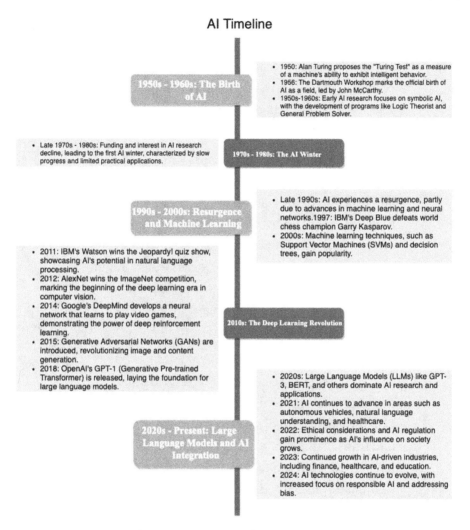

***Figure 1-1.***  *AI timeline*

**Key Concepts in AI: Algorithms, Neural Networks, and Data Processing**

To understand AI fully, it's essential to grasp some key concepts that underpin the field. These concepts include algorithms, neural networks, and data processing.

**Algorithms**: Algorithms are step-by-step sets of instructions designed to solve specific problems or perform particular tasks. In AI, algorithms are crucial for decision-making and problem-solving. They are the building blocks of AI systems, guiding how data is processed, analyzed, and acted upon.

**Neural Networks**: Neural networks are computational models inspired by the structure and function of the human brain. They consist of interconnected nodes, or "neurons," organized in layers. Neural networks are capable of learning patterns from data through a process called training, making them central to many AI applications, including image recognition, natural language processing, and speech recognition.

**Data Processing**: Data is the lifeblood of AI. Machine learning algorithms[1] rely on large datasets to learn and make predictions or decisions. Data processing involves collecting, cleaning, and transforming data into a format suitable for AI models. The quality and quantity of data significantly impact AI performance.

---

[1] Algorithms are automated instructions that can vary in complexity based on their depth. Machine learning and artificial intelligence are both based on sets of algorithms, with the key difference being how they handle structured vs. unstructured data

**The Role of AI in Modern Technology and Society**

AI's role in modern technology and society is profound and far-reaching. It has permeated various aspects of our lives, from the devices we use to the services we access. Here are some key areas where AI plays a pivotal role:

1. **Healthcare**: AI is revolutionizing healthcare by enabling faster and more accurate diagnosis, drug discovery, and personalized treatment plans. Machine learning models can analyze medical images, detect anomalies, and predict patient outcomes.

2. **Finance**: In the financial industry, AI is used for fraud detection, algorithmic trading, and risk assessment. AI-driven chatbots and virtual assistants also enhance customer service and support.

3. **Education:** AI-powered educational tools offer personalized learning experiences, adapt to individual student needs, and provide valuable insights to educators. This promotes more effective learning outcomes.

4. **Natural Language Processing**: AI models excel in understanding and generating human language. This capability drives advancements in virtual assistants like Siri and Alexa, as well as language translation services.

5. **Autonomous Vehicles**: Self-driving cars rely on AI algorithms to navigate and make split-second decisions based on sensor data. This technology has the potential to reshape transportation systems.

6.  **Entertainment**: AI is used in content recommendation systems, video game design, and even the creation of art and music.

As AI continues to advance, it poses both exciting opportunities and ethical challenges. It is essential to strike a balance between innovation and responsible use to harness the full potential of AI for the benefit of society.

# 1.2 The Journey from Traditional Machine Learning to Generative AI

**Fundamentals of Machine Learning: Supervised, Unsupervised, and Reinforcement Learning**

Machine learning (ML) serves as the foundation upon which Generative AI and Large Language Models are built. ML is a subset of AI that focuses on developing algorithms capable of learning from data and making predictions or decisions without explicit programming.

There are several categories of machine learning, with three primary paradigms being supervised learning, unsupervised learning, and reinforcement learning:

**Supervised Learning**: In supervised learning, algorithms are trained on labeled datasets, where the correct answers are provided. The goal is to learn a mapping from inputs to outputs, allowing the model to accurately predict unseen data. This paradigm is used for tasks like classification and regression.

**Unsupervised Learning**: Unsupervised learning deals with unlabeled data and aims to discover patterns, structures, or groupings within the data. Common techniques include clustering and dimensionality reduction. Unsupervised learning can uncover hidden insights and relationships in data.

**Reinforcement Learning**: Reinforcement learning is centered around agents that interact with an environment and learn to make decisions by receiving feedback in the form of rewards or penalties. It is commonly used in robotics, game playing, and autonomous systems.

These fundamental ML paradigms laid the groundwork for the transition to more complex and capable AI systems.

**Transition to Deep Learning: Importance and Impact**

Deep learning, a subfield of machine learning, emerged as a game-changer in the world of AI. At its core, deep learning leverages neural networks with multiple layers, often referred to as deep neural networks. This architecture enables models to automatically learn hierarchical features from data, making them capable of handling tasks that were previously challenging for traditional ML algorithms.

The importance of deep learning lies in its ability to extract high-level representations from raw data. This feature is particularly valuable for tasks such as image recognition, speech recognition, and natural language processing. Convolutional neural networks (CNNs) and recurrent neural networks (RNNs) are examples of deep learning architectures that have revolutionized computer vision and sequential data processing.

The impact of deep learning can be observed in applications like autonomous vehicles, where CNNs analyze images from cameras mounted on vehicles to make real-time driving decisions. Additionally, deep learning has fueled breakthroughs in speech recognition technology, enabling virtual assistants to understand and respond to spoken commands accurately.

**Emergence of Generative AI: Characteristics and Capabilities**

Generative AI represents a significant leap in AI capabilities. Unlike traditional AI systems that focus on specific tasks, Generative AI aims to create new content, whether it's text, images, or other forms of data. These systems have the remarkable ability to generate human-like content, making them a cornerstone of natural language generation and creative applications.

The emergence of Generative AI is marked by the development of Large Language Models (LLMs), which have set new standards for AI performance. LLMs are neural network–based models with a vast number of parameters, enabling them to understand and generate human language at a level

# 1.3  Exploring Large Language Models: A Paradigm Shift in AI

**What Are Large Language Models (LLMs)?**

Large Language Models (LLMs) are a type of deep learning model that has gained immense popularity and attention in recent years. These models are characterized by their enormous size, often comprising hundreds of millions or even billions of parameters. LLMs are specifically designed for natural language understanding and generation tasks.

The key defining feature of LLMs is their ability to process and generate human language and interpret and generate images. They can understand the context of text, answer questions, translate languages, summarize documents, and even create creative written content. Some of the models like Dall-E can generate images. This paradigm shift in AI has led to advancements in fields such as chatbots, language translation, content generation, and more.

**Understanding the Mechanism: How LLMs Process and Generate Language**

The mechanism behind Large Language Models is rooted in deep learning and neural networks. These models utilize a variant of neural networks known as Transformer architectures. The Transformer architecture introduced the concept of self-attention mechanisms, allowing the model to weigh the importance of different words in a sentence when making predictions. This was articulated in the paper "Attention Is All You Need" `https://arxiv.org/abs/1706.03762`.

The training process of LLMs involves exposing the model to vast amounts of text data. Through this exposure, the model learns the statistical patterns, grammar, semantics, and context of human language. This knowledge is encoded in the model's parameters, which are fine-tuned during training.

When generating language, LLMs take an input sequence of text and use their learned knowledge to predict the next word or sequence of words. This process is repeated iteratively, resulting in coherent and contextually relevant text generation. LLMs can be used for various tasks, from completing sentences to generating entire articles.

**Comparing LLMs with Traditional Machine Learning Models**

To appreciate the significance of LLMs, it's essential to compare them with traditional machine learning models, especially in the context of natural language processing (NLP) tasks.

> **Traditional NLP Models**: Traditional NLP models often rely on handcrafted features and linguistic rules. They require substantial manual effort for feature engineering, making them less adaptable to different languages and domains. These models may struggle with understanding context and generating coherent text.

**Large Language Models (LLMs)**: LLMs, on the other hand, excel at capturing complex language patterns without the need for extensive feature engineering. They are pretrained on massive text corpora, enabling them to generalize across languages and domains. LLMs are highly versatile and can be fine-tuned for specific tasks with relatively little data.

The comparison between LLMs and traditional NLP models underscores the transformative impact of LLMs on AI and language-related applications. Their ability to process and generate language with human-like fluency has opened new horizons for AI-powered communication and content creation. Figure 1-2 shows the comparison between traditional machine learning and LLMs.

| Feature | Traditional Machine Learning | Large Language Models (LLMs) |
|---|---|---|
| Data Requirements | Generally, requires less data. Models are often trained on specific datasets tailored to a particular task. | Requires massive amounts of data, often sourced from diverse and extensive text corpora to learn language patterns. |
| Training Complexity | Relatively simpler models that can be trained on modest hardware depending on the complexity and size of the dataset. | Requires significant computational resources (often GPUs or TPUs) due to the complexity and size (billions of parameters). |
| Task Specialization | Models are usually task-specific and need to be retrained or finely tuned for each new task. | Designed to handle multiple tasks with a single model, often without task-specific tuning (zero-shot or few-shot learning). |
| Interpretability | Often more interpretable, especially with models like decision trees and linear regression. | Less interpretable due to their complexity and the 'black box' nature of deep neural networks. |
| Generalization | Depends on the model and the feature engineering; some models generalize better than others. | Excellent at generalizing from the training data to a wide range of natural language tasks due to extensive pre-training. |
| Performance on New Tasks | Requires retraining or adaptation to handle new tasks effectively. | Can perform new language tasks they were not explicitly trained on, demonstrating adaptability and flexibility. |
| Deployment | Often lighter and easier to deploy on limited resources depending on the model. | Due to their size, deployment can be resource-intensive and may require specialized infrastructure like cloud services. |
| Development and Maintenance Cost | Lower development costs and maintenance can be manageable depending on the application and model complexity. | High development cost due to data acquisition, computational resources, and ongoing training requirements. |
| Model Updates | Models may need periodic retraining and updates based on new data or changes in the data distribution. | Continuous updates may be necessary to incorporate new information, refine responses, and improve model performance. |

*Figure 1-2.  Traditional machine learning vs. LLMs*

Large Language Models (LLMs) are highly adaptable and can be extended with ease to perform a variety of tasks. Their ability to process and generate human-like text allows them to be fine-tuned or adapted for specific domains, making them versatile for numerous applications.

Extending LLMs typically involves adjusting them to handle new types of data, integrating them with other systems, or enhancing their capabilities through additional training or customization. This flexibility makes LLMs a powerful tool in AI-driven solutions.

# 1.4 Overview of Prominent LLMs: GPT, BERT, and Beyond

Large Language Models (LLMs) have revolutionized the field of artificial intelligence, especially in natural language processing (NLP) and generation tasks. These models are characterized by their vast size, measured in billions of parameters, and their ability to understand, generate, and interpret human language with remarkable accuracy. Let's take a look into some of the most prominent LLMs, highlighting their development, capabilities, and impact. See Figure 1-3.

1. **GPT Series (OpenAI) (`https://platform.openai.com/docs/models`)**

   - **Overview**: The Generative Pretrained Transformer (GPT) series by OpenAI is among the most well-known LLMs. Starting with GPT-1, the series has evolved significantly over time, with GPT-3, and its successors setting new standards for language model capabilities.

   - **Capabilities**: GPT models are pretrained on a diverse range of Internet text. They excel in tasks such as text generation, conversation, translation, and answering questions without specific fine-tuning for each task.

- **Impact**: GPT-3 and its successors have been widely adopted across industries for applications like content creation, coding assistance, and customer support, showcasing the versatile potential of LLMs in real-world applications.

- Notes[2] on GPT-4:

- **Release Date**: GPT-4's release in 2023 marked another significant leap in the capabilities of language models, showcasing OpenAI's continued innovation in AI.

- While the exact number of parameters for GPT-4 has not been disclosed, it is known to be substantially larger than GPT-3, indicating a further increase in complexity and understanding capabilities.

- **Capabilities and Applications**: GPT-4 advances the state of the art with more sophisticated text generation, improved context understanding, and enhanced performance across a broad range of language tasks. It has been applied to even more complex and nuanced applications than its predecessors, demonstrating the ongoing evolution of AI's potential to mimic and augment human intelligence in writing, conversation, and analysis tasks.

---

[2] At the time of this publication

2. **BERT (Google) (`https://huggingface.co/docs/transformers/en/model_doc/bert`)**

   - **Overview**: Bidirectional Encoder Representations from Transformers (BERT) is a breakthrough model introduced by Google. Unlike GPT, BERT focuses on understanding the context of words in sentences from both directions (left and right of a word), which is a departure from previous models that processed text in one direction.

   - **Capabilities**: BERT's bidirectional training improves its performance on a variety of language understanding tasks, including question answering, language inference, and named entity recognition.

   - **Impact**: BERT has been integrated into Google Search, enhancing the search engine's understanding of the nuances and context of user queries.

3. **T5 (Google) (`https://huggingface.co/docs/transformers/en/model_doc/t5`)**

   - **Overview**: Text-to-Text Transfer Transformer (T5) converts all NLP problems into a unified text-to-text format, where both input and output are always text strings. This approach simplifies the NLP pipeline and allows for a more generalized application of the model.

   - **Capabilities**: T5 has shown strong performance across a range of tasks, including translation, summarization, question answering, and classification tasks.

- **Impact**: T5's versatility and effectiveness have made it a popular choice for researchers and practitioners looking for a flexible and powerful model for various NLP tasks.

4. **ERNIE (Baidu) (`https://huggingface.co/docs/transformers/en/model_doc/ernie`)**

    - **Overview**: Enhanced Representation through Knowledge Integration (ERNIE) is a language model developed by Baidu. ERNIE is designed to better understand the semantics of language by integrating world knowledge and linguistic context into its pretraining.

    - **Capabilities**: ERNIE performs well on tasks requiring semantic understanding, such as sentiment analysis, named entity recognition, and question answering.

    - **Impact**: ERNIE's ability to incorporate external knowledge and context has helped improve the performance of language models on tasks requiring a deeper understanding of language and world knowledge.

5. **XLNet (Google/CMU) (`https://huggingface.co/docs/transformers/en/model_doc/xlnet`)**

    - **Overview**: XLNet is an advanced model that outperforms BERT on several benchmarks by using a permutation-based training strategy. This approach allows XLNet to learn the bidirectional context of a word more effectively.

- **Capabilities**: XLNet excels in tasks requiring understanding of complex sentence structures and has set new records in performance for tasks like text classification, question answering, and textual entailment.

- **Impact**: XLNet's innovative training strategy and its resulting performance gains have contributed to the ongoing research and development in the field, pushing the boundaries of what's possible with LLMs.

6. **LLaMA (Meta) (`https://llama.meta.com/docs/get-started/`)**

- **Overview**: LLaMA, developed by Meta, is one of the latest advancements in the field of Large Language Models. It stands out for its efficiency and adaptability, designed to perform a wide range of language understanding and generation tasks with fewer parameters compared to its predecessors, making it more accessible for research and practical applications.

- **Capabilities**: LLaMA excels in various NLP tasks such as text generation, translation, and complex reasoning. Its smaller model variants allow for use in environments with limited computational resources while maintaining high performance.

- **Impact**: The versatility and efficiency of LLaMA make it suitable for both academic researchers and industry practitioners. It opens up new possibilities for deploying advanced NLP models in more diverse settings, including on devices with lower processing power.

7. **Mistral AI (https://docs.mistral.ai/getting-started/models/)**

   - **Overview**: Mistral AI represents a step forward in democratizing access to powerful language models. It aims to provide scalable solutions that are adaptable to a wide array of tasks, maintaining high performance without the extensive resource requirements typically associated with such models.

   - **Capabilities**: Mistral AI models are known for their general-purpose language understanding and generation, capable of performing tasks ranging from summarization and translation to more complex reasoning and content creation.

   - **Impact**: The adaptability and scalability of Mistral AI's models facilitate their integration into various applications, making advanced NLP capabilities accessible to a broader range of users and developers across industries.

8. **IBM Granite (https://www.ibm.com/products/watsonx-ai/foundation-models?utm_content =SRCWW&p1=Search&p4=43700078747002614&p5 =e&p9=58700008385933274&gbraid=0AAAAAD-_ QsSKeLfOGDy8HjRfPsKdeUR-n&gclid=CjO KCQjwz7C2BhDkARIsAA_SZKY4xgajHusdNGngUbre8 IaTrSCJYp67GIjgcZBwrr8dxRH4XuoAdSYaAv6 eEALw_wcB&gclsrc=aw.ds)**

- **Overview**: IBM's Granite series of models are part of their broader initiative to integrate AI more deeply into enterprise solutions. These models are designed to be robust and scalable, addressing specific needs in large-scale business applications.

- **Capabilities**: Granite models are particularly noted for their ability to handle enterprise-level tasks such as language translation, content generation, and complex data analysis, all within a framework that emphasizes security and compliance with industry standards.

- **Impact**: IBM Granite significantly enhances the ability of enterprises to leverage AI for improving decision-making processes, enhancing customer interactions, and automating complex tasks, thereby driving efficiency and innovation in business operations.

| Model | Developer | Release Date | Parameters | Main Capabilities | Typical Applications |
|---|---|---|---|---|---|
| Granite Foundation Models (e.g., granite.13b) | IBM | 2023 | 13 billion | Generative AI tasks, multi-query attention, instruction following, chat enhancements, large context handling, fine-tuning | Enterprise tasks, content generation, chatbots, prompt engineering |
| GPT-4 | OpenAI | 2023 | ~ 1.7 trillion | Advanced text generation, deeper understanding of context and nuances, improved accuracy in language translation and question answering | Advanced content creation, more nuanced AI chatbots, professional-grade language translation, coding and debugging assistance |
| LLaMA | Meta | 2023 | Varied, including models from 7 billion to 65 billion parameters | Efficient text generation and understanding, with strong performance across a wide range of tasks including NLP and code generation | Research, content generation, complex NLP tasks, and code-related applications |
| Mistral | Mistral AI | 2023 | Models scaling up to 10s of billions of parameters | General-purpose language understanding and generation, adaptable to various tasks including summarization and translation | General NLP tasks, custom AI tool creation, educational content, and creative writing |
| Titan | Amazon | 2023 | ~45 Billion | Generative AI tasks, multi-query attention, instruction following, chat enhancements, large context handling, fine-tuning | Enterprise tasks, content generation, chatbots, prompt engineering |
| Claude | Anthropic | 2023 | 137 Billion | Ethical oriented Generative AI tasks, multi-query attention, instruction following, chat enhancements, large context handling, fine-tuning | Enterprise tasks, content generation, chatbots, prompt engineering |
| Gemini | Google | 2023 | 1.8 to 3.5 Billion | Multimodel LLM | Mix of text, picture, video, and audio |
| GPT-3 | OpenAI | 2020 | 175 billion | Text generation, conversation, language translation, question answering | Content creation, AI chatbots, language translation, coding assistance |
| T5 | Google | 2019 | Up to 11 billion | Text-to-text tasks: translation, summarization, question answering, classification | Text summarization, language translation, information extraction |
| ERNIE | Baidu | 2019 | Varied across versions, up to billions | Semantic understanding, sentiment analysis, question answering | Enhanced search, sentiment analysis, question answering |
| XLNet | Google/CMU | 2019 | 340 million | Text classification, question answering, textual entailment | Document summarization, question answering, classification tasks |
| BERT | Google | 2018 | 110 million (Base), 340 million (Large) | Text understanding, question answering, language inference | Search engines, sentiment analysis, named entity recognition |

*Figure 1-3. Prominent LLMs as of 2024[3]*

---

[3] At the time of this publication

Figure 1-4 shows the releases of LLMs in a chronological order.

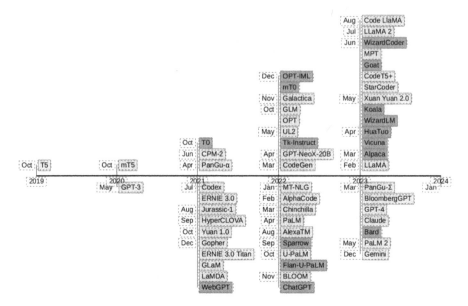

***Figure 1-4.*** *Chronological display of LLM releases: light blue rectangles represent "pretrained" models, while dark rectangles correspond to "instruction-tuned" models. Models on the upper half signify open source availability, whereas those on the bottom half are closed source. The chart illustrates the increasing trend toward instruction-tuned models and open source models, highlighting the evolving landscape and trends in natural language processing research. (Source:* https://arxiv.org/pdf/2307.06435.pdf*)*

# 1.5  Real-World Applications and Impact of LLMs

Large Language Models (LLMs) like GPT-4 have revolutionized various sectors by providing advanced natural language understanding and generation capabilities. Their applications span across industries, offering significant benefits and transforming how businesses, educational institutions, and healthcare providers operate. Here are several real-world applications and impacts of LLMs, along with specific use cases:

1. **Content Creation and Journalism**

   **Use Case**: Automated article and content generation for blogs, news summaries, and reports. LLMs can produce draft articles, which editors can then refine to ensure accuracy and alignment with editorial standards.

   **Impact**: Increases content production speed, helps meet the growing demand for fresh content, and supports journalists by providing initial drafts or research summaries.

2. **Customer Support and Virtual Assistance**

   **Use Case**: Powering chatbots and virtual assistants to offer instant customer support across various platforms. LLMs can understand and respond to customer inquiries, provide recommendations, and automate routine tasks.

   **Impact**: Enhances customer experience through 24/7 support, reduces wait times, and decreases the workload on human support teams.

3. **Education and Learning**

   **Use Case**: Personalized learning experiences and tutoring. LLMs can generate custom educational content, assist with homework, and explain complex concepts in a simplified manner.

**Impact**: Supports personalized education at scale, addresses diverse learning needs, and offers students additional resources outside the classroom.

4. **Programming and Code Generation**

**Use Case**: Automating coding tasks and generating code listings through platforms like GitHub Copilot. Developers can describe the functionality they need, and the LLM generates code listings in various programming languages.

**Impact**: Increases developer productivity, accelerates the software development process, and helps beginners learn coding more efficiently.

5. **Language Translation and Localization**

**Use Case**: High-quality, context-aware translation of texts between natural languages, aiding communication and content localization for global audiences.

**Impact**: Breaks down language barriers, enables businesses to reach a wider audience, and facilitates cross-cultural communication.

6. **Legal and Compliance Documentation**

**Use Case**: Generating and reviewing legal documents, contracts, and compliance reports. LLMs can draft initial versions of legal texts, which legal professionals can then review and finalize.

**Impact**: Streamlines the legal documentation process, reduces the time and cost associated with legal drafting, and helps nonexperts understand complex legal language.

7. **Healthcare Information Management**

   **Use Case**: Summarizing medical records and literature to support healthcare professionals in decision-making. LLMs can analyze vast amounts of medical texts to provide concise summaries or answer specific questions.

   **Impact**: Assists in clinical decision-making, supports research by summarizing the latest studies, and enhances patient care by providing quick access to relevant information.

8. **Creative Writing and Entertainment**

   **Use Case**: Generating creative content such as stories, scripts, and game dialogues. LLMs can produce original creative texts, offering inspiration and a starting point for human creators.

   **Impact**: Fosters creativity, supports the entertainment industry by generating new content ideas, and offers novel ways to engage audiences.

9. **Ecommerce and Marketing**

   **Use Case**: Producing product descriptions, generating marketing copy, and personalizing customer interactions on ecommerce platforms.

   **Impact**: Enhances online shopping experiences, improves engagement through personalized content, and streamlines the creation of marketing materials.

10. **Accessibility and Assistive Technologies**

   **Use Case**: Developing tools to assist individuals with disabilities, such as generating real-time captions for the hearing impaired or reading text aloud for the visually impaired.

   **Impact**: Improves accessibility to information and services, supports independence for individuals with disabilities, and promotes inclusivity.

LLMs are reshaping industries by providing scalable solutions to complex problems, enhancing productivity, and creating new opportunities for innovation. Their ability to understand and generate human-like text has opened up new avenues for application, making technology more accessible and efficient across various domains.

# 1.6 Ethical Considerations and Challenges in the Use of LLMs

The use of Large Language Models (LLMs) such as GPT-4 brings numerous benefits across various fields, yet it also raises significant ethical considerations and challenges. As these models become more integrated into societal functions, it's crucial to address these ethical aspects to ensure their responsible and equitable use. Here are key ethical considerations and challenges associated with LLMs:

1. **Bias and Fairness**

   **Issue**: LLMs can inherit and amplify biases present in their training data, leading to outputs that may be discriminatory or biased against certain groups.

**Challenge**: Ensuring fairness and mitigating bias in LLM outputs require continuous efforts in model training, data selection, and output monitoring.

2. **Privacy and Data Security**

**Issue**: LLMs trained on vast datasets may inadvertently memorize and reproduce sensitive information, posing risks to individual privacy and data security.

**Challenge**: Implementing robust data handling practices and developing techniques to prevent the leakage of personal information are crucial for maintaining privacy.

3. **Misinformation and Manipulation**

**Issue**: The ability of LLMs to generate convincing text can be exploited to produce misinformation, fake news, or manipulate public opinion.

**Challenge**: Developing and enforcing ethical guidelines for content generation, along with mechanisms to identify and label AI-generated content, are essential to combat misinformation.

4. **Intellectual Property Concerns**

**Issue**: LLMs can generate content that may infringe on existing copyrights or intellectual property rights, raising questions about originality and ownership.

**Challenge**: Establishing clear legal frameworks and ethical guidelines to address copyright and intellectual property issues in AI-generated content is necessary.

5.  **Transparency and Accountability**

    **Issue**: The complex nature of LLMs can make it difficult to understand how decisions are made, leading to challenges in transparency and accountability.

    **Challenge**: Developing explainability standards and methods for LLMs to ensure that their operations can be understood and scrutinized by humans is critical.

6.  **Employment and Economic Impact**

    **Issue**: Automation through LLMs could disrupt job markets, especially in fields reliant on language-based tasks, potentially leading to job displacement.

    **Challenge**: Creating policies that support workforce transition, retraining, and education to prepare for changes in job requirements due to AI advancements is vital.

7.  **Dependence and De-skilling**

    **Issue**: Overreliance on LLMs for tasks such as writing, decision-making, or learning can lead to skill degradation in critical thinking and creativity among users.

    **Challenge**: Encouraging balanced use of LLMs, emphasizing human oversight, and fostering skills development alongside AI tools are important.

8.  **Accessibility and Inclusivity**

    **Issue**: There's a risk that the benefits of LLMs may not be equally accessible to all, exacerbating digital divides and inequality.

**Challenge**: Ensuring equitable access to AI technologies and their benefits requires targeted efforts to include underrepresented communities in their development and deployment.

9. **Environmental Impact**

   **Issue**: The significant computational resources required to train and run LLMs have environmental impacts, contributing to carbon emissions.

   **Challenge**: Improving the energy efficiency of AI research and deployment and using sustainable energy sources for computational tasks are steps toward reducing the environmental footprint of LLMs.

To better understand the ethical considerations and challenges in the use of Large Language Models (LLMs) across various industries, including healthcare, retail, law, automotive, and oil and gas, let's explore the specific issues and challenges faced by each sector:

### Healthcare

**Bias and Fairness**: Biases in training data can lead to unequal healthcare outcomes for different demographic groups.

**Privacy and Data Security**: Handling sensitive health records requires robust privacy protections to comply with regulations like the Health Insurance Portability and Accountability Act (HIPAA).

**Misinformation and Manipulation**: Accuracy in medical information is crucial; misinformation can have serious health consequences.

**Retail**

> **Bias and Fairness**: Recommendation algorithms might promote products in a discriminatory manner, affecting sales diversity and fairness.

> **Privacy and Data Security**: Customer data, including shopping habits and personal preferences, must be protected to prevent misuse.

> **Transparency and Accountability**: Retailers must be transparent about how AI is used in marketing and customer interactions to maintain trust.

**Law**

> **Intellectual Property Concerns**: LLMs in law might generate documents that infringe on copyrighted legal arguments or presentations.

> **Transparency and Accountability**: In legal applications, the reasoning provided by LLMs must be interpretable by lawyers to ensure it aligns with legal standards.

> **Misinformation and Manipulation**: Accuracy is critical in legal advice; errors can lead to judicial missteps or unfair rulings.

**Automotive**

> **Employment and Economic Impact**: Automation of tasks like customer support and manual documentation could displace jobs in the automotive sector.

**Dependence and De-skilling**: Overreliance on automated systems can reduce skills in engineering and design areas, leading to a loss of craftsmanship.

**Environmental Impact**: The automotive industry must consider the carbon footprint of training LLMs used in designing more efficient vehicles.

## Oil and Gas

**Environmental Impact**: The energy-intensive nature of LLMs contrasts with the industry's need to reduce its carbon footprint.

**Transparency and Accountability**: Decision-making processes informed by LLMs must be clear, especially when they impact environmental policies.

**Bias and Fairness**: There's a need to ensure that AI-driven decisions in resource allocation do not favor certain regions or groups unfairly.

## Cross-Industry Challenges

**Intellectual Property Concerns**: Across all industries, LLMs can generate outputs that potentially violate intellectual property laws, necessitating clear guidelines.

**Accessibility and Inclusivity**: Ensuring that the benefits of LLMs are accessible across different regions and socioeconomic groups is critical to avoid widening the digital divide.

**Privacy and Data Security**: Each industry must develop stringent data governance frameworks to prevent data breaches and ensure user trust.

Addressing these ethical considerations requires a tailored approach for each industry, ensuring that the deployment of LLMs enhances value without compromising ethical standards or societal norms. This involves cooperation among technologists, ethicists, industry specialists, and policymakers to develop and enforce industry-specific guidelines and standards.

# 1.7 Future Trends and Potential Developments in LLM Technology

The landscape of Large Language Models (LLMs) is rapidly evolving, driven by advances in artificial intelligence, machine learning algorithms, and computational hardware. As we look to the future, several trends and potential developments are likely to shape the trajectory of LLM technology. These advancements promise to expand the capabilities, efficiency, and applications of LLMs while also addressing some of the current limitations and ethical concerns. Here are key future trends and potential developments in LLM technology:

1. **Increased Model Efficiency and Environmental Sustainability**

   Future LLMs are expected to become more energy-efficient, reducing the environmental impact associated with their training and operation. Techniques like pruning, quantization, and more efficient algorithms will help in creating models that require less computational power.

2. **Improved Understanding and Generation of Multimodal Content**

   Advances in multimodal LLMs, which can understand and generate not just text but also images, audio, and video. This will enable more sophisticated applications that can seamlessly integrate various forms of media, enhancing user experiences and enabling new forms of content creation.

3. **Greater Focus on Bias Mitigation and Ethical AI**

   As awareness of the ethical implications of LLMs grows, we can expect a stronger focus on developing methods to detect, mitigate, and prevent biases in these models. This includes more diverse and inclusive data collection, ethical AI training practices, and the incorporation of fairness metrics in model evaluation.

4. **Enhanced Personalization and Contextual Understanding**

   LLMs will likely achieve better personalization and contextual understanding, tailoring responses and content generation to individual users' preferences, history, and situational context. This will be crucial for applications in education, customer service, and personalized content recommendations.

5. **Advancements in AI Safety and Robustness**

   Ensuring the safety and robustness of LLMs in diverse and sometimes adversarial environments will be a key area of development. Techniques to improve model interpretability, prevent malicious use, and ensure that LLMs adhere to ethical guidelines will become increasingly sophisticated.

6. **Expansion of Low-Resource Language Support**

   Efforts to expand the capabilities of LLMs in understanding and generating text in low-resource languages will continue. This includes not only major global languages but also indigenous and minority languages, helping to preserve cultural heritage and improve global accessibility.

7. **Integration of LLMs with IoT and Edge Computing**

   The integration of LLMs with Internet of Things (IoT) devices and edge computing infrastructure will enable smarter, context-aware applications. This could revolutionize fields such as smart homes, healthcare monitoring, and autonomous vehicles by providing real-time, natural language processing capabilities at the edge.

8. **Advances in Domain-Specific LLMs**

   We will see more specialized LLMs tailored for specific professional domains, such as law, medicine, and engineering. These models will offer more accurate and relevant assistance, leveraging domain-specific knowledge to improve decision-making and productivity.

9. **Interactive and Conversational AI Improvements**

   Future LLMs are expected to engage in more natural, dynamic, and contextually rich conversations with users. This involves better memory, understanding of nuance, and the ability to manage complex interactions over extended periods.

10. **Regulatory and Ethical Framework Development**

The evolution of LLM technology will likely be accompanied by the development of more comprehensive regulatory and ethical frameworks. These frameworks will aim to ensure responsible use, protect user rights, and address societal concerns related to privacy, security, and the impact on employment.

As LLM technology continues to advance, it will be important to balance innovation with ethical considerations, ensuring that the benefits of LLMs are accessible to all segments of society while minimizing potential harms. Collaboration across industries, academia, and regulatory bodies will be key to shaping a future where LLMs contribute positively to societal progress.

11. **Small Language Models**

Small Language Models (SLMs) represent a promising future direction in AI, focusing on creating efficient models with fewer parameters. Unlike Large Language Models (LLMs), which have billions of parameters and require significant computational resources, SLMs are designed to be much smaller in size, often with millions or even fewer parameters. This reduction in size makes them more accessible for deployment in resource-limited environments, such as edge devices and

mobile platforms, while still delivering effective
performance for specific tasks. As AI continues
to evolve, SLMs offer a scalable and sustainable
alternative, balancing capability with efficiency.

# 1.8  How Can Spring AI Contribute

The Spring AI project represents a significant and innovative step toward
making artificial intelligence (AI) functionalities more accessible and
easier to integrate into a broad range of applications, beyond the Python
ecosystem. Here's how Spring AI can contribute to the development and
ethical use of Large Language Models (LLMs) and AI in general:

### Streamlining AI Application Development

Spring AI aims to simplify the incorporation of
AI functionalities into applications by providing
abstractions that facilitate the development process.
This approach allows developers across various
programming languages to leverage AI technologies
without needing to dive deep into the complexities
often associated with AI implementations.

### Promoting Cross-Language AI Development

By drawing inspiration from Python projects while
not being a direct port, Spring AI underscores the
importance of making Generative AI applications
accessible to developers who work in languages
other than Python. This inclusivity promotes a more
diverse development ecosystem, where AI benefits
can be realized across different platforms and
applications.

### Enhancing Flexibility Through Abstractions

The introduction of core abstractions, such as the ChatClient interface with implementations for OpenAI and Azure OpenAI, enables developers to easily swap components with minimal code changes. This flexibility is crucial for adapting to evolving AI technologies and integrating various AI services into applications efficiently.

### Addressing Common Use Cases

Spring AI focuses on providing higher-level functionalities to address common use cases like "Q&A over your documentation" or "Chat with your documentation." These functionalities can greatly enhance user experiences by making interactions with applications more intuitive and informative.

### Integration with the Spring Ecosystem

The integration with other projects in the Spring ecosystem, such as Spring Integration, Spring Batch, and Spring Data, allows for handling more complex use cases. This integration ensures that applications can leverage the robust, scalable infrastructure provided by the Spring ecosystem while incorporating AI capabilities.

### Simplifying Setup and Exploration

The availability of Spring Boot starters and a collection of sample applications facilitates easy setup and exploration of AI features. This lowers the barrier to entry for developers new to AI, encouraging experimentation and innovation.

Overall, Spring AI's contributions to the AI field are poised to democratize access to AI technologies, making it easier for developers across different programming environments to build sophisticated, AI-powered applications. By focusing on simplicity, flexibility, and integration, Spring AI not only promotes the development of Generative AI applications across various languages but also ensures that ethical considerations and best practices can be more readily implemented within the AI development process.

# 1.9  Conclusion

In this chapter, we have embarked on a journey to understand the foundations, evolution, and significance of Generative AI and Large Language Models. We've explored the basics of artificial intelligence, the transition from traditional machine learning to Generative AI, the mechanisms behind Large Language Models, and the impact of prominent models like GPT-4 and BERT. We've also examined real-world applications, ethical considerations, and future trends in LLM technology. We also touched on how Spring AI can contribute to the Generative AI revolution.

In the next chapter, we will deep dive into Spring ecosystem of tools and see how they can contribute to AI.

# CHAPTER 2

# Exploring Spring.io, Spring Components for GenAI: The Developer's Backbone

We've conquered the fundamentals of LLMs and Generative AI in Chapter 1. However, for Java developers, venturing into Generative AI often meant navigating workarounds and unfamiliar territory. In this chapter, we'll delve into the world of Spring.io through the lens of Generative AI, exploring the core Spring components that act as the developer's backbone in this new domain.

Get ready to discover how Spring.io's principles, like dependency injection and the Spring Boot framework, become powerful tools for building robust Generative AI applications. We'll explore how these components provide a solid foundation for managing dependencies, streamlining development, and ensuring the maintainability of your code. Buckle up, as we unlock the potential of Spring.io for Generative AI and empower you to build the future of creative applications!

© Banu Parasuraman 2024
B. Parasuraman, *Mastering Spring AI*, https://doi.org/10.1007/979-8-8688-1001-5_2

# 2.1 Introduction to Spring.io

Spring.io's contribution to Generative AI can be understood by exploring
how its framework and ecosystem support the development, deployment,
and scaling of Generative AI applications. Generative AI involves creating
models that can generate new data that is similar to the training data,
such as text, images, or videos. Here's how Spring.io can facilitate the
development and operation of such systems:

> **Facilitating Model Serving**: Spring Boot can be
> used to quickly create standalone, production-grade
> applications that serve AI models. This is crucial
> for Generative AI applications that need to provide
> real-time or near-real-time responses. For instance,
> a Spring Boot application could serve as a text-
> generation model, handling requests and responses
> efficiently. This is addressed this in detail in my
> previous book available in Amazon: `https://www.`
> `amazon.com/Practical-Spring-Cloud-Function-`
> `Cloud-Native/dp/1484289129`.
>
> **Scalability**: Generative AI models, especially those
> like GPT (Generative Pretrained Transformer)
> or image generation models, require substantial
> computational resources. Spring Cloud can help
> manage these applications across multiple servers
> or services, enabling them to scale out according
> to demand. This scalability is vital for handling the
> variable loads that Generative AI applications might
> experience.

**Integration with Data Stores**: Generative AI models often require large datasets for training and may generate significant amounts of data. Spring Data provides a consistent, easy-to-use API for accessing a wide range of data stores, from relational databases to NoSQL options. This makes it easier to manage the data needed for training and generated by AI models.

**Microservices for Modular AI Systems**: Spring's support for microservice architectures allows developers to build Generative AI systems as a suite of small, independently deployable services. This modular approach can be particularly beneficial for complex AI systems, enabling independent scaling and updating of different components, such as data processing, model training, and model serving.

**Reactive Programming Support**: Generative AI applications often require handling a large number of concurrent requests and streaming data. Spring WebFlux offers a reactive programming model that can help build nonblocking, asynchronous applications, improving performance and resource utilization in such scenarios.

**Security:** With Spring Security, Generative AI applications can be secured to protect sensitive data and ensure that only authorized users can access certain AI capabilities. This is especially important for applications that generate or handle sensitive or proprietary information.

**Robust Deployment Options**: Spring Boot
applications can be containerized and deployed on
various platforms, including cloud environments
that provide the computational power needed for
Generative AI. This flexibility allows organizations
to choose the most cost-effective and efficient
environment for their AI applications.

**Community and Resources**: The Spring
community is large and active, offering extensive
documentation, tutorials, and support. This can be
invaluable for developers working on Generative
AI projects, as they can find resources and help for
integrating AI models with Spring applications.

In summary, Spring.io can significantly contribute to Generative AI
by offering a robust, scalable, and flexible development ecosystem. Its
support for microservices, data management, reactive programming, and
security provides a solid foundation for building, deploying, and scaling
Generative AI applications.

# 2.2  Data Management for AI with Spring Data

Data management is a critical aspect of developing and operating
Generative AI applications, as these systems often rely on large datasets
for training and generate new data that must be processed and stored
efficiently. Spring Data provides a comprehensive, integrated approach
to data access and management, simplifying the interaction with a
wide variety of data sources. Here's how Spring Data can support data
management for Generative AI applications:

1. **Unified Data Access API**

   Spring Data offers a unified API for accessing various
   data stores, including SQL databases, NoSQL
   databases, map-reduce frameworks, and cloud data
   services. This abstraction layer allows developers to
   work with different data sources using a consistent
   programming model, which is particularly useful for
   Generative AI applications that may need to aggregate
   data from diverse sources for training and operation.

2. **Repository Abstraction**

   The repository abstraction simplifies CRUD
   (Create, Read, Update, Delete) operations, making
   it easier to manage the datasets used for training
   Generative AI models and handling the data they
   generate. By defining repository interfaces, Spring
   Data automatically provides implementations at
   runtime, reducing boilerplate code and speeding up
   development.

3. **Custom Query Methods**

   Spring Data repositories support custom query
   methods, enabling developers to define complex
   queries using method names or annotations. This
   feature is essential for Generative AI applications that
   need to perform sophisticated queries to select training
   data, filter generated content, or manage metadata.

4. **Data Store–Specific Extensions**

   Spring Data offers extensions for various data stores,
   such as Spring Data JPA for relational databases,
   Spring Data MongoDB for document databases,

and Spring Data Redis for key/value stores.
These extensions provide additional features and
optimizations tailored to each data store, allowing
Generative AI applications to leverage the unique
capabilities and performance characteristics of their
underlying databases.

5. **Transaction Management**

   Spring Data supports declarative transaction
   management, simplifying the process of managing
   transactions across multiple data sources. This is
   crucial for ensuring data integrity and consistency,
   especially in complex Generative AI applications
   that may involve multiple steps of data manipulation
   and storage.

6. **Stream Processing**

   For Generative AI applications that process
   streaming data, Spring Data provides integrations
   with stream processing libraries and platforms.
   This allows for real-time data processing and
   analysis, which can be used to dynamically adjust
   model parameters, filter incoming data streams for
   training, or process data generated by the AI models.

7. **Data Migration and Versioning**

   Spring Data can facilitate data migration and
   schema versioning, which are important for
   Generative AI applications as models evolve and
   require changes to the data structure. Tools like
   Flyway or Liquibase can be integrated with Spring
   Data to manage database migrations seamlessly.

8. **Scalability and Performance**

Finally, Spring Data's support for advanced data
access features, such as caching, batch processing,
and asynchronous queries, can help optimize
the performance and scalability of Generative AI
applications. Efficient data access and management
are critical for training and running Generative AI
models, especially when dealing with large datasets
and high request volumes.

In summary, Spring Data provides a powerful and flexible framework
for managing the data needs of Generative AI applications, from
simplifying data access and CRUD operations to supporting advanced
querying, transaction management, and performance optimization. Its
comprehensive support for a wide range of data stores and its integration
with the broader Spring ecosystem make it an excellent choice for
developers building data-intensive AI applications.

# 2.2.1 Let's Code

Let's create a simple example implementation demonstrating how Spring
Data can be used in a Generative AI application. In this scenario, imagine
we're building a system that generates and stores custom news articles
based on user inputs. We'll use Spring Boot for the application framework,
Spring Data JPA for database interactions, and an H2 in-memory database
for simplicity. We will be leveraging GPT 3.5 as our LLM for much of
the code.

**Prerequisites**

- **OpenAI API Key**: This can be obtained at
  `https://platform.openai.com/docs/quickstart`.

- **An IDEA for Spring**

**Step 1: Project Setup**

First, ensure your **pom.xml** (for Maven) includes the necessary
dependencies for Spring Boot, Spring Data JPA, and H2 (see Listing 2-1).

*Listing 2-1.* pom.xml

```
<dependencies>
    <dependency>
        <groupId>org.springframework.boot</groupId>
        <artifactId>spring-boot-starter-data-jpa</artifactId>
    </dependency>
    <dependency>
        <groupId>org.springframework.boot</groupId>
        <artifactId>spring-boot-starter-web</artifactId>
    </dependency>
    <dependency>
        <groupId>com.h2database</groupId>
        <artifactId>h2</artifactId>
        <scope>runtime</scope>
    </dependency>
</dependencies>
```

**Step 2: Define Configuration Properties**

Add configuration properties for the ChatGPT API endpoint and
any necessary authentication details in **application.properties** or
**application.yml** as shown in Listing 2-2.

*Listing 2-2.* application.properties file

```
# application.properties
chatgpt.api.url=https://api.example.com/generate
chatgpt.api.key=your_api_key_here
```

**Step 3: Define the Entity**

Create an **Article** entity (see Listing 2-3) that represents the news articles
generated by your AI model.

***Listing 2-3.*** Article.java

```java
import javax.persistence.Entity;
import javax.persistence.GeneratedValue;
import javax.persistence.GenerationType;
import javax.persistence.Id;

@Entity
public class Article {

    @Id
    @GeneratedValue(strategy = GenerationType.AUTO)
    private Long id;

    private String title;
    private String content;

    // Constructors, getters and setters
    public Article() {}

    public Article(String title, String content) {
        this.title = title;
        this.content = content;
    }

    // standard getters and setters
}
```

## Step 4: Repository Interface

Define a repository interface (see Listing 2-4) for accessing the **Article**
entities. Spring Data JPA will provide the implementation automatically:

```
import org.springframework.data.jpa.repository.JpaRepository;
```

***Listing 2-4.*** ArticleRepository.java

```
public interface ArticleRepository extends
JpaRepository<Article, Long> {
    // Custom query methods can be defined here if needed
}
```

## Step 5: Create a RestTemplate Bean

In your main application class or a configuration class, define a
**RestTemplate** (see Listing 2-5) bean for making HTTP requests.

***Listing 2-5.*** RestTemplate in AppConfig.java

```
import org.springframework.context.annotation.Bean;
import org.springframework.context.annotation.Configuration;
import org.springframework.web.client.RestTemplate;

@Configuration
public class AppConfig {

    @Bean
    public RestTemplate restTemplate() {
        return new RestTemplate();
    }
}
```

## Step 6: Implement the ChatGPT Service

Create a service class (see Listing 2-6) to handle communication with
the ChatGPT API. This service will use RestTemplate to send requests to
the API.

***Listing 2-6.*** ChatGptSerice.java

```java
import org.springframework.beans.factory.annotation.Autowired;
import org.springframework.beans.factory.annotation.Value;
import org.springframework.http.HttpEntity;
import org.springframework.http.HttpHeaders;
import org.springframework.http.HttpMethod;
import org.springframework.http.ResponseEntity;
import org.springframework.stereotype.Service;
import org.springframework.web.client.RestTemplate;

@Service
public class ChatGptService {

    @Autowired
    private RestTemplate restTemplate;

    @Value("${chatgpt.api.url}")
    private String apiUrl;

    @Value("${chatgpt.api.key}")
    private String apiKey;

    public String generateText(String prompt) {
        HttpHeaders headers = new HttpHeaders();
        headers.set("Authorization", "Bearer " + apiKey);
        HttpEntity<String> entity = new HttpEntity<>(prompt,
        headers);

        ResponseEntity<String> response = restTemplate.
        exchange(apiUrl, HttpMethod.POST, entity, String.class);

        return response.getBody();
    }
}
```

**Step 7: Service Layer**

Implement a service layer (see Listing 2-7) to handle the business logic,
including interacting with the AI model and the database.

***Listing 2-7.*** ArticleService.java

```java
import org.springframework.beans.factory.annotation.Autowired;
import org.springframework.stereotype.Service;

import java.util.List;

@Service
public class ArticleService {

    @Autowired
    private ArticleRepository articleRepository;

    @Autowired
    private ChatGptService chatGptService;

    public Article generateAndSaveArticle(String seedText) {
        String generatedContent = chatGptService.
        generateText(seedText);
        String generatedTitle = "Generated Title: " + seedText.
        substring(0, Math.min(10, seedText.length())) + "...";

        Article article = new Article(generatedTitle,
        generatedContent);
        return articleRepository.save(article);
    }

    public List<Article> getAllArticles() {
        return articleRepository.findAll();
    }
}
```

**Step 8: REST Controller**

Finally, create a REST controller (see Listing 2-8) to expose endpoints for
generating and retrieving articles.

***Listing 2-8.*** ArticleController.java

```java
import org.springframework.beans.factory.annotation.Autowired;
import org.springframework.web.bind.annotation.GetMapping;
import org.springframework.web.bind.annotation.PostMapping;
import org.springframework.web.bind.annotation.RequestParam;
import org.springframework.web.bind.annotation.RestController;

import java.util.List;

@RestController
public class ArticleController {

    @Autowired
    private ArticleService articleService;

    @PostMapping("/articles")
    public Article generateArticle(@RequestParam String
    seedText) {
        return articleService.generateAndSaveArticle(seedText);
    }

    @GetMapping("/articles")
    public List<Article> getAllArticles() {
        return articleService.getAllArticles();
    }
}
```

**Step 9: Execute and Test the Service**

1.  Do some posts to inject data into the database (see
    Figure 2-1).

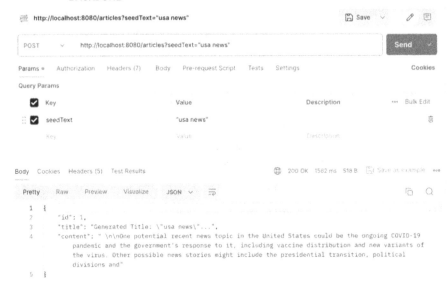

*Figure 2-1.* *POST call with seedText in Postman*

2.    Check the database for the entry (see Figure 2-2).

H2 Console can be accessed at localhost:8080/h2.

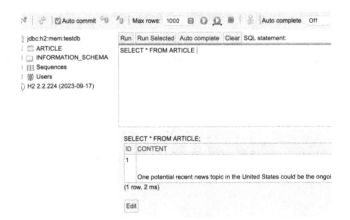

*Figure 2-2.* *H2 Console showing content in the database*

3.  View the generated content with a Get operation in
    Postman (see Figure 2-3).

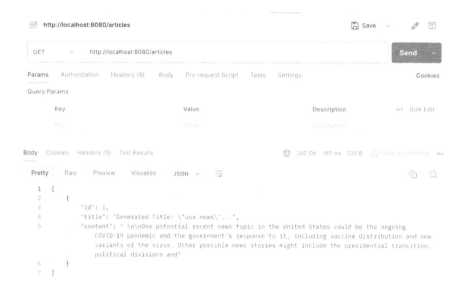

***Figure 2-3.***  *Get operation in Postman showing the content from the*
*database*

With the spring code that we created, we saw that we can query
ChatGPT, get the response back, store it in a database with a Post
operation, and later with a Get operation view the generated content that
was stored in the database.

# 2.3  Reactive Programming with Spring WebFlux for AI Streams

Reactive programming with Spring WebFlux can be particularly effective
when dealing with AI streams for Generative AI applications. This
approach enables the handling of large amounts of data with nonblocking

backpressure, which is crucial for efficiently managing the data flows that
Generative AI models often require. Here's an overview of how you can use
Spring WebFlux for AI streams in a Generative AI context:

1. **Understanding Reactive Programming**

   Reactive programming is a programming paradigm
   oriented around data flows and the propagation of
   change. It allows for the creation of nonblocking,
   asynchronous applications that can handle a large
   number of concurrent data streams efficiently.

2. **Spring WebFlux**

   Spring WebFlux is a reactive web framework part
   of the Spring Framework 5, designed to build
   reactive applications. It enables the development
   of nonblocking, asynchronous applications
   using a reactive programming model. Spring
   WebFlux supports backpressure, which is a way
   to control how much data is processed to prevent
   overwhelming the consumer.

3. **Handling AI Streams**

   In the context of Generative AI, streams can refer
   to the input data fed into the model for generation
   tasks or the output stream of generated data.
   Handling these streams efficiently is crucial due to
   the potentially large volume of data and the need for
   real-time processing.

4. **Implementation Steps**

   **Define a Reactive Stream**: You can define a reactive
   stream for your AI data using Flux or Mono types
   from Project Reactor (the reactive library used by

Spring WebFlux). For instance, a Flux<Data> could
represent a stream of input data for your AI model.

**Nonblocking Data Operations**: Ensure that all
operations on the data stream are nonblocking. This
includes data fetching, transformation, and sending
it to the Generative AI model.

**Backpressure Management**: Utilize Spring
WebFlux's backpressure management to control
the flow of data and prevent the consumer (e.g., a
Generative AI model) from being overwhelmed by
too much data at once.

**Integration with AI Models**: Integrate your reactive
stream with the Generative AI model. This could
involve sending data to the model for generation
tasks and handling the model's output reactively.

**Asynchronous and Event-Driven**: Make your
application asynchronous and event-driven to
efficiently handle the operations without blocking
the main thread. This is particularly important for
real-time AI applications where latency is critical.

**Error Handling**: Implement error handling in your
reactive streams to deal with any issues that may
arise during the data processing or interaction with
the Generative AI model.

**Security**: Ensure that your application is secure,
especially if you are handling sensitive data.
Spring Security offers reactive support that can be
integrated with Spring WebFlux.

# 2.3.1 Let's Code

Let's look at an example implementation.

To create a reactive, nonblocking AI service leveraging Spring WebFlux and the ChatGPT API, you would typically follow these steps:

> **Set Up Spring Boot with WebFlux**: Start by setting up a Spring Boot project with WebFlux dependency for reactive programming support.
>
> **Integrate ChatGPT API**: You'll need to integrate the OpenAI ChatGPT API. This involves making HTTP requests to the OpenAI API endpoints and handling the responses.
>
> **Implement Real-Time Data Processing**: Utilize Spring WebFlux's support for reactive streams to process data in real time. This can be used to stream data to and from the ChatGPT API.
>
> **Secure and Configure the Application**: Ensure your application is secure and properly configured, especially in handling API keys for OpenAI.

**Prerequisites**

- **OpenAI API Key**: This can be obtained at `https://platform.openai.com/docs/quickstart`.

- **An IDEA for Spring**

**Step 1: Add WebFlux Dependency**

In your build.gradle or pom.xml, add the Spring Boot starter WebFlux dependency (see Listing 2-9).

*Listing 2-9.* pom.xml

```
<dependency>
    <groupId>org.springframework.boot</groupId>
    <artifactId>spring-boot-starter-webflux</artifactId>
</dependency>
```

**Step 2: Create a Service for ChatGPT API That Uses Data Streams**

Create a service that makes nonblocking calls to the ChatGPT API.
Listing 2-10 shows an example using Spring's WebClient.

*Listing 2-10.* ChatGptService.java

```
import org.springframework.beans.factory.annotation.Value;
import org.springframework.stereotype.Service;
import org.springframework.web.reactive.function.client.
WebClient;
import reactor.core.publisher.Flux;
import reactor.core.publisher.Mono;

import java.util.Map;

@Service
public class ChatGptService {

    private final WebClient webClient;

    public ChatGptService(WebClient.Builder webClientBuilder,
                          @Value("${chatgpt.api.url}") String
                          chatGptApiUrl,
                          @Value("${chatgpt.api.key}") String
                          apiKey) {
        this.webClient = webClientBuilder.baseUrl(chatGptApiUrl)
                .defaultHeader("Authorization", "Bearer "
                + apiKey)
```

```java
                .build();
    }

    // Enrich a single data item
    public Flux<String> enrichData(Flux<String> dataStream) {
        return dataStream.flatMap(this::enrichSingleItem);
    }

    public Mono<String> enrichSingleItem(String data) {
        String prompt = "Provide a summary and sentiment
        analysis for the following text: \"" + data + "\"";

        return this.webClient.post()
                .bodyValue(Map.of("model", "gpt-3.5-turbo-
                instruct", "prompt", prompt, "temperature",
                0.5, "max_tokens", 100))
                .retrieve()
                .bodyToMono(String.class)
                .map(response -> "Original: " + data + " |
                Enrichment: " + response);
    }
}
```

**Step 3: Adapt the Controller for Streaming Data**

Next, adjust the controller to accept a stream of data for enrichment. In a real-world scenario, this stream might come from a message broker (like Kafka or RabbitMQ), a database change stream, or a batch file process. For simplicity, this example will simulate a stream of data items received as a list, but in practice, you'd adapt this to your specific source (see Listing 2-11).

*Listing 2-11.* ChatGptController.java

```java
import org.springframework.web.bind.annotation.*;
import reactor.core.publisher.Flux;
import reactor.core.publisher.Mono;

@RestController
public class ChatGptController {

    private final ChatGptService chatGptService;

    public ChatGptController(ChatGptService chatGptService) {
        this.chatGptService = chatGptService;
    }

    @PostMapping("/enrich-data")
    public Flux<String> enrichData(@RequestBody Flux<String>
    dataStream) {
        return chatGptService.enrichData(dataStream);
    }
}
```

**Step 4: Execute and Test the Service**

To use this service, clients would send a stream of data items to the
/enrich-data endpoint. The service enriches each item with insights from
the ChatGPT API and returns a stream of enriched data.

It is best to use an external data.json file to input sample data for
sentiment analysis as shown in Listing 2-12.

*Listing 2-12.* Data.json

```json
[
    "I absolutely love the new features in your app! They've
    made my experience so much better.",
    "I had some issues with the latest update. It crashed a few
    times on my device.",
```

```
"Your customer service is outstanding. I got help within
minutes of asking.",
"I'm disappointed with the product durability. It broke
after a week of use."
]
```

Run curl command as shown in Listing 2-13.

***Listing 2-13.*** Curl to enrich-data api

```
curl -X POST http://localhost:8080/enrich-data \-H "Content-
Type: application/json" \ --data-binary @data.json
```

The output is as shown in Listing 2-14.

***Listing 2-14.*** Output showing the sentiment analysis

```
      Original: ]' | Enrichment: {
  "id": "cmpl-8z7pdz1JpE1DyowBAskaXvOJMJ9nZ",
  "object": "text_completion",
  "created": 1709578805,
  "model": "gpt-3.5-turbo-instruct",
  "choices": [
    {
      "text": "\n\nThe given text is a single character, which
      does not provide any meaningful information to summarize.
      Therefore, no sentiment analysis can be performed.",
      "index": 0,
      "logprobs": null,
      "finish_reason": "stop"
    }
  ],
  "usage": {
    "prompt_tokens": 13,
```

```
      "completion_tokens": 28,
      "total_tokens": 41
   }
}
Original: -H "Content-Type: application/json" \ | Enrichment: {
   "id": "cmpl-8z7pdgGqvQ2c1I9cV1JubudF8CWGl",
   "object": "text_completion",
   "created": 1709578805,
   "model": "gpt-3.5-turbo-instruct",
   "choices": [
     {
       "text": "\n\nThe text is a command line argument that
       specifies the content type of a request being made, which
       is JSON. It does not contain any specific information or
       sentiment.",
       "index": 0,
       "logprobs": null,
       "finish_reason": "stop"
     }
   ],
   "usage": {
     "prompt_tokens": 21,
     "completion_tokens": 33,
     "total_tokens": 54
   }
}
Original: curl -X POST http://localhost:8080/enrich-data \ |
Enrichment: {
   "id": "cmpl-8z7pdSSshW4VD44PLdEOz6RFO6AsN",
   "object": "text_completion",
   "created": 1709578805,
```

```json
  "model": "gpt-3.5-turbo-instruct",
  "choices": [
    {
      "text": "\n\nThe text is a command for the curl
tool, which is used to transfer data from or to a server.
Specifically, the command is instructing the tool to perform a
POST request to a local server at port 8080, with the endpoint
being \"enrich-data\". The sentiment of the text is neutral, as
it is simply providing instructions for a technical task. ",
      "index": 0,
      "logprobs": null,
      "finish_reason": "stop"
    }
  ],
  "usage": {
    "prompt_tokens": 26,
    "completion_tokens": 76,
    "total_tokens": 102
  }
}
```

Original: -d '[ "I absolutely love the new features in your
app! They have made my experience so much better., I had some
issues with the latest update. It crashed a few times on my
device., Your customer service is outstanding. I got help
within minutes of asking.,I am disappointed with the product
durability. It broke after a week of use." | Enrichment: {

```json
  "id": "cmpl-8z7pd0OLR220jzbOJIlFKfnGa6TxC",
  "object": "text_completion",
  "created": 1709578805,
  "model": "gpt-3.5-turbo-instruct",
  "choices": [
```

```
{
    "text": "\n\nSummary: The text contains a mix of positive
and negative feedback for an app. The speaker expresses love
for the new features and praises the customer service, but also
mentions issues with the latest update and disappointment with
the product durability.\n\nSentiment analysis: The overall
sentiment of the text is mixed, with a slightly positive
tone due to the positive feedback for the app's features
and customer service. However, the negative feedback about
the update and product durability brings down the overall
sentiment.",
        "index": 0,
        "logprobs": null,
        "finish_reason": "stop"
    }
  ],
  "usage": {
    "prompt_tokens": 82,
    "completion_tokens": 95,
    "total_tokens": 177
  }
}
```

This approach demonstrates how Spring WebFlux can be used to
build reactive, nonblocking services for real-time data processing and
enrichment with AI models like ChatGPT. Depending on the volume
of data and complexity of the enrichment, you might also consider rate
limiting, batching requests to the ChatGPT API, or caching to optimize
performance and costs.

# 2.4  Spring Security for GenAI Applications

In the era of Generative AI, securing applications becomes not just a
necessity but a pivotal element of trust and reliability. Generative AI
applications, which can create new content or data based on their training,
face unique security challenges. These range from safeguarding the data
they learn from to ensuring the integrity of the generated content. Spring
Security, a robust framework for securing Java applications, offers a flexible
solution tailored to the complex needs of Generative AI. We will look at
the process of integrating Spring Security into Generative AI applications,
highlighting key steps and considerations to enhance their security
posture.

## 2.4.1  Let's Code

### Step 1: Add Spring Security Dependencies

First, add the Spring Security dependency to your build.gradle or pom.xml
file to include it in your project (see Listing 2-15).

***Listing 2-15.***  pom.xml

```
<dependency>
    <groupId>org.springframework.boot</groupId>
    <artifactId>spring-boot-starter-security</artifactId>
</dependency>
```

### Step 2: Configure Web Security

Create a configuration class that extends WebSecurityConfigurerAdapter
to configure security aspects of your application. In a reactive application
with WebFlux, you will extend SecurityWebFilterChain instead.

Listing 2-16 shows an example configuration that secures your
application with HTTP Basic authentication.

*Listing 2-16.* SecurityConfig.java

```java
import org.springframework.context.annotation.Bean;
import org.springframework.context.annotation.Configuration;
import org.springframework.security.config.annotation.web.
reactive.EnableWebFluxSecurity;
import org.springframework.security.config.web.server.
ServerHttpSecurity;
import org.springframework.security.core.userdetails.
MapReactiveUserDetailsService;
import org.springframework.security.core.userdetails.User;
import org.springframework.security.core.userdetails.UserDetails;
import org.springframework.security.web.server.
SecurityWebFilterChain;
@Configuration
@EnableWebFluxSecurity
public class SecurityConfig {

    @Bean
    public SecurityWebFilterChain securityWebFilterChain(Server
    HttpSecurity http) {
        return http
                .authorizeExchange()
                .pathMatchers("/enrich-data").
                authenticated()  // Secure this endpoint
                .anyExchange().permitAll()  // Allow all other
                endpoints
                .and().httpBasic()  // Use HTTP Basic
                authentication
                .and().csrf().disable()  // Disable CSRF for
                simplicity in this example
                .build();
    }
```

```
@Bean
public MapReactiveUserDetailsService userDetailsService() {
    // Define a default user for testing purposes
    UserDetails user = User.withDefaultPasswordEncoder()
            .username("user")
            .password("password")
            .roles("USER")
            .build();
    return new MapReactiveUserDetailsService(user);
}
}
```

**Step 3: Testing Security**

After applying these configurations, any request to /enrich-data will require HTTP Basic authentication. You can test this using curl by providing the username and password (see Listing 2-17).

*Listing 2-17.* Accessing enrich-data api with authentication

```
curl -u user:password -X POST http://localhost:8080/
enrich-data \
-H "Content-Type: application/json" \
-d @data.json
```

If you try to access the /enrich-data endpoint without authentication, you will receive a 401 Unauthorized response.

**Additional Security Considerations**

1.  **Password Storage:** Utilize secure hash functions like BCrypt for password storage, a best practice supported out of the box by Spring Security.

2. **SSL/TLS**: Implement SSL/TLS to safeguard data transmission, particularly vital when employing basic authentication.

3. **Roles and Permissions**: For nuanced access control, define roles and permissions tailored to your application's requirements.

4. **JWT Authentication**: In scenarios demanding stateless authentication, JSON Web Tokens offer a robust solution, enabling advanced security configurations.

This basic example sets the foundation for securing your Spring WebFlux application. As your application's security requirements become more complex, you may explore additional features and capabilities offered by Spring Security.

# 2.5  Spring Cloud for AI Microservices

Spring Cloud is an ideal framework for building scalable and resilient microservice architectures, including those that incorporate AI capabilities. Leveraging Spring Cloud for AI microservices involves several key components and practices that ensure your services are robust, scalable, and easily manageable. Below, we'll discuss how Spring Cloud can be used to build AI microservices, focusing on service discovery, configuration management, and load balancing.

**Using Spring Cloud for AI Microservices**

**Overview of Spring Cloud**: Spring Cloud provides tools for developers to quickly build some of the common patterns in distributed systems (e.g., configuration management, service discovery, circuit breakers, intelligent routing, micro-proxy, control bus). It is built on top of Spring Boot, making it easy to develop JVM applications for the cloud.

**AI Microservices**: AI microservices involve breaking down AI functionalities into smaller, independent services that can be developed, deployed, and scaled independently. This can include services for data preprocessing, model training, inference, and post-processing of results.

**Key Components for AI Microservices**

- **Service Discovery:** In a microservice architecture, services need to communicate with each other. However, due to the dynamic nature of cloud environments, where services can move around and change IP addresses, a robust service discovery mechanism is essential. Spring Cloud provides service discovery via Netflix Eureka or HashiCorp Consul, which allows services to register themselves and discover other services dynamically.

- **Configuration Management:** Managing configuration across multiple environments and services can be challenging. Spring Cloud Config provides server- and client-side support for externalized configuration in a distributed system. This allows AI microservices to fetch their configurations from a central place, making it easier to manage and change configurations without redeploying or restarting services.

- **Load Balancing:** Load balancing is crucial for distributing incoming network traffic across multiple instances of microservices, ensuring no single service is overwhelmed. Spring Cloud LoadBalancer provides client-side load balancing in calls to another microservice. It simplifies the call to the services by providing a higher level of abstraction over the discovery and client-side load balancing mechanisms.

**Best Practices**

- **Decoupling Services:** Ensure your AI microservices are loosely coupled so that they can be developed, deployed, and scaled independently. This includes separating concerns between services (e.g., separating data processing from inference services).

- **Stateless Services:** Design your microservices to be stateless wherever possible. This makes scaling out services much simpler, as any instance of a service can handle the request.

- **Continuous Delivery:** Implement continuous integration and continuous delivery (CI/CD) pipelines to automate testing and deployment of your microservices. This is crucial for maintaining high velocity in development and ensuring reliability.

- **Monitoring and Logging:** Implement comprehensive monitoring and logging to track the health and performance of your microservices. Spring Cloud Sleuth and Zipkin can be used for distributed tracing to understand the behavior of your microservices and identify bottlenecks.

- **Security:** Secure your microservices using Spring Security, which provides authentication and authorization mechanisms. This is particularly important for AI services that may access sensitive data.

In summary, Spring Cloud offers a robust framework for building scalable AI microservices by providing essential features such as service discovery, configuration management, and load balancing. By adhering to best practices and leveraging Spring Cloud's capabilities, you can build efficient, scalable, and resilient AI microservice architectures.

# 2.5.1 Let's Code

Creating a Spring Cloud application for data interpretation and trend analysis
using the ChatGPT API involves several steps, including setting up a Spring
Boot application, integrating with the ChatGPT API, and implementing the
logic for data interpretation and trend analysis. This example will guide you
through setting up the application, making API calls to ChatGPT for text-based
data interpretation, and performing simple trend analysis.

**Step 1: Create a Spring Boot Application**

Use Spring Initializr (start.spring.io) or your IDE to create a new Spring
Boot application. Choose Maven or Gradle as your build tool and Java as
the programming language.

**Step 2: Add Dependencies**

In your pom.xml, add dependencies for Spring Web, Eureka Client, and
any other dependencies you might need as shown in Listing 2-18.

***Listing 2-18.*** Pom.xml

```xml
<dependencies>
    <!-- Spring Web -->
    <dependency>
        <groupId>org.springframework.boot</groupId>
        <artifactId>spring-boot-starter-web</artifactId>
    </dependency>
    <!-- Eureka Client -->
    <dependency>
        <groupId>org.springframework.cloud</groupId>
        <artifactId>spring-cloud-starter-netflix-eureka-
        client</artifactId>
    </dependency>
    <!-- Add other dependencies as needed -->
</dependencies>
```

```
<dependencyManagement>
    <dependencies>
        <dependency>
            <groupId>org.springframework.cloud</groupId>
            <artifactId>spring-cloud-dependencies</artifactId>
            <version>${spring-cloud.version}</version> <!--
            Replace with the correct Spring Cloud version -->
            <type>pom</type>
            <scope>import</scope>
        </dependency>
    </dependencies>
</dependencyManagement>
```

**Step 3: Enable Eureka Client**

In your application.properties or application.yml, configure your
application to register with Eureka Server (see Listing 2-19).

*Listing 2-19.* application.yml

```
spring:
  application:
    name: data-analysis-service
eureka:
  client:
    serviceUrl:
      defaultZone: http://localhost:8761/eureka/

chatgpt:
  api:
    key: "Your-OpenAI-API-Key"
    endpoint: https://api.openai.com/v4/completions
```

**Step 4: Enable RestTemplate**

Configure a RestTemplate bean (see Listing 2-20) to make HTTP requests.
This can be done in any configuration class or directly in the main
application class.

*Listing 2-20.* PredictiveChatServiceApplication.java

```java
package com.example.predictivechatservice;

import org.springframework.boot.SpringApplication;
import org.springframework.boot.autoconfigure.
SpringBootApplication;
import org.springframework.context.annotation.Bean;
import org.springframework.web.client.RestTemplate;

@SpringBootApplication
public class PredictiveChatServiceApplication {

    public static void main(String[] args) {
        SpringApplication.run(PredictiveChatServiceApplication.
        class, args);
    }

    @Bean
    public RestTemplate restTemplate() {
        return new RestTemplate();
    }
}
```

**Step 5: Implement the Service to Call ChatGPT API**

Create a service class (see Listing 2-21) that uses RestTemplate to send
requests to the ChatGPT API and process responses.

*Listing 2-21.*  ChatGPTService.java

```java
import org.springframework.beans.factory.annotation.Value;
import org.springframework.http.*;
import org.springframework.stereotype.Service;
import org.springframework.web.client.RestTemplate;
import java.util.Collections;

@Service
public class ChatGPTService {

    private final RestTemplate restTemplate;

    @Value("${chatgpt.api.key}")
    private String apiKey;

    @Value("${chatgpt.api.endpoint}")
    private String apiEndpoint;

    public ChatGPTService(RestTemplate restTemplate) {
        this.restTemplate = restTemplate;
    }

    public String interpretData(String prompt) {
        HttpHeaders headers = new HttpHeaders();
        headers.setContentType(MediaType.APPLICATION_JSON);
        headers.setAccept(Collections.singletonList(MediaType.
        APPLICATION_JSON));
        headers.set("Authorization", "Bearer " + apiKey);

        String requestBody = "{\"model\": \"text-davinci-003\",
        \"prompt\": \"" + prompt + "\", \"temperature\": 0.5,
        \"max_tokens\": 100}";

        HttpEntity<String> entity = new
        HttpEntity<>(requestBody, headers);
```

```
ResponseEntity<String> response = restTemplate.
exchange(apiEndpoint, HttpMethod.POST, entity,
String.class);

    return response.getBody();
    }
}
```

**Step 6: Create a REST Controller**

Add a controller (see Listing 2-22) to expose an endpoint where users can
submit their data for interpretation.

***Listing 2-22.*** DataAnalysisController.java

```
import com.example.dataanalysisservice.service.ChatGPTService;
import org.springframework.beans.factory.annotation.Autowired;
import org.springframework.web.bind.annotation.*;

@RestController
@RequestMapping("/analyze")
public class DataAnalysisController {

    private final ChatGPTService chatGPTService;

    @Autowired
    public DataAnalysisController(ChatGPTService
    chatGPTService) {
        this.chatGPTService = chatGPTService;
    }

    @GetMapping("/interpret")
    public String interpretData(@RequestParam String prompt) {
        return chatGPTService.interpretData(prompt);
    }
}
```

**Step 7: Run and Test Your Application**

Start your Eureka server.

Run your Spring Boot application.

Use a tool like Postman or a simple curl command (see Listing 2-23) to test the /analyze/interpret endpoint by sending a prompt for interpretation.

***Listing 2-23.*** Curl to interpret API

```
curl -X GET "http://localhost:8080/analyze/
interpret?prompt=Your prompt here"
```

**Conclusion**

This example sets up a basic Spring Cloud application that uses the ChatGPT API for data interpretation and trend analysis. You can expand this application by adding more sophisticated data processing, analysis capabilities, or integrating additional services for comprehensive data analytics solutions. Remember, using the ChatGPT API requires an API key from OpenAI, and you should adhere to their usage policies and rate limits.

# 2.6 Integrating LLMs with Spring Applications

Integrating large language models (LLMs) like LLAMA or BERT into a Spring application involves several steps, from setting up the model environment to interfacing with the Spring application. Here's a practical guide to help you get started, along with example architectures and code listings for integration.

1. **Environment Setup**

   - First, ensure you have the environment necessary to run your chosen LLM. This typically involves Python environment (for LLMs like BERT or LLAMA, which are often accessed via Python libraries)

- Dependency management tools like pip for
  Python libraries and Maven or Gradle for Java
  dependencies in Spring

2. **Choose an Integration Approach**

   There are several approaches to integrating LLMs
   with Spring, including

   - **Direct API Calls**: If your LLM is hosted as a service
     (either by yourself using something like TensorFlow
     Serving or via cloud providers), your Spring
     application can make HTTP requests to the API.

   - **Python–Java Integration**: Tools like Jython, Py4J, or
     GraalVM allow you to run Python code directly from
     Java, which is useful for integrating Python-based
     models directly into your Spring application.

   **Example Architectural Components**
   **Direct API Calls**

   - **Spring Boot Application:** Handles web requests,
     business logic, etc. **Figure STYLEREF 1 \s 2 SEQ
     Figure \* ARABIC \s 1 4: Direct API call from
     spring boot**

LLMs (BERT, GPT, Llama ..)

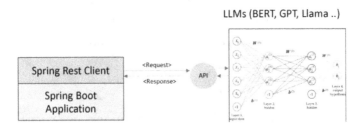

- **REST Client:** A component within the Spring application (e.g., using RestTemplate or WebClient) that makes HTTP requests to the LLM API.

- LLM Service: The hosted LLM (e.g., BERT, LLAMA) accessible via HTTP endpoints.

**Python–Java Integration**

- **Spring Boot Application**: Manages the overall application.

- **Python Service Interface**: A Java interface that communicates with Python code using Py4J or a similar tool.

- **LLM Python Script:** The actual LLM code running in a Python environment, callable from Java.

3. **Code Listings**

Listing 2-24 shows how to use a Direct API Call using WebClient.

***Listing 2-24.*** Direct API calls using WebClient

```
import org.springframework.web.reactive.function.client.WebClient;

public class LlmService {
    private final WebClient webClient;

    public LlmService(WebClient.Builder webClientBuilder) {
        this.webClient = webClientBuilder.baseUrl("http://llm-
        service-endpoint").build();
    }

    public Mono<String> queryModel(String prompt) {
        return this.webClient.post()
                .uri("/query")
```

```
                .bodyValue(new Query(prompt))
                .retrieve()
                .bodyToMono(String.class);
    }

    private static class Query {
        private String prompt;

        public Query(String prompt) {
            this.prompt = prompt;
        }

        // getters and setters
    }
}
```

Listing 2-25 shows how to use Py4J for the Python
and Java integration.

***Listing 2-25.*** Python–Java integration with Py4J

```python
import requests
from py4j.java_gateway import JavaGateway, GatewayServer

class LLMModel:
    def getResponse(self, prompt):
        # Replace 'YOUR_LLM_API_URL' with the actual API URL
        # Replace 'YOUR_API_KEY' with your actual API key
        headers = {
            "Authorization": "Bearer YOUR_API_KEY"
        }
        data = {
            "prompt": prompt,
            "max_tokens": 50
        }
```

```
        response = requests.post("YOUR_LLM_API_URL", json=data,
        headers=headers)
        return response.json()['choices'][0]['text']

if __name__ == '__main__':
    gateway = JavaGateway()  # Default port is 25333
    gateway.entry_point.registerModel(LLMModel())
    gateway.entry_point.run()
```

Listing 2-26 shows how to use the py4j
GatewayServer to serve the model.

***Listing 2-26.*** Invoking the gateway in Spring Boot

```
import py4j.GatewayServer;

public class Application {
    public static void main(String[] args) {
        LlmModel llmModel = new LlmModel();
        GatewayServer server = new GatewayServer(llmModel);
        server.start();
        System.out.println("Gateway Server Started");
    }
}
```

   4.  **Running the Example**

       1. **Start the Python Script (LLMModel.py)**: This initiates
          the Py4J gateway server and waits for connections.

       2. **Run the Spring Boot Application**: It connects to the
          Python server at startup.

       3. **Test the Endpoint**: Access **http://localhost:8080/
          api/llm/response?prompt=YourPromptHere** to get
          responses from the LLM based on your prompts.

5.  **Deployment Considerations**

**Security:** Ensure secure communication between
your Spring application and the LLM, especially if
using API calls over the network.

**Performance:** Test the performance impact of
integrating the LLM into your application, especially
for real-time responses.

**Scalability:** Plan for scalability, as LLM queries
can be resource-intensive. Consider asynchronous
processing if appropriate.

# 2.7 Deploying and Scaling AI Services with Spring

In the dynamic landscape of today's technology, the deployment and
scalability of AI services are paramount. The Spring Framework emerges
as a formidable ally in this arena, offering robustness and versatility for
Java developers. This section delves into advanced strategies for deploying
and scaling AI applications with Spring, emphasizing containerization via
Docker, orchestration through Kubernetes, and Spring's integration within
these paradigms.

**Deploying AI Services with Spring: A Strategic Overview**

- **Leveraging Microservices with Spring Boot**

    - **Rationale**: Spring Boot stands out for
      constructing microservices, aligning perfectly
      with AI applications due to their inherent need
      for scalability and modular flexibility. This
      architectural style allows each AI component to
      be finely tuned, deployed, and scaled in isolation,
      promoting agility and resilience.

- **Implementation**: Deploy individual AI
  functionalities as microservices using Spring Boot,
  enabling independent development cycles and
  facilitating granular scalability.

- **Discovering Services with Spring Cloud**

  - **Rationale**: Efficient communication between
    microservices is vital, especially in a distributed AI
    ecosystem. Spring Cloud introduces service discovery
    mechanisms, streamlining the interaction among AI
    services.

  - **Implementation**: Utilize Spring Cloud for dynamic
    service discovery, ensuring AI services can
    seamlessly locate and communicate with each
    other, enhancing operational coherence.

- **Data Management with Spring Data**

  - **Rationale**: The backbone of AI applications is data.
    Spring Data enriches these applications by offering
    streamlined data access and management, crucial
    for both training AI models and inferencing.

  - **Implementation**: Adopt Spring Data to facilitate
    interactions with various data sources, simplifying
    the CRUD operations and data processing tasks
    inherent in AI applications.

**Containerization with Docker** (You can leverage other forms of
containerization such as podman or rancher desktop based on your needs)

- **Dockerizing Spring Boot for AI**

  - **Rationale**: Containerization encapsulates AI
    services within a consistent environment, ensuring
    dependency isolation and deployment uniformity.

  - **Implementation**: Package Spring Boot AI services
    into Docker containers, bundling them with their
    dependencies to achieve environment consistency
    across development, testing, and production.

- **Local Development with Docker Compose**

  - **Rationale**: AI services often rely on external
    services (e.g., databases, message brokers). Docker
    Compose facilitates the orchestration of these
    multicontainer setups for development.

  - **Implementation**: Define a Docker Compose file
    to manage AI services and their dependencies,
    streamlining local development and testing
    workflows.

**Orchestration with Kubernetes**

- **Scaling AI with Kubernetes**

  - **Rationale**: Kubernetes excels in managing
    containerized applications, offering features
    like auto-scaling, load balancing, and self-
    healing, essential for AI services demanding high
    availability and scalability.

  - **Implementation**: Deploy AI services on
    Kubernetes, leveraging its auto-scaling capabilities
    to dynamically adjust resources based on demand,
    ensuring optimal performance.

- **Integrating Spring Cloud Kubernetes**

  - **Rationale**: For seamless operation within
    Kubernetes, Spring applications need to interact
    with its ecosystem effectively.

  - **Implementation**: Use Spring Cloud Kubernetes for
    tight integration, enabling Spring Boot applications
    to utilize Kubernetes' features like ConfigMaps
    and Secrets for externalized configurations and
    sensitive data management.

**Advanced Deployment and Scaling Strategies**

- **Horizontal Scaling Techniques**

  - Implement Kubernetes horizontal pod auto-scaling
    to automatically adjust the number of AI service
    instances based on real-time demand, ensuring
    efficiency and responsiveness.

- **Streamlined Continuous Deployment**

  - Utilize Kubernetes rolling updates in tandem
    with Spring Boot's externalized configuration for
    seamless, downtime-minimal deployment cycles,
    facilitating rapid iteration and resilience.

- **Comprehensive Monitoring and Management**

  - Combine Spring Boot Actuator with Kubernetes-
    native monitoring solutions like Prometheus and
    Grafana for in-depth application insights, crucial
    for informed scaling decisions and maintaining
    service health.

# 2.8 Conclusion: Spring—A Solid Foundation for the Future

This chapter has delved into the substantial utility and adaptability of Spring.io components in the construction of enterprise-grade Java applications. It has illuminated how foundational principles of Spring, such as dependency injection and the Spring Boot framework, facilitate streamlined development processes and foster the creation of maintainable code architectures. Although employing Spring to interface with Generative AI models necessitates certain improvisations, it has not traditionally been the most streamlined approach for engaging with this burgeoning and dynamic domain.

Nonetheless, Spring is in a continuous state of evolution, with its developers perpetually exploring avenues to broaden its utility. This brings us to the advent of Spring AI: an innovative initiative aimed at the seamless incorporation of Generative AI functionalities within Java applications.

Spring AI is poised to transpose the quintessential paradigms of Spring into the realm of Generative AI. Envision the development of sophisticated chatbots, the generation of inventive text constructs, or even the creation of imagery—all executed within the familiar confines of the Java ecosystem. By offering a modular and intuitively accessible framework, Spring AI endeavors to eliminate the complexities traditionally associated with Generative AI development.

In the ensuing chapter, we shall venture further into the captivating domain of Spring AI. We will scrutinize its principal functionalities, elucidate how it simplifies interactions with Generative AI models, and demonstrate its harmonious integration within the extant Spring ecosystem.

# CHAPTER 3

# Spring AI and LLMs

As artificial intelligence continues to evolve, the integration of advanced AI capabilities into enterprise applications has become increasingly vital. Among the most transformative developments in AI are Large Language Models (LLMs), which are capable of understanding and generating human-like text, performing complex tasks, and facilitating seamless interaction between users and machines.

Spring AI, an extension of the widely adopted Spring Framework, emerges as a powerful solution for embedding these AI capabilities into enterprise applications. By providing a structured, developer-friendly environment, Spring AI enables the integration of LLMs into Spring-based architectures with minimal friction. This fusion of LLMs and Spring AI opens new avenues for creating intelligent, context-aware applications that can respond dynamically to user inputs and deliver more personalized and effective solutions.

In this chapter, we will embark on a detailed exploration of Spring AI and its synergy with LLMs. We will start by introducing the foundational abstractions of Spring AI, which simplify the development process by abstracting the complexity of AI integration. From there, we will delve into hands-on examples, demonstrating how to build applications that harness the full potential of LLMs for tasks such as text generation, image creation, audio transcription, and more.

By the end of this chapter, you will have a comprehensive understanding of how to leverage Spring AI to seamlessly incorporate LLMs into your applications. Whether you are a seasoned developer or

© Banu Parasuraman 2024
B. Parasuraman, *Mastering Spring AI*, https://doi.org/10.1007/979-8-8688-1001-5_3

new to AI, this chapter will equip you with the tools and knowledge to develop cutting-edge, AI-powered solutions using the combined strengths of Spring AI and LLMs.

# 3.1 Introduction to Spring AI

### Origins and Inspiration

Spring AI emerges from a vision to revolutionize AI application development by streamlining complexity without compromising functionality, drawing inspiration from notable Python projects like LangChain and LlamaIndex.

### Foundational Abstractions

Spring AI provides a robust framework built on a foundation of abstractions, enabling developers to seamlessly integrate AI functionality into their applications. These abstractions are meticulously designed to facilitate agile development and effortless component swapping, minimizing development overhead.

### Comprehensive Model Support

Spring AI boasts extensive support for leading model providers, including OpenAI, Microsoft, Amazon, Google, and Hugging Face. Covering a diverse range of model types such as Chat and Text to Image, Spring AI empowers developers with a versatile toolkit for diverse AI applications.

### Portable API and Easy Integration

With a portable API across AI providers, Spring AI simplifies the process of accessing and integrating AI models into applications. Whether developers opt for synchronous or stream API options, Spring AI ensures seamless integration with minimal effort.

### Robust Vector Database Compatibility

In addition to model support, Spring AI offers compatibility with major vector database providers such as Azure Vector Search, Chroma, Milvus, Neo4j, PostgreSQL/pgvector, Pinecone, Redis, and Weaviate.

This compatibility extends to a portable API for vector stores, enabling developers to harness the power of vector-based data storage across different platforms.

**Empowering Frameworks and Tools**

Spring AI equips developers with a suite of tools and frameworks, including Spring Boot Auto Configuration, Starters for AI Models, and Vector Stores. Additionally, an Extract, Transform, Load (ETL) framework facilitates seamless data engineering tasks.

**Addressing Common Use Cases**

By offering a comprehensive feature set, Spring AI enables developers to tackle common use cases effortlessly. From Q&A over documentation to conversational interfaces, Spring AI empowers developers to unlock the full potential of AI-driven innovation.

In this chapter, we will deep dive into the workings of Spring AI and cover topics such as embeddings, chat, vector databases, and prompts with some specific examples that will get your feet wet.

# 3.2 Headfirst into Spring AI

As we dive headfirst into this exploration of the capabilities of Spring AI, we uncover the seamless integration between Spring AI's streamlined application development process and ChatGPT's advanced AI functionalities.

This introduction sets the stage for a deep dive into practical implementations, beginning with foundational concepts and gradually advancing to complex applications. Whether you're aiming to build sophisticated chatbots, implement natural language understanding in your applications, or generate content dynamically, this guide provides the insights and tools necessary to bring your AI-driven projects to life.

Through hands-on examples, detailed walkthroughs, and clear explanations, we'll navigate the process of integrating ChatGPT with Spring AI. This includes setting up your development environment, understanding the core components of Spring AI, and making the most of ChatGPT's capabilities within your Spring applications. By the end of this journey, you'll be equipped with the knowledge and skills to create applications that not only respond intelligently to user input but also anticipate needs and offer solutions in ways previously unimagined.

# 3.2.1  A Simple "Hello World" Application with Spring AI

**Introduction**

Starting with the basics, we'll outline the steps to set up a Spring Boot project configured to communicate with the ChatGPT API. This exercise will not only illustrate the simplicity of initiating a project with Spring AI but also highlight how effortlessly it can be configured to interact with one of the most powerful language processing APIs available today.

**Start Coding**

**Step 1:** Download and configure Spring CLI Release from `https://github.com/spring-projects/spring-cli/releases`.

**Step 2:** Run the following command (see Listing 3-1). This will generate the simple application and the project. This can be modified to suit your needs.

*Listing 3-1.*  Creating a new project

```
spring boot new --from ai --name helloai
```

This command will create the following project structure with sample code (see Figure 3-1).

**Figure 3-1.** *Spring AI project structure*

Note the additions in POM.xml (see Listing 3-2) that are specific to
Spring AI.

**Listing 3-2.** POM.xml with Spring AI 0.8.1[1]

```
<dependencyManagement>
    <dependencies>
        <dependency>
            <groupId>org.springframework.ai</groupId>
            <artifactId>spring-ai-bom</artifactId>
            <version>0.8.1</version>
            <type>pom</type>
            <scope>import</scope>
        </dependency>
    </dependencies>
</dependencyManagement>
```

The spring-ai-bom matches the CLI that you downloaded in Step 1.
Change the package name to suit.

The generated SimpleAIControler is as shown in Listing 3-3.

---

[1] At the time of writing, 0.8.1 was the latest stable version

*Listing 3-3.* SimpleAiController.java

```java
import org.springframework.ai.chat.ChatClient;
import org.springframework.beans.factory.annotation.Autowired;
import org.springframework.web.bind.annotation.GetMapping;
import org.springframework.web.bind.annotation.RequestParam;
import org.springframework.web.bind.annotation.RestController;

import java.util.Map;

@RestController
public class SimpleAiController {

    private final ChatClient chatClient;

    @Autowired
    public SimpleAiController(ChatClient chatClient) {
        this.chatClient = chatClient;
    }

    @GetMapping("/ai/simple")
    public Map<String, String> completion(@RequestParam(value =
"message", defaultValue = "Tell me a joke") String message) {
        return Map.of("generation", chatClient.call(message));
    }
}
```

**Step 3:** Run the application and test.

The application is accessible at localhost:8080/ai/simple.

The Postman results (see Figure 3-2) show the joke that has been generated.

**Figure 3-2.** *Postman run of GET against localhost:8080/ai/simple*

Change the value of the "message" parameter to "give me a Shakespeare quote" and test (see Figure 3-3).

**Figure 3-3.** *Run the endpoint with a Shakespeare quote*

Remarkably, ChatGPT has not only retrieved the desired quote but has also identified it as originating from Shakespeare's *As You Like It*. This adds a layer of usefulness to the response.

Let's dig a bit deeper into the code. This will help us understand how Spring AI accomplishes with little Java code.

First, observe the inclusion of the ChatClient library as in Listing 3-4.

***Listing 3-4.*** ChatClient library in Spring Framework

```
import org.springframework.ai.chat.ChatClient;
```

This library simplifies the intricacies involved in establishing connections to your Large Language Models (LLMs). A closer examination of the ChatClient code within the library (spring.ai.core-0.8.1.jar), as shown in Figure 3-4, reveals that it has been preprogrammed to handle the tasks of sending prompts and processing responses. This enhancement significantly boosts your productivity by streamlining development processes.

***Figure 3-4.*** *ChatClient class in spring-ai-core-0.8.1.jar*

Upon further examination of the auto-configuration JAR file within **spring-ai-spring-boot-autoconfigure**, you'll find that default settings for the OpenAI URL, models, and other configurations have already been established (see Figure 3-5). Should you wish to alter these defaults, modifications can be made by specifying your preferences in the **application.properties** or **application.yaml** file.

**Figure 3-5.** *OpenAIConnectionProperties class*

The model for OpenAI defaults to gpt-3.5-turbo as shown in Figure 3-6.

**Figure 3-6.** *OpenAIChatProperties class*

Table 3-1 provides a comprehensive overview of the preset configurations for every Large Language Model (LLM) supported by Spring AI.

***Table 3-1.*** *Default settings in Spring AI jar files*

| PROVIDERS | ADITIONAL LLM SUPPORT | DEFAULT MODEL | DEFAULT URL |
|---|---|---|---|
| OpenAI | Need to specify in configurations files | gpt-3.5-turbo | https://api.openai.com |
| Azure.OpenAI | Need to specify in configurations files | gpt-35-turbo | Need to specify in configurations files |
| Amazon bedrock | Anthropic | Need to specify in configurations files | Need to specify in configurations files |
| | Cohere | | AWS default region: us-east-1 |
| | Llama2 | | |
| | titan | | |
| Huggingface | Need to specify in configurations files | Need to specify in configurations files | Need to specify in configurations files |
| Ollama | Need to specify in configurations files | Need to specify in configurations files | http://localhost:11434 |
| Mistralai | Need to specify in configurations files | Need to specify in configurations files | https://api.mistral.ai |
| Stabilityai | Need to specify in configurations files | Need to specify in configurations files | https://api.stability.ai/v1 |
| vertexAI – Gemini | Gemini | Need to specify in configurations files | Need to specify in configurations files |
| VertexAI – palm2 | Palm2 | Need to specify in configurations files | https://generativelanguage.googleapis.com/v1beta3 |

For most providers, additional LLM support and default settings require custom specifications in the configuration files (e.g., **Application. yaml** or **application.properties**). Only a few providers have a preset default URL, and even fewer have a specified default model.

Listing 3-5 is an example **application.yaml file** configured to access Bedrock llama2.

***Listing 3-5.*** Application.yaml for bedrock

```
spring:
  ai:
    bedrock:
      aws:
        region: eu-central-1
        access-key: ${AWS_ACCESS_KEY_ID} # You'll need to
        set this environment variable with your actual AWS
        access key ID.
        secret-key: ${AWS_SECRET_ACCESS_KEY} # You'll need to
```

```
set this environment variable with your actual AWS
secret access key.

llama2:
  chat:
    enabled: true
    options:
      temperature: 0.8
```

**Section Summary**

This section provided a comprehensive guide on creating a simple "Hello World" application using Spring AI, illustrating the ease of integrating advanced AI functionalities into a Spring Boot application. The process was broken down into clear, manageable steps, starting from downloading the Spring CLI Release, generating a new project tailored to AI applications, and configuring it to meet specific development needs.

Key highlights included

- **Downloading and Configuring Spring CLI**: A straightforward initial step that sets the foundation for Spring AI projects.

- **Project Generation and Structure**: Utilizing the **spring boot new** command to create a project, emphasizing the importance of the project structure and specific additions to the **POM.xml** file that are essential for Spring AI development.

- **Code Implementation**: Detailed code listings, such as the **SimpleAiController**, showcased the implementation of a basic AI-driven endpoint. The controller utilized the **ChatClient** library to connect to Large Language Models (LLMs), demonstrating how to send prompts and process AI-generated responses with minimal coding effort.

- **Running and Testing the Application**: Steps to launch the application and test its functionality were provided, with examples showing how to use Postman to verify the AI's response capability. The section illustrated how changing the input parameter affects the AI's output, offering practical insights into the application's versatility.

- **Exploring the Code and Libraries**: An examination of the **ChatClient** library and its role in simplifying connections to LLMs highlighted the streamlining of development processes. This was complemented by a look at the auto-configuration JAR file, which predefines settings for the OpenAI URL and models, further easing the development process.

- **Configuration Flexibility**: The discussion on modifying default settings by adjusting the **application. properties** or **application.yaml** file underscored the application's adaptability to different project requirements.

The section concluded with insights into configuring the application to connect with specific models and services, such as Bedrock llama2, illustrating the comprehensive support Spring AI offers for various LLMs. This "Hello World" example served as a foundation for integrating AI into Spring applications, setting the stage for more complex implementations.

# 3.2.2 Simple Image Generation

**Introduction**

Venturing further into the capabilities of Spring AI and its integration with OpenAI's powerful tools, we delve into the realm of image generation in this segment. Building upon the foundational knowledge established in previous sections, we now explore how ChatGPT can be leveraged, not just for textual responses but for generating images based on textual descriptions. This introduces an exciting dimension to our applications, where the synthesis of visual content from language becomes possible.

In this section, we'll guide you through setting up a simple application capable of interfacing with OpenAI's image generation API via ChatGPT. We'll cover the essential steps from crafting descriptive prompts that articulate the desired image characteristics, to sending these prompts through our Spring AI application, and finally, to receiving and handling the generated images.

The focus here is on demystifying the process of connecting to and utilizing an LLM for image creation, showcasing how easily text can be transformed into visuals. This example will not only illustrate the practical application of image generation APIs but also emphasize the versatility of ChatGPT when combined with Spring AI's streamlined development framework.

### Start Coding

Creating images with Spring AI is remarkably straightforward and requires minimal coding effort.

Add the following code to the SimpleAIController that we created earlier in Listing 3-6.

***Listing 3-6.*** Generate image section on SimpleAIController

```
@Autowired
public ImageClient openaiImageClient;

@GetMapping("/ai/generateimage")
public Image getImage() {
    ImageResponse response = openaiImageClient.call(
            new ImagePrompt("Orange Tabby cat. The mood is
            excited. wearing boots",
                OpenAiImageOptions.builder()
```

```
                        .withQuality("hd")
                        .withN(1)
                        .withHeight(1024)
                        .withWidth(1024).build())

    );
    return response.getResult().getOutput();

}
```

In Listing 3-6, when a GET request is made to the /**ai/generateimage**
endpoint of the web service, the **getImage()** method is called. It uses
**openaiImageClient** to send a request to an image generation API, asking
for a high-quality image of an "excited Orange Tabby cat wearing boots,"
and then returns the generated image as the response to the request.

When you use Postman to make a request to the URL, you will receive
a response that includes a URL. This URL directs you to the image that has
been generated.

To view the generated image, you can either

1. Copy the URL from the response and paste it into
   the address bar of your web browser (Figure 3-7).

2. Utilize Postman's "Visualize" tab, which can display
   the image directly within Postman, as in Figure 3-8.

***Figure 3-7.*** *Postman output of* `http://localhost:8080/ai/`
*generateimage with GET*

***Figure 3-8.***  *Output of generate image*

Please note that each time you make a request, a new image will be generated.

**Section Summary**

In this section, we explored the integration of Spring AI with OpenAI's powerful tools for image generation. Leveraging ChatGPT, we demonstrated how to create visual content from textual descriptions, adding a dynamic layer to applications. The process involves crafting descriptive prompts, interfacing with OpenAI's image generation API through a Spring AI application, and handling the generated images.

We detailed the steps to set up a simple image generation functionality within the Spring AI framework, emphasizing the ease and minimal coding effort required. Specifically, we added code to the SimpleAIController, illustrating how a GET request to the **/ai/generateimage** endpoint triggers the **getImage()** method. This method calls the **openaiImageClient** to request an image based on a specified prompt, such as an "excited Orange Tabby cat wearing boots," and returns the generated image.

To view the generated image, users have two options: directly accessing the image via a provided URL in a web browser or using Postman's "Visualize" tab for in-app visualization, as shown in Figures 3-7 and 3-8. It's highlighted that each request results in the generation of a new image, showcasing the API's dynamic capability.

This section not only illustrated the practical application of image generation APIs but also highlighted the versatility of combining ChatGPT with the Spring AI framework, making the development of AI-powered visual content creation straightforward and accessible.

# 3.2.3  Audio Transcription

**Introduction**

In the evolving landscape of artificial intelligence applications, audio transcription stands out as a transformative tool, converting spoken words into precise textual representations. The integration of Spring AI and ChatGPT brings this capability to new heights, offering a seamless and efficient pathway to transcribe audio content. This synergy not only enhances the accessibility and usability of audio data but also leverages the power of cutting-edge language models to ensure accuracy and context awareness in transcriptions.

This section will guide you through harnessing Spring AI alongside ChatGPT for audio transcription tasks. By tapping into this potent combination, developers can effortlessly implement audio to text conversion in their applications, benefitting from the advanced natural language processing (NLP) capabilities of ChatGPT and the robust, developer-friendly framework of Spring AI. Whether it's for creating searchable archives, generating subtitles, or enabling content analysis, audio transcription with Spring AI and ChatGPT opens up a realm of possibilities, making audio content more accessible and versatile than ever before.

**Start Coding**

Here again, the implementation of OpenAI's transcription API is quite simple.

Add the following code (see Listing 3-7) to the SimpleAIController that we created earlier in Listing 3-3.

***Listing 3-7.*** Audio transcription section in SimpleAIController

```
// this file is from https://www.kaggle.com/datasets/
pavanelisetty/sample-audio-files-for-speech-recognition
@Value("classpath:/speech/harvard.wav")
private Resource audioFile;

@Autowired
public OpenAiAudioTranscriptionClient
openAiTranscriptionClient;

@PostMapping("/ai/transcribe")
public String transcribe(){

    OpenAiAudioApi.TranscriptResponseFormat responseFormat =
    OpenAiAudioApi.TranscriptResponseFormat.VTT;

    OpenAiAudioTranscriptionOptions transcriptionOptions =
    OpenAiAudioTranscriptionOptions.builder()
            .withLanguage("en")
            .withPrompt("Ask not this, but ask that")
```

```
        .withTemperature(0f)
        .withResponseFormat(responseFormat)
        .build();
    AudioTranscriptionPrompt transcriptionRequest = new AudioTr
    anscriptionPrompt(audioFile, transcriptionOptions);

    AudioTranscriptionResponse response =
    openAiTranscriptionClient.call(transcriptionRequest);
    return response.getResults().get(0).getOutput().
    toLowerCase();
}
```

Please note the audio file **harward.wav**. This is available at https://
www.kaggle.com/datasets/pavanelisetty/sample-audio-files-for-
speech-recognition.

Listing 3-7 exposes a **post** endpoint **/ai/transcribe**.

When you execute this endpoint through Postman, the response will
resemble what is depicted in Figure 3-9.

***Figure 3-9.*** *Execution of transcribe endpoint in Postman*

You'll observe that the transcription accuracy is notably high.

**Section Summary**

In this section, we explored the integration of Spring AI and ChatGPT for audio transcription, a powerful application of artificial intelligence that converts spoken language into text. This combination enhances the accuracy and usability of transcribed audio data, leveraging advanced NLP capabilities for a wide range of applications, from creating searchable archives to generating subtitles and enabling content analysis.

The implementation process involves utilizing the OpenAI transcription API, which is straightforward within the Spring AI framework. A detailed walkthrough was provided on adding the necessary code to a SimpleAIController, illustrating how to set up and execute audio transcription tasks. The example used **harvard.wav**, an audio file available on Kaggle, to demonstrate the transcription capabilities and the high accuracy of the results.

Executing the **/ai/transcribe** endpoint through Postman, as detailed in Listing 3-7 and illustrated in Figure 3-9, shows the practical application of these concepts. This hands-on example reinforces the potential and accessibility of using Spring AI alongside ChatGPT for efficient and precise audio transcription, making this technology an invaluable asset for developers aiming to enrich their applications with AI-driven features.

# 3.2.4  Prompting with Spring AI

**Introduction**

In Generative AI, prompts serve as crucial navigational tools, guiding AI models to generate specific and relevant outputs. Much like a compass directs a traveler, the design and phrasing of prompts significantly influence the direction and quality of an AI model's responses. This section delves into the art and science of crafting effective prompts within the Spring AI framework, likening the process to managing views in Spring MVC or constructing SQL statements with placeholders for dynamic content.

- **Understanding Prompts and Messages**

  At the heart of interaction with AI models in Spring AI lies the sophisticated management of prompts. This involves creating detailed texts with placeholders that dynamically adapt based on user requests or application code, providing a flexible and powerful means to communicate with AI models.

- **The Evolution of Prompt Structure**

  Over time, the structure of prompts has transitioned from simple text strings to more complex formats incorporating placeholders for specific inputs. OpenAI has further refined this approach by categorizing messages within prompts into distinct roles, enhancing the model's ability to process and respond to inputs with greater context and clarity.

- **API Overview and Key Components**

  - **Prompt**: The "generate" method of **ChatClient** uses a **Prompt** instance, serving as a container for a series of **Message** objects. Each message within the prompt plays a unique role, contributing to a nuanced dialogue with the AI model.

  - **Message**: This interface represents a textual message and can include attributes, a message type, and media objects for multimodal models. It encapsulates the essence of communication with AI, distinguishing between different categories of messages through the **MessageType**.

- **Roles**: The introduction of roles in prompts marks a significant advancement, with specific categories such as system, user, assistant, and function roles. These roles delineate the purpose and context of each message, facilitating more structured and effective interactions with AI models.

- **Prompt Templating and Engineering**

  - Spring AI introduces the **PromptTemplate** class, utilizing the StringTemplate engine for constructing prompts. This class, along with its associated actions interfaces, supports the creation of both simple and complex prompts, demonstrating the versatility of prompt management in Spring AI.

In this section, we will look at a sample use case of motivational quotes using a prompt template and tweaking parameters such as intensity to change the GenAI response

**Start Coding**

Let's begin by adding the following code (see Listing 3-8).

*Listing 3-8.* Generate motivational quote

```
@Value("classpath:/prompts/motivational-quote-prompt.st")
private Resource motivationalQuoteResource;

@GetMapping("/ai/motivation")
public String generateMotivationalQuote(@RequestParam
(value = "theme", defaultValue = "perseverance") String theme,
                                        @RequestParam
                                        (value = "intensity",
                                        defaultValue = "high")
                                        String intensity) {
```

101

```
PromptTemplate promptTemplate = new PromptTemplate(motivati
onalQuoteResource);
Prompt prompt = promptTemplate.create(Map.of("theme",
theme, "intensity", intensity));
return chatClient.call(prompt).getResult().getOutput().
getContent();
}
```

Add the following file (see Listing 3-9) with the .st extension, that has the prompt template. This can be saved under the prompts folder as shown in Figure 3-10.

***Listing 3-9.*** motivational-quote-prompt.st

The theme of today's motivation is {theme}. In times of challenge, it's essential to remember that {intensity} effort and dedication lead to breakthroughs. Here's a quote to inspire you:

"If you're going through hell, keep going. The virtue of {theme} is not in falling, but in rising every time we fall. With {intensity} determination, nothing is impossible."

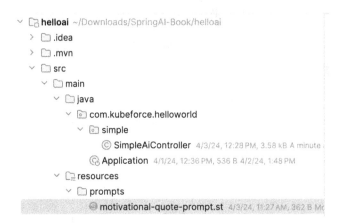

***Figure 3-10.*** *prompts folder*

**For the Curious**

*The .st extension in the prompt template file (**motivational-quote-prompt. st**) signifies that it is a StringTemplate file. StringTemplate is a Java template engine used for generating source code, web pages, emails, or any other formatted text output. It is designed around the philosophy that a template should be strictly a view and should not contain application logic, which promotes a clear separation of concerns.*

*The choice of StringTemplate and the **.st** file extension offer several benefits:*

1. ***Clarity and Simplicity**: StringTemplate enforces a model-view separation, making the templates easy to understand and maintain. Templates focus solely on formatting the output, receiving data from your application to fill in placeholders without embedding complex logic.*

2. ***Reusability**: Templates can be reused across different parts of an application or even across projects, as they define a standard way of rendering data into a textual format.*

3. ***Powerful Formatting Options**: Despite its simplicity, StringTemplate provides powerful formatting capabilities, including conditional expressions, loops, and the ability to include other templates. This makes it suitable for generating complex text outputs.*

4. ***Language Neutrality**: While StringTemplate is a Java library, the template files themselves (.st files) are essentially plain text files with placeholders. This means that the templates can be easily adapted or used as a basis for templates in other languages that have similar concepts.*

*Using a .st file for prompts, especially in applications like Spring AI, allows developers to define complex, dynamic text outputs in a clean, organized manner. The template serves as a blueprint for generating responses, with placeholders filled in by the application at runtime based on user input or other contextual data. This approach facilitates the dynamic generation of text, such as motivational quotes, with varying themes and intensities, enhancing the flexibility and interactivity of AI-driven applications.*

Run the application and test with Postman (see Figure 3-11).

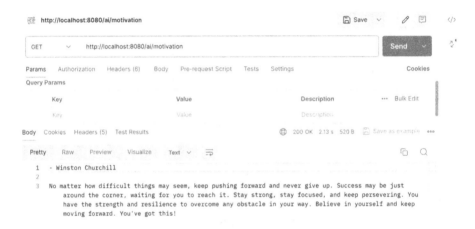

***Figure 3-11.*** *Results of execution with Postman*

Interestingly, you will see that quote and the person whom this quote is attributed to, in this case, Winston Churchill.

To change this to a structured format (JSON), do the following.

Modify the .st file as shown in Listing 3-10.

***Listing 3-10.*** Modified motivational-quote-prompt.st

```
The theme of today's motivation is {theme}.  In times of
challenge, it's essential to remember that {intensity} effort and
dedication lead to breakthroughs. Here's a quote to inspire you:
```

"If you're going through hell, keep going. The virtue of
{theme} is not in falling, but in rising every time we fall.
With {intensity} determination, nothing is impossible."
the output should be in JSON and include author
{format}

Add a class for speaker (see Listing 3-11) to structure the content.

***Listing 3-11.*** Speaker class

```
public class Speaker {
    private String quote;
    private String author;

    // Getters and setters
    public String getQuote() {
        return quote;
    }

    public void setQuote(String quote) {
        this.quote = quote;
    }

    public String getAuthor() {
        return author;
    }

    public void setAuthor(String author) {
        this.author = author;
    }
}
```

Modify the generateMotivationalQuote method to include the
outputParser as shown in Listing 3-12.

***Listing 3-12.*** Modified generateMotivationalQuote in
SimpleAIController

```
@GetMapping("/ai/motivation")
public Speaker generateMotivationalQuote(@RequestParam(value =
"theme", defaultValue = "perseverance") String theme,
                                    @RequestParam(value =
"intensity", defaultValue = "high") String intensity) {
    var outputParser = new BeanOutputParser<>(Speaker.class);
    PromptTemplate promptTemplate = new
    PromptTemplate(motivationalQuoteResource);
    Prompt prompt = promptTemplate.create(Map.of("theme",
    theme, "intensity", intensity,"format",outputParser.
    getFormat()));
    String output = chatClient.call(prompt).getResult().
    getOutput().getContent();

    return outputParser.parse(output);

}
```

On executing the API in Postman, you can observe that the output (see Figure 3-12) is generated in a structured format. Compare this with the output in Figure 3-11.

**Figure 3-12.** *Structured output*

### Section Summary

In the realm of Generative AI, the efficacy of interaction with AI models significantly hinges on the art of prompt crafting. This section has delved into the nuances of constructing effective prompts within the Spring AI framework, illustrating the parallel between managing views in Spring MVC and curating prompts to guide AI models toward generating specific, contextually relevant outputs.

#### Core Insights

- **The Essence of Prompts**: Prompts act as the steering wheel for AI models, directing them to produce desired responses. Their design and composition are pivotal, requiring thoughtful consideration to ensure clarity and relevance.

- **Prompt Structure Evolution**: Over time, the format of prompts has evolved from simple text strings to sophisticated structures incorporating dynamic placeholders. This evolution reflects in OpenAI's method of categorizing messages within prompts, enhancing the AI's contextual understanding and response accuracy.

107

- **Spring AI's Approach to Prompting**: Spring AI leverages the **PromptTemplate** class, utilizing the StringTemplate engine for prompt construction. This enables developers to craft complex, dynamic prompts efficiently, fostering a clean and organized method for generating AI responses.

- **Practical Implementation**: Through examples, this section illustrated the process of using **PromptTemplate** for creating nuanced, context-aware prompts. The discussion underscored the significance of prompt engineering—the strategic design of prompts to optimize AI outputs.

### Implementation Steps

1. **Prompt Template Creation**: The guide provided a straightforward example of defining a motivational quote prompt within a **.st** file, setting the stage for generating themed, intensity-tailored quotes.

2. **Generating Motivational Quotes**: The **generateMotivationalQuote** method demonstrated how to dynamically create prompts using **PromptTemplate**, generating inspirational quotes based on user-defined themes and intensities.

3. **Adjusting for Structured Output**: Further refinement was suggested to structure the output, including modifications to the **.st** file and the introduction of the **Speaker** class for organizing the quote and author information.

4. **Enhanced Interaction with Spring AI**: By modifying the **.st** file and the **generateMotivationalQuote** method, the section showcased how to evolve from plain text to structured (JSON) outputs, enhancing the flexibility and interactivity of AI-driven applications.

# 3.3  Practical Value of Spring AI in Prompt Engineering

Prompt engineering is crucial for guiding AI models to generate relevant and accurate outputs. Spring AI significantly enhances this process through its various features and capabilities. Here are examples illustrating the practical value of Spring AI in prompt engineering:

1. **Abstraction and Simplification**

   **Example**: Imagine you're building a customer support chatbot that helps users troubleshoot common issues. With Spring AI, you can create a simple prompt like:

   ```
   String userQuery = "My internet is slow"; Prompt prompt
   = new Prompt("You are a helpful assistant. " + "The
   user has a problem: " + userQuery + ". Provide a step-
   by-step solution.");
   ```

   ```
   String response =chatClient.call(prompt).getResult().
   getOutput().getContent();
   ```

   In this example, Spring AI abstracts the complexity of interacting with the LLM, allowing you to focus on crafting the prompt rather than managing API calls or handling responses manually.

2.  **Reusable Prompt Templates**

    **Example**: If you're developing an application that
    generates motivational quotes based on user input,
    you can create a reusable prompt template:

    ```
    @Value("classpath:/prompts/motivational-quote-
    prompt.st")
    private Resource motivationalQuoteResource;
    @GetMapping("/ai/motivation")
    public String generateMotivationalQuote(@
    RequestParam(value = "theme", defaultValue =
    "perseverance") String theme) {
        PromptTemplate promptTemplate = new PromptTemplate(
        motivationalQuoteResource);
        Prompt prompt = promptTemplate.create(Map.
        of("theme", theme));
        return chatClient.call(prompt).getResult().
        getOutput().getContent();
    }
    ```

    By using a template, you can quickly generate different
    motivational quotes based on various themes, making
    your application more versatile and efficient.

3.  **Enhanced Prompt Structuring**

    **Example**: Consider building a chatbot that categorizes
    different types of user input. With Spring AI, you can
    structure prompts to include specific roles:

    ```
    Prompt prompt = new Prompt(List.of(
        new Message(MessageType.SYSTEM, "You are an
        assistant that categorizes user requests."),
    ```

```
    new Message(MessageType.USER, "How do I reset my
    password?")
));
String response = chatClient.call(prompt).getResult().
getOutput().getContent();
```

Here, the system and user roles help the model understand the context better, leading to more accurate categorizations of user requests.

4. **Token Management and Cost Efficiency**

**Example**: When generating long-form content, token management becomes crucial. Suppose you're developing a content generator that needs to summarize long documents:

```
Prompt prompt = new Prompt("Summarize the following
text: " + longText.substring(0, 2000));
String summary = chatClient.call(prompt).getResult().
getOutput().getContent();
```

By managing the length of the input text (and hence the tokens), you can optimize the cost while ensuring the summary remains accurate. Spring AI helps you efficiently manage token usage without compromising the quality of the generated content.

# 3.4  Chapter Summary

Throughout this chapter, we embarked on an insightful journey into the realm of Spring AI, unraveling its potential to revolutionize AI application development. From the foundational abstractions inspired by leading Python projects to the seamless integration of diverse AI models and the innovative use of prompt engineering, we've explored the depth and breadth of what Spring AI offers to the developer community.

**Key Takeaways**

- **Streamlined AI Integration**: Spring AI's robust framework and foundational abstractions have demonstrated how effortlessly AI functionalities can be woven into applications, enabling a seamless bridge between cutting-edge AI capabilities and the agile development process.

- **Extensive Model Support**: The comprehensive coverage of leading model providers like OpenAI, Microsoft, and Google, among others, highlights Spring AI's commitment to offering a versatile toolkit that caters to a wide array of AI-driven applications.

- **Advanced Prompting Techniques**: The dive into prompting with Spring AI has illuminated the critical role of effective prompt crafting in steering AI models toward generating specific, contextually relevant outputs. This section underscored the strategic importance of prompt engineering in optimizing AI interactions.

- **Practical Implementations**: From generating simple "Hello World" applications to sophisticated image generation and audio transcription tasks, the hands-on examples provided actionable insights into leveraging Spring AI for creating dynamic, AI-powered solutions.

**Empowering Developers for AI-Driven Innovation**

As we conclude this chapter, it's clear that Spring AI stands at the forefront of AI application development, empowering developers with the tools and knowledge needed to harness the power of Generative AI. The framework's ease of use, combined with its ability to cater to both foundational and complex AI use cases, positions Spring AI as a catalyst for innovation in the AI landscape.

In the next chapter, we will explore some advanced features that Spring AI offers including prompting with roles, tokens, function calling, embeddings, and ETL pipelines. This will prepare us to explore some useful enterprise use cases that we will address in later chapters.

# CHAPTER 4

# Spring AI and RAG (Retrieval-Augmented Generation)

## 4.1 Introduction

In the rapidly evolving field of artificial intelligence, the ability to retrieve and process information accurately and efficiently is paramount. Large Language Models (LLMs) like GPT-3 and GPT-4 have shown remarkable capabilities in generating human-like text based on extensive training on public domain data. However, these models face limitations when it comes to handling proprietary, enterprise-specific data that they have not been pretrained on. This is where Retrieval-Augmented Generation (RAG) steps in.

RAG is an advanced technique designed to augment the capabilities of LLMs by integrating them with external knowledge sources. This approach mitigates several challenges inherent in LLMs, such as hallucinations, outdated knowledge, and limited context windows. By combining the intrinsic knowledge of LLMs with dynamic retrieval of relevant information from external databases, RAG significantly enhances the accuracy and relevance of generated content.

© Banu Parasuraman 2024
B. Parasuraman, *Mastering Spring AI*, https://doi.org/10.1007/979-8-8688-1001-5_4

In this chapter, we will explore the following:

1. **Token Limits and Context Windows in LLMs**:
   Understanding the constraints of LLMs in terms of
   token processing and context management.

2. **What Is Retrieval-Augmented Generation (RAG)**:
   A comprehensive overview of RAG, its evolution
   from Naive RAG to Advanced and Modular RAG,
   and its key components.

3. **RAG in the Enterprise Context**: Examining the
   benefits, challenges, and mitigation strategies for
   deploying RAG in enterprise environments.

4. **RAG Pipelines**: Analyzing the structure and
   application of RAG pipelines, from basic to
   advanced, and their role in enhancing information
   retrieval and response generation.

5. **RAG with Spring AI**: Practical implementation of
   RAG using the Spring AI framework, including ETL
   (Extract, Transform, Load) processes and querying
   structured and unstructured data.

By the end of this chapter, you will have a robust understanding of
how to leverage RAG and Spring AI to overcome the limitations of LLMs,
enabling them to process proprietary data effectively. This knowledge will
equip you with the tools to build more accurate, contextually relevant,
and up-to-date AI-driven solutions, tailored to the specific needs of your
enterprise.

In the previous chapter, we explored how Spring AI facilitates the
creation of prompts and prompt templates for use with various Large
Language Models (LLMs). This method of prompt tuning is efficient and
productive, allowing us to query a vast array of public domain data that

LLMs are pretrained on. However, when it comes to querying specific, proprietary data that LLMs have not been trained on, prompt tuning alone falls short. This limitation arises due to the token limits and context window constraints inherent in LLMs.

# 4.2 Token Limits and Context Windows in LLMs[1]

Each LLM has specific limits on the number of tokens it can process in a single request and the size of the context window it uses. Below is a comparison of token limits and context windows for various LLMs.

*Table 4-1.* *Token limits and context windows for popular LLMs (compiled from the respective LLM pages)*

| Language Model | Context Window | Context Window |
| --- | --- | --- |
| davinci-002 | 16,000 tokens | https://platform.openai.com/docs/models |
| Babbage-002 (GPT-3.5) | 16,000 tokens | https://platform.openai.com/docs/models |
| GPT-4 | 32,768 tokens | https://platform.openai.com/docs/models |
| GPT-4o | 128,000 tokens | https://www.anthropic.com/news/claude-2 |
| Claude (Claude-2) | 100,000 tokens | https://github.com/meta-llama/llama-models/blob/main/models/llama3_1/MODEL_CARD.md |

*(continued)*

---

[1] The token limits are constantly evolving and are subject to change

***Table 4-1.*** (*continued*)

| Language Model | Context Window | Context Window |
|---|---|---|
| LLaMA 3.1 | 128,000 tokens | `https://blog.google/technology/ai/` `google-gemini-next-generation-model-` `february-2024/#gemini-15` |
| Gemini 1.5 | 128,000 tokens | `https://platform.openai.com/docs/` `models` |

# 4.2.1  Understanding Tokens and Context Windows

**Token Limits**

- **Definition**: Token limits refer to the maximum number of tokens in NLP model can process in a single input. Tokens can be words, sub words, or characters, depending on the model's tokenization strategy.

- **Impact**: Token limits define how much text the model can handle at once. For instance, if a model has a token limit of 2048 tokens, it cannot process text exceeding this limit in a single pass.

- **Truncation and Splitting**: When input text exceeds the token limit, it must be truncated or split into multiple segments. This affects how the text is fed into the model and can impact the model's ability to understand long documents or conversations.

**Context Windows**

- **Definition**: The context window refers to the specific span of text the model considers when generating a response or making a prediction. It is a subset of the total tokens being processed, focused on the relevant portion of text at any given moment.

- **Relevance**: The context window is crucial for the model's comprehension and coherence. It determines how much context the model uses to generate each part of its output.

- **Sliding Window Technique**: In some applications, a sliding window technique is used, where the context window moves across the text to include different parts of the input over multiple passes. This helps in processing long texts by maintaining relevant context throughout the generation process.

## 4.2.2 Key Differences Between Token Limits and Context Windows

1. **Scope**

    - **Token Limits**: Refer to the overall capacity of the model in terms of how many tokens it can process at once

    - **Context Windows**: Refer to the portion of text the model actively uses for generating responses at any given point within the token limit

2. **Function**

- **Token Limits**: Set the boundary for input size, beyond which the text must be truncated or split

- **Context Windows**: Determine the active context for the model's operations, influencing how well the model understands and generates text

3. **Usage**

- **Token Limits**: Are a hard constraint imposed by the model's architecture

- **Context Windows**: Are more about the model's operational strategy within the given token limits, impacting the quality and relevance of the output

Understanding both token limits and context windows is essential for effectively utilizing NLP models, especially when dealing with large datasets or generating long-form content. In the following sections, we will delve deeper into how Spring AI and Retrieval-Augmented Generation (RAG) can address these challenges and enhance the capabilities of LLMs.

# 4.3 What Is Retrieval-Augmented Generation or RAG?

## 4.3.1 Introduction

Retrieval-Augmented Generation (RAG)[2] is an advanced technique designed to enhance the capabilities of Large Language Models (LLMs) by integrating them with external knowledge sources. This approach

---

[2] Retrieval-Augmented Generation for Knowledge-Intensive NLP Tasks: https://arxiv.org/abs/2005.11401

addresses several challenges inherent to LLMs, such as hallucinations, outdated knowledge, and a lack of transparent, traceable reasoning processes. By combining intrinsic knowledge from LLMs with external databases, RAG significantly improves the accuracy and credibility of generated content, making it particularly effective for knowledge-intensive tasks.

### Key Components of RAG

1. **Retrieval**: The system retrieves relevant information from an external knowledge base using semantic similarity calculations. This step is crucial in reducing the likelihood of the model generating factually incorrect content.

2. **Generation**: The retrieved information is then combined with the user's query to generate a more accurate and contextually relevant response. This process leverages the strengths of both the LLM and the external knowledge sources.

3. **Augmentation**: This involves continuous updates and the integration of domain-specific information to ensure the LLM remains current and capable of handling a wide range of queries.

### Evolution of RAG (Yunfan Gao, 2024)

- **Naive RAG**: The initial stage, characterized by a straightforward retrieval-read approach. This involved basic indexing, retrieval, and generation processes but faced limitations in retrieval precision and generation relevance.

- **Advanced RAG**: Introduced improvements such as preretrieval and postretrieval optimization, fine-grained segmentation, and the incorporation of metadata to enhance indexing and retrieval quality.

- **Modular RAG**: The most flexible and adaptable stage, which includes various specialized modules to refine retrieval and processing capabilities. This approach supports iterative and adaptive retrieval, allowing for more sophisticated and contextually aware responses.

RAG has rapidly developed into a key technology for advancing LLMs, making them more suitable for real-world applications, including chatbots, question answering, and various domain-specific tasks. The ongoing evolution of RAG focuses on overcoming current challenges and exploring new research avenues to further enhance its capabilities and applicability.

## 4.3.2 Detailed Overview of Naive RAG, Advanced RAG, and Modular RAG[3]

### Naive RAG

**Overview:** Naive RAG represents the earliest implementation of Retrieval-Augmented Generation. This approach primarily focuses on enhancing LLMs by incorporating additional knowledge from external sources through a simple retrieve-read mechanism. It consists of three main steps: indexing, retrieval, and generation (see Figure 4-1).

---

[3] Retrieval-Augmented Generation for Large Language Models: A Survey: https://arxiv.org/abs/2312.10997

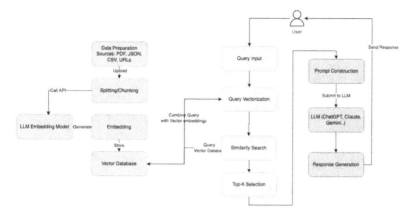

***Figure 4-1.*** *Naive RAG process*

**Process**

1. **Indexing**

   - Raw data from various formats (PDF, HTML, Word, etc.) is cleaned and converted into a uniform plain text format.

   - Text is segmented into smaller chunks to fit the context limitations of LLMs.

   - Chunks are encoded into vector representations using an embedding model and stored in a vector database.

2. **Retrieval**

   - Upon receiving a user query, the system transforms the query into a vector representation.

   - The system computes similarity scores between the query vector and the stored vectors of text chunks.

   - It retrieves the top K chunks most relevant to the query based on these similarity scores.

3. **Generation**

- The retrieved documents and the user query are combined into a prompt.

- The LLM generates a response based on this expanded prompt, potentially including conversational history for multiturn dialogues.

**Challenges**

- **Retrieval Precision:** The system might select misaligned or irrelevant chunks, missing crucial information.

- **Generation Quality:** The model can produce hallucinations or irrelevant, biased outputs.

- **Augmentation:** Integrating retrieved information can lead to redundancy, disjointed outputs, or repetitive responses.

# Advanced RAG

**Overview:** Advanced RAG introduces specific optimizations to address the limitations of Naive RAG. It enhances the retrieval quality by employing preretrieval and postretrieval strategies, optimizing indexing techniques, and improving the overall efficiency of the RAG system (see Figure 4-2).

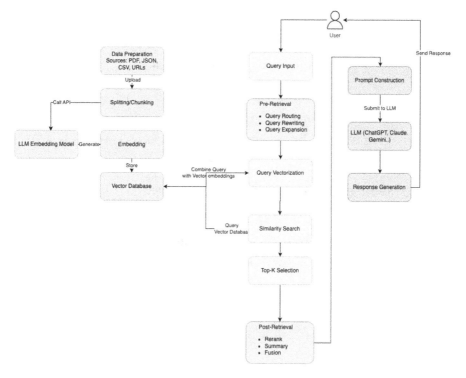

***Figure 4-2.*** *Advanced RAG process*

**Improvements**

1. **Preretrieval Optimization**

   - **Indexing Enhancements:** Improved data granularity, optimized index structures, added metadata, alignment optimization, and mixed retrieval

   - **Query Optimization:** Techniques like query rewriting, query transformation, and query expansion to make the user's query clearer and more suitable for retrieval tasks

2. **Postretrieval Optimization**

- **Re-ranking:** Re-ordering the retrieved information to prioritize the most relevant content

- **Context Compression:** Selecting essential information and emphasizing critical sections to avoid information overload and focus on key details

**Techniques**

- **Sliding Window Approach:** Fine-grained segmentation for better indexing

- **Metadata Utilization:** Adding metadata like timestamps, authors, and categories for more precise retrieval

- **Context Summarization:** Using smaller language models to summarize and compress the retrieved context before feeding it to LLMs

# Modular RAG

**Overview:** Modular RAG advances beyond Naive and Advanced RAG by offering enhanced adaptability and versatility. It incorporates various strategies for improving retrieval and processing capabilities, introducing new specialized modules and enabling end-to-end training across components.

**Features**

1. **New Modules**

- **Search Module:** Adapts to specific scenarios, enabling direct searches across diverse data sources

- **RAG-Fusion:** Uses a multiquery strategy for expanded user queries, employing parallel vector searches and intelligent re-ranking

- **Memory Module:** Creates an unbounded memory pool to guide retrieval

- **Routing:** Selects optimal pathways for queries, whether involving summarization, specific database searches, or merging different information streams

- **Predict Module:** Reduces redundancy by generating context directly through LLM

- **Task Adapter Module:** Tailors RAG to various downstream tasks, automating prompt retrieval for zero-shot inputs and creating task-specific retrievers through few-shot query generation

2. **New Patterns**

- **Rewrite-Retrieve-Read:** Leverages LLM's capabilities to refine retrieval queries through a rewriting module and a LM-feedback mechanism

- **Generate-Read:** Replaces traditional retrieval with LLM-generated content

- **Recite-Read:** Emphasizes retrieval from model weights for knowledge-intensive tasks

- **Hybrid Retrieval Strategies:** Integrates keyword, semantic, and vector searches to cater to diverse queries

**Advantages**

- **Flexibility:** Modular RAG supports both sequential processing and integrated end-to-end training, allowing for dynamic adjustments based on specific needs.

- **Adaptability:** It can integrate with other technologies like fine-tuning or reinforcement learning, enhancing the overall effectiveness of the RAG system.

- **Scalability:** Modular architecture allows for easy scalability and integration of new modules, facilitating continuous improvement and adaptation to emerging challenges.

**Overall, Modular RAG represents the cutting edge of Retrieval-Augmented Generation, offering a robust framework that can adapt to various tasks and scenarios with improved accuracy, efficiency, and scalability.**

# 4.4  RAG in the Context of Private Data (Enterprise Context)

**Introduction**

In an enterprise context, Retrieval-Augmented Generation (RAG) systems offer significant potential to enhance productivity, decision-making, and customer service by leveraging both internal and external data. Here are some key advantages.

## 4.4.1  Benefits of RAG in Enterprise Context

1. **Enhanced Information Accuracy and Relevance**

   - **Access to Proprietary Data**: RAG allows enterprises to integrate their specific, proprietary data into the model's responses, ensuring that the information provided is accurate and tailored to the organization's unique needs.

- **Up-to-Date Information**: By dynamically retrieving the latest data, RAG ensures that the information used in responses is current, avoiding the pitfalls of outdated or irrelevant pretrained data.

2. **Improved Decision-Making**

   - **Contextualized Responses**: RAG combines the context of the query with relevant documents or data points, providing more comprehensive and contextually relevant answers. This aids in better decision-making processes by giving employees access to precise and relevant information.

   - **Comprehensive Analysis**: The ability to retrieve and integrate data from multiple sources allows for a more holistic view, supporting more thorough analysis and informed decisions.

3. **Scalability and Efficiency**

   - **Handling Large Data Volumes**: RAG can efficiently handle large volumes of data, making it suitable for enterprises with extensive datasets. It can retrieve relevant information quickly without being limited by the model's token limits or context windows.

   - **Reduced Manual Effort**: Automating the retrieval and generation process reduces the need for manual data searches and analyses, saving time and resources for employees.

4. **Personalization and Customization**

- **Tailored Responses**: By leveraging specific enterprise data, RAG can generate responses that are highly personalized and relevant to the particular needs of the business, enhancing customer service and internal support.

- **Adaptability**: RAG systems can be fine-tuned and customized to meet the unique requirements of different departments or use cases within the enterprise, ensuring that each team gets the most relevant information for their needs.

5. **Enhanced Knowledge Management**

- **Knowledge Retention**: RAG systems can be integrated with enterprise knowledge bases, ensuring that valuable information is easily retrievable and not lost over time.

- **Improved Training and Onboarding**: New employees can benefit from instant access to relevant information and context, improving training and onboarding processes.

6. **Cost Efficiency**

- **Optimized Resource Utilization**: By automating data retrieval and generation tasks, RAG helps optimize the use of human resources, allowing employees to focus on higher-value tasks.

- **Reduced Operational Costs**: Efficient information retrieval can lead to significant cost savings in terms of time and effort required to gather and analyze data.

7. **Enhanced Collaboration**

- **Unified Information Access**: RAG systems can provide a unified platform for accessing information across different departments, improving collaboration and ensuring that all team members have access to the same, up-to-date data.

- **Cross-Departmental Insights**: By integrating data from various sources, RAG can provide insights that are beneficial across different departments, fostering a more collaborative and informed working environment.

# 4.4.2  Challenges in Deploying RAG

However, deploying RAG in enterprise settings comes with unique challenges related to accuracy, relevancy, and privacy.

**Issues with Accuracy**

1. **Data Quality**

- **Inconsistent Data**: Enterprise data is often collected from various sources and formats, leading to inconsistencies that can affect the accuracy of the retrieval and generation processes.

- **Outdated Information**: Internal databases might contain outdated information, which can lead to inaccurate or irrelevant responses.

2. **Model Limitations**

- **Hallucinations**: Even with RAG, LLMs can generate information that seems plausible but is factually incorrect, which can be problematic in critical enterprise applications.

- **Context Misunderstanding**: The model might misinterpret the context of a query, especially in specialized domains, leading to inaccurate responses.

## Issues with Relevancy

1. **Query Understanding**

   - **Ambiguous Queries**: Enterprise queries often involve complex, domain-specific language that can be ambiguous, leading to less relevant retrieval results.

   - **Incomplete Queries**: Users might provide incomplete information in their queries, making it difficult for the RAG system to retrieve the most relevant data.

2. **Document Relevance**

   - **Noise in Data**: Large volumes of internal data can include irrelevant documents that clutter search results, reducing the relevancy of retrieved information.

   - **Redundancy**: Multiple documents containing similar information can be retrieved, causing redundancy and inefficiency in the response generation process.

3. **Context Sensitivity**

   - **Dynamic Contexts**: Enterprise environments are dynamic, with context changing rapidly. Ensuring the relevancy of retrieved information in such a fluid setting can be challenging.

- **User-Specific Relevance**: Different users might require different information based on their roles and tasks, necessitating personalized retrieval mechanisms.

**Issues with Privacy**

1. **Data Security**

   - **Confidential Information**: Enterprises handle sensitive information (e.g., financial data, personal employee details) that must be protected from unauthorized access.

   - **Data Breaches**: Integrating RAG with enterprise data systems increases the risk of data breaches if not properly secured.

2. **Compliance**

   - **Regulatory Requirements**: Enterprises must comply with regulations like the General Data Protection Regulation (GDPR), HIPAA, and others that mandate strict data handling and privacy practices.

   - **Audit Trails**: Maintaining comprehensive audit trails for data access and usage is essential to meet compliance requirements but can be complex in a RAG system.

3. **User Privacy**

   - **Anonymization**: Ensuring that personal data is anonymized in the retrieval process to protect user privacy while still providing relevant information

- **Access Controls**: Implementing robust access controls to ensure that only authorized personnel can retrieve sensitive information

# 4.4.3 Mitigation Strategies

1. **Improving Data Quality**

   - **Data Cleaning**: Regularly cleaning and updating internal databases to ensure high-quality, consistent data

   - **Automated Data Validation**: Implementing automated tools to validate data integrity and accuracy before it is used in the RAG system

2. **Enhancing Model Accuracy**

   - **Domain-Specific Training**: Fine-tuning LLMs with domain-specific data to improve understanding and accuracy in specialized contexts

   - **Human-in-the-Loop**: Incorporating human oversight in the generation process to verify and correct the model's outputs

3. **Optimizing Relevance**

   - **Advanced Query Processing**: Using advanced natural language processing techniques to better understand and disambiguate complex queries

   - **Relevance Feedback**: Implementing mechanisms for users to provide feedback on the relevance of retrieved information, which can be used to improve future retrievals

- **Context-Aware Retrieval**: Developing context-aware retrieval models that adapt to changing enterprise contexts and user-specific needs

4. **Ensuring Privacy and Security**

- **Data Encryption**: Encrypting data both in transit and at rest to protect against unauthorized access

- **Access Controls and Audits**: Implementing strict access controls and regular audits to monitor data access and ensure compliance with privacy regulations

- **Privacy-Preserving Techniques**: Using techniques like differential privacy to ensure that sensitive information is protected during the retrieval and generation processes

- **Compliance Management**: Establishing a compliance management framework to continuously monitor and enforce regulatory requirements

**Conclusion**

While RAG offers powerful capabilities for leveraging private enterprise data, addressing issues related to accuracy, relevancy, and privacy is crucial for its effective deployment. By implementing robust data management, model optimization, and privacy-preserving strategies, enterprises can harness the full potential of RAG systems while safeguarding their critical information assets.

# 4.5 RAG Pipelines

## 4.5.1 What Is a RAG Pipeline?

A RAG pipeline consists of several sequential stages that together form a robust framework for enhancing the performance of Large Language Models (LLMs). The core idea is to augment the generative capabilities of LLMs by incorporating relevant information retrieved from external knowledge sources. This process involves three primary steps: retrieval, generation, and integration.

1. **Retrieval**

    - The pipeline begins by retrieving relevant documents or information chunks from an external database or knowledge source. This is typically done using a vector search based on semantic similarity, ensuring that the retrieved information closely matches the query's context and content.

2. **Generation**

    - Once the relevant information is retrieved, it is combined with the original query to create a comprehensive prompt. This prompt is then fed into a generative model, such as GPT-3 or GPT-4, which produces a response that leverages both its pretrained knowledge and the retrieved context.

3. **Integration**

    - The final step involves integrating the generated response with the retrieved information to produce a coherent and contextually accurate answer. This step may include additional processing, such as re-ranking retrieved documents, filtering irrelevant information, or fine-tuning the generative model to align with the specific requirements of the task.

## Advantages of RAG Pipelines

- **Enhanced Accuracy:** By leveraging external knowledge sources, RAG pipelines can significantly improve the accuracy of generated responses, reducing the likelihood of hallucinations and incorrect information.

- **Contextual Relevance:** The retrieval component ensures that the information used in generation is highly relevant to the query, leading to more contextually appropriate responses.

- **Up-to-Date Information:** RAG pipelines can access the latest information from external sources, making them suitable for tasks that require current and dynamic knowledge.

- **Flexibility and Adaptability:** The modular nature of RAG pipelines allows for easy integration of different retrieval and generative models, enabling customization for various applications and domains.

## Applications of RAG Pipelines

- **Question Answering:** Providing precise answers to complex queries by retrieving relevant information from large knowledge bases

- **Document Summarization:** Generating concise summaries of long documents by incorporating key points retrieved from the text

- **Interactive Dialogues:** Enhancing conversational agents and chatbots by supplying them with relevant information to produce more engaging and informative dialogues

- **Research and Content Creation:** Assisting researchers and content creators by providing accurate and contextually relevant information on demand

In summary, RAG pipelines represent a significant advancement in the field of NLP, offering a powerful framework for combining the strengths of retrieval systems and generative models. Their ability to produce accurate, relevant, and up-to-date responses makes them an invaluable tool for a wide range of applications, from customer service to academic research.

# 4.5.2  RAG Pipelines: From Simple to Complex

## Basic RAG Pipeline

**Components**

- **Prompt Creation**: A simple prompt is generated based on user input.

- **Retrieval System**: Basic keyword-based search retrieves relevant documents from a predefined dataset.

- **Generation Model**: A language model (e.g., GPT-3) generates responses using the retrieved documents and the initial prompt.

**Process**

1. **User Query**: The user inputs a query.

2. **Keyword Search**: The system performs a keyword-based search on a fixed dataset.

3. **Document Retrieval**: Relevant documents are retrieved based on keyword matching.

4. **Response Generation**: The language model uses the retrieved documents to generate a response.

**Example Use Case**: Customer service FAQs where common questions are matched with preexisting answers.

# Intermediate RAG Pipeline

**Components**

- **Advanced Query Processing**: NLP techniques such as named entity recognition (NER) and part-of-speech tagging enhance the query.

- **Vector Search**: A vector database (e.g., FAISS) retrieves documents based on semantic similarity rather than keywords.

- **Contextual Response Generation**: The generation model takes both the user query and the retrieved documents into account for a more coherent response.

**Process**

1. **User Query**: The user inputs a query.

2. **Query Enhancement**: NLP techniques process the query to extract key entities and context.

3. **Semantic Search**: The enhanced query is used to perform a semantic search in a vector database.

4. **Document Retrieval**: Documents with high semantic similarity are retrieved.

5. **Response Generation**: The language model generates a response using both the query and the retrieved documents.

**Example Use Case**: Technical support where specific details and context from user queries need to be understood and matched with relevant documentation.

# Advanced RAG Pipeline

**Components**

- **Complex Query Understanding**: Utilizes deep learning models for query understanding, capable of handling ambiguous and incomplete queries

- **Hybrid Retrieval System**: Combines keyword search, semantic search, and domain-specific databases for comprehensive document retrieval

- **Context-Aware Generation**: Incorporates user history, context, and personalization for generating highly relevant responses

- **Feedback Loop**: Continuous learning from user feedback to improve the retrieval and generation processes

**Process**

1. **User Query**: The user inputs a query.

2. **Advanced Query Processing**: Deep learning models process the query to understand intent, context, and entities.

3. **Hybrid Search**: The query is used to perform both keyword and semantic searches across multiple databases.

4. **Document Retrieval**: A diverse set of documents from various sources are retrieved and ranked by relevance.

5. **Contextual Integration**: The user's history and current context are integrated into the response generation process.

6. **Response Generation**: The language model generates a personalized and context-aware response.

7. **Feedback Incorporation**: User feedback is used to refine future responses and improve the system.

**Example Use Case**: Personalized virtual assistants for enterprises, where the system needs to understand complex queries, integrate various data sources, and provide tailored responses based on user history and preferences.

## Summary

- **Basic RAG Pipeline**: Suitable for straightforward applications with limited complexity, relying on keyword-based search and simple prompt generation

- **Intermediate RAG Pipeline**: Enhances retrieval with semantic search and better query processing, suitable for more detailed and context-sensitive applications

- **Advanced RAG Pipeline**: Incorporates deep learning, hybrid retrieval, and personalization, ideal for complex, dynamic environments requiring highly relevant and tailored responses

By understanding and implementing RAG pipelines from simple to complex, enterprises can progressively enhance their information retrieval and response generation capabilities, leading to better decision-making, improved customer service, and greater overall efficiency.

# 4.6  RAG with Spring AI

## 4.6.1  Introduction

Spring AI[4] simplifies the development of Retrieval-Augmented Generation (RAG) pipelines by providing a clear, structured approach. It divides the RAG process into two distinct phases:

1. **ETL (Extract, Transform, Load)**

2. **Query (Chat)**

**ETL Process**

The ETL process involves three key steps:

- **Reading Documents:** Collecting and loading documents from various sources

- **Transforming Documents:** Splitting and chunking the documents into manageable pieces

---

[4] Spring AI Docs: https://docs.spring.io/spring-ai/reference/index.html

- **Writing to the Vector Store:** Encoding these chunks into vector representations and storing them in a vector database

This ETL process is typically performed offline, separate from the query process, ensuring that the data is preprocessed and ready for efficient retrieval.

**Query Process**

The query process consists of the following steps:

- **User Input:** Receiving a user query through a prompt

- **Combining with Relevant Embeddings:** Retrieving relevant document chunks from the vector store based on the query

- **Generating Response:** Submitting the combined prompt to the LLM and generating a contextually accurate and relevant response

This method aligns with the principles of Naive RAG, ensuring a straightforward yet effective approach to integrating external knowledge with generative models.

Illustration of Spring AI's Implementation of Naive RAG

Spring AI's implementation of Naive RAG streamlines the process of building powerful and efficient RAG pipelines. By clearly separating the ETL and query phases, Spring AI allows developers to focus on optimizing each step, resulting in enhanced performance and accuracy in generating responses.

Figure 4-3 is an illustration of Spring AI's implementation of Naive RAG.

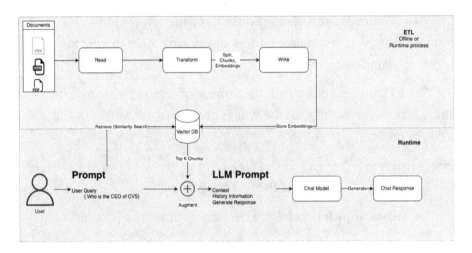

***Figure 4-3.*** *Spring AI's implementation of Naive RAG*

# 4.6.2 Let's Code

**Prerequisites**

Before we begin coding, ensure you have the following prerequisites set up:

1. **Postgres Database with pgvector**: Information on installation and configuration is available at `https://github.com/pgvector/pgvector`.

2. **OpenAI API Key**: Ensure you have a valid API key.

3. **Spring CLI**: Installation instructions are available at `https://docs.spring.io/spring-cli/reference/installation.html`.

4. **Latest JDK 17 and Above**[5]: Ensure you have the latest version of JDK installed.

---

[5] Spring Boot 3.x supports only Java 17 and above: `https://github.com/spring-projects/spring-boot/wiki/Spring-Boot-3.0-Release-Notes`

5. **Project Repository**: Clone the project from
   https://github.com/banup-kubeforce/
   health-rag.git.

**Creating a Project**

With Spring CLI, creating a project for RAG is straightforward since Spring AI provides a template project. You can create the project with a single line of code (see Listing 4-1).

***Listing 4-1.*** Spring Boot project generator for ai-rag

```
spring boot new  -- from ai-rag  -- name <name of your project>
```

Figure 4-4 shows the output after running *Listing 4-1*.

```
banup@banus-MacBook-Pro-2 Downloads % spring boot new --from ai-rag --name healthrag
Getting project from https://github.com/ai-7833/ai-examples
Created project in directory 'healthrag'
```

***Figure 4-4.*** *Execution of Spring Boot project generator*

The project structure as shown in Figure 4-5 gets created automatically.

***Figure 4-5.*** *Project structure upon execution of the Spring command using the Spring CLI*

The project structure will be automatically generated. You will need to modify the package name, prompts, and data to suit your needs.

### Customizing the Code

1. **Configuration File**

   Update the `application.yaml` or `application.properties` (shown in file with your connection parameters for your vector store).

   For Postgres:

***Listing 4-2.*** Application.yaml properties for data source

```
datasource:
    url: jdbc:postgresql://localhost:5432/vector_store
    username: postgres
    password: postgres
```

For Redis vector store:

***Listing 4-3.*** Application.yaml properties for Redis vector store

```
spring.ai.vectorstore.redis.uri=<your redis instance uri>
spring.ai.vectorstore.redis.index=<your index name>
spring.ai.vectorstore.redis.prefix=<your prefix>
```

2. **Add Data as PDFs**

   In the sample code, there is a PDF file Medicaid-wa-faqs.pdf that contains information on a healthcare tech company called Carina. You can use any PDF. In my example, I downloaded CVS's annual report as a PDF file and ran queries against it.

3. **Modifying the Prompt Template**

   Customize the prompt template (see Figure 4-6) to fit your use case. The default prompt template file is system-stuff.st.

***Figure 4-6.*** *Default prompt template system-stuff.st*

If you want to use CVS information instead of the default, you can copy and paste CVS's details into the data folder.

4. **Running the Spring Boot Application**

Start your Spring Boot application and call the /data/load endpoint using Postman.

This will the load the data in the vector database. See Figure 4-7.

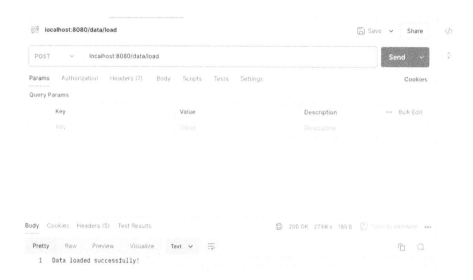

***Figure 4-7.*** *Postman UI showing the execution of the load method*

Verify that the data has been loaded into the vector
database by going to the Postgres admin console as
shown in Figure 4-8.

***Figure 4-8.*** *Postgres vector_store table contents view via pgAdmin UI*

Now you can run queries/prompts against the llm with the vector embeddings.

5. **Running Queries**

Run your query using GET from this URL: `http://localhost:8080/qa` (see Figure 4-9).

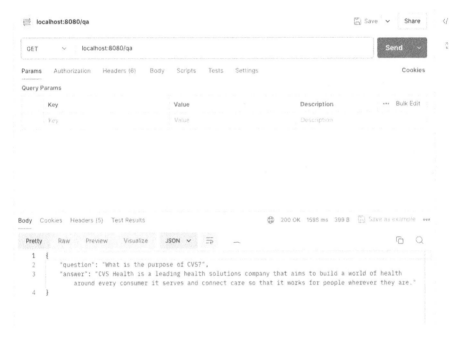

***Figure 4-9.*** *Postman UI showing the execution of the /qa api*

To modify your query, add parameters like this: localhost:8080/qa?question="Who is the CEO of CVS".

Figure 4-10 is an example of the output.

***Figure 4-10.*** *Postman UI showing the execution of /qa with parameters*

While the model can answer obvious questions, it may not handle more complex queries perfectly (e.g., "Who is Roger N. Farah?"). Nonetheless, Spring AI effectively processes documents into a vector store and facilitates querying without significant coding effort.

**Deep Dive into the Generated Code**

Let's review the key elements of the generated code and understand how it can be modified to meet our requirements.

**1) Dependencies**

Update the POM.xml file with the following key elements (see Listing 4-4).

***Listing 4-4.*** POM.xml showing the spring-ai-bom version

```
<artifactId>healthrag</artifactId>
      <version>0.0.1-SNAPSHOT</version>
      <name>healthrag</name>
      <description>Simple AI Application using OpenAPI Service
      for RAG</description>
      <properties>
            <java.version>17</java.version>
      </properties>
...
<dependency>
<groupId>org.springframework.ai</groupId>
<artifactId>spring-ai-bom</artifactId>
<version>0.8.1</version>
<type>pom</type>
<scope>import</scope>
</dependency>
```

Additional dependencies including pgvector and OpenAI libraries need to be added as shown in Listing 4-5.

***Listing 4-5.*** POM.xml with additional dependencies including starters for OpenAI, pgvector, and PDF document reader

```
<dependency>
<groupId>org.springframework.ai</groupId>
<artifactId>spring-ai-openai-spring-boot-starter</artifactId>
</dependency>
```

```
<dependency>
<groupId>org.springframework.ai</groupId>
<artifactId>spring-ai-pgvector-store-spring-boot-starter</
artifactId>
</dependency>

<dependency>
<groupId>org.springframework.ai</groupId>
<artifactId>spring-ai-pdf-document-reader</artifactId>
</dependency>
```

---

**Note**    You can change the pgvector store to the vector store of
your choice.

---

## 2) Relevant Code from GitHub

Of the code that is pulled from the GitHub via the Spring CLI command,
we will discuss the most relevant ones as these should be sufficient to run
your code. The Spring team has introduced additional code that handles
scenarios like prompt templates, VectorStoreRetriever, and other advanced
methods that are not relevant for our current example. The code will work
just fine with the following code bits.

### 2.1 Data Handlers

There are two classes that used to handle data. The DataLoadingService
and DataController.

### 2.1.1 DataLoadingService

This service loads data from a specified PDF document into a VectorStore
(see Listing 4-6).

***Listing 4-6.*** DataLoadingService.java code that uses the method load() to load data into vector_store

```
import org.slf4j.Logger;
import org.slf4j.LoggerFactory;
import org.springframework.ai.reader.ExtractedTextFormatter;
import org.springframework.ai.reader.pdf.PagePdfDocumentReader;
import org.springframework.ai.reader.pdf.config.
PdfDocumentReaderConfig;
import org.springframework.ai.transformer.splitter.
TokenTextSplitter;
import org.springframework.ai.vectorstore.VectorStore;
import org.springframework.beans.factory.annotation.Autowired;
import org.springframework.beans.factory.annotation.Value;
import org.springframework.core.io.Resource;
import org.springframework.stereotype.Service;
import org.springframework.util.Assert;

@Service
public class DataLoadingService {

        private static final Logger logger = LoggerFactory.
        getLogger(DataLoadingService.class);

        @Value("classpath:/data/CVS-Health-2023-Annual-
        Report.pdf")
        private Resource pdfResource;

        private final VectorStore vectorStore;

        @Autowired
        public DataLoadingService(VectorStore vectorStore) {
                Assert.notNull(vectorStore, "VectorStore must not
                be null.");
```

```java
        this.vectorStore = vectorStore;
    }

    public void load() {
        PagePdfDocumentReader pdfReader = new
        PagePdfDocumentReader(this.pdfResource,
                    PdfDocumentReaderConfig.builder()
                            .withPageExtractedTextFormatter(E
                            xtractedTextFormatter.builder()
                                    .withNumberOfBottom
                                    TextLinesToDelete(3)
                                    .withNumberOfTopPages
                                    ToSkipBeforeDelete(1)
                                    .build())
                            .withPagesPerDocument(1)
                            .build());

        var tokenTextSplitter = new TokenTextSplitter();

        logger.info(
                    "Parsing document, splitting, creating
                    embeddings and storing in vector
                    store...  this will take a while.");
        this.vectorStore.accept(tokenTextSplitter.
        apply(pdfReader.get()));
        logger.info("Done parsing document, splitting,
        creating embeddings and storing in vector store");

    }

}
```

This Java code defines a `DataLoadingService` class that loads data from a specified PDF document into a `VectorStore`. Let's break down what each part of the code does:

1. **Imports**

    - Imports necessary classes from various packages, including logging (`org.slf4j.Logger`, `org.slf4j.LoggerFactory`), PDF reading (`org.springframework.ai.reader.pdf.PagePdfDocumentReader`, `org.springframework.ai.reader.pdf.config.PdfDocumentReaderConfig`), text processing (`org.springframework.ai.transformer.splitter.TokenTextSplitter`), and Spring Framework components (`org.springframework.beans.factory.annotation.Autowired`, `org.springframework.beans.factory.annotation.Value`, `org.springframework.core.io.Resource`, `org.springframework.stereotype.Service`)

2. **Service Annotation (@Service)**

    - Marks the class `DataLoadingService` as a service component that should be automatically detected and registered as a Spring bean

3. **Logger Declaration**

    - Defines a static logger (`private static final Logger logger`) using SLF4J for logging messages related to `DataLoadingService`

4. **Field Declaration**

- Declares a field pdfResource annotated with @Value, which injects a classpath resource (classpath:/data/CVS-Health-2023-Annual-Report.pdf). This is where the PDF file to be processed is specified.

5. **Constructor**

- Constructor injection (@Autowired) is used to inject a VectorStore instance into the service. It ensures that the VectorStore dependency is not null.

6. **Method load()**

- This method performs the actual data loading process:

  - Creates a PagePdfDocumentReader instance (pdfReader) to read the PDF document specified by pdfResource. It configures how text extraction should be handled (e.g., skipping pages, deleting lines).

  - Initializes a TokenTextSplitter instance (tokenTextSplitter) to split extracted text into tokens.

  - Logs an info message indicating the start of the parsing and embedding process.

  - Applies the tokenTextSplitter to the data extracted by pdfReader and stores the result in vectorStore.

  - Logs a message indicating the completion of the data loading process.

**Summary**

The DataLoadingService class is designed to load textual data from a specific PDF document (CVS-Health-2023-Annual-Report.pdf). It uses Spring Framework components for dependency injection (@Autowired, @Value) and PDF handling (PagePdfDocumentReader). The extracted text is split into tokens and stored in a VectorStore. Logging (logger) is used to provide information about the progress and completion of the data loading process. This service is likely intended to be used in an application where PDF data needs to be processed and stored for further analysis or manipulation.

### 2.1.2 DataController

This piece of code (see Listing 4-7) exposes endpoints for loading, counting, and deleting of data.

***Listing 4-7.*** DataController.java that exposes endpoints for data loading, deleting, and counting of rows

```
import org.springframework.beans.factory.annotation.Autowired;
import org.springframework.http.HttpStatus;
import org.springframework.http.ResponseEntity;
import org.springframework.jdbc.core.JdbcTemplate;
import org.springframework.web.bind.annotation.*;

@RestController
@RequestMapping("/data")
public class DataController {

    private final DataLoadingService dataLoadingService;

    private final JdbcTemplate jdbcTemplate;

    @Autowired
    public DataController(DataLoadingService
    dataLoadingService, JdbcTemplate jdbcTemplate) {
```

```java
        this.dataLoadingService = dataLoadingService;
        this.jdbcTemplate = jdbcTemplate;
}

@PostMapping("/load")
public ResponseEntity<String> load() {
        try {
                this.dataLoadingService.load();
                return ResponseEntity.ok("Data loaded
                successfully!");
        }
        catch (Exception e) {
                return ResponseEntity.status(HttpStatus.
                INTERNAL_SERVER_ERROR)
                        .body("An error occurred while loading
                        data: " + e.getMessage());
        }
}

@GetMapping("/count")
public int count() {
        String sql = "SELECT COUNT(*) FROM vector_store";
        return jdbcTemplate.queryForObject(sql,
        Integer.class);
}

@PostMapping("/delete")
public void delete() {
        String sql = "DELETE FROM vector_store";
        jdbcTemplate.update(sql);
}

@ExceptionHandler(Exception.class)
```

```
public ResponseEntity<String> handleException
(Exception e) {
        return ResponseEntity.status(HttpStatus.INTERNAL_
        SERVER_ERROR)
                .body("An error occurred in the controller: "
                + e.getMessage());
    }

}
```

This Java code defines a RESTful controller (DataController) that interacts with a DataLoadingService to load data from a PDF into a database using JDBC operations. Here's a breakdown of what each part of the code does:

1. **Imports**

   - Imports necessary classes from Spring Framework (org.springframework.beans.factory. annotation.Autowired, org.springframework. http.HttpStatus, org.springframework.http. ResponseEntity, org.springframework.jdbc. core.JdbcTemplate, org.springframework.web. bind.annotation.*) for dependency injection, HTTP response handling, JDBC operations, and request mapping

2. **RestController Annotation (@RestController)**

   - Indicates that this class is a REST controller, which means it handles HTTP requests and automatically serializes responses as JSON/XML (typically JSON by default)

3. **RequestMapping Annotation** (`@RequestMapping("/data")`)

   - Maps all HTTP requests with the base URL `/data` to this controller

4. **Constructor**

   - Constructor injection (`@Autowired`) is used to inject dependencies into the controller:

     - `DataLoadingService dataLoadingService`: An instance of `DataLoadingService` used to initiate the data loading process

     - `JdbcTemplate jdbcTemplate`: An instance of `JdbcTemplate` used to execute JDBC operations

5. **Method** `load()`

   - HTTP POST endpoint (`@PostMapping("/load")`) mapped to `/data/load`

   - Calls `dataLoadingService.load()` to trigger the data loading process

   - If successful, returns a `ResponseEntity` with status OK (200) and a success message

   - If an exception occurs during loading, catches the exception (`Exception e`) and returns a `ResponseEntity` with an internal server error status (500) and an error message including the exception message

6. **Method** `count()`

   - HTTP GET endpoint (`@GetMapping("/count")`) mapped to `/data/count`

- Executes a SQL query (SELECT COUNT(*) FROM vector_store) using jdbcTemplate. queryForObject() to retrieve the count of records in the vector_store table

- Returns the count as an integer

7. **Method** delete()

- HTTP POST endpoint (@PostMapping("/delete")) mapped to /data/delete

- Executes a SQL delete statement (DELETE FROM vector_store) using jdbcTemplate.update() to delete all records from the vector_store table

8. **ExceptionHandler Method** handleException()

- An exception handler (@ExceptionHandler (Exception.class)) that catches any Exception thrown within the controller

- Returns a ResponseEntity with an internal server error status (500) and an error message including the exception message

**Summary**

The DataController class provides a REST API to manage data loading from a PDF document into a database (vector_store) using Spring Framework components:

- It has endpoints for loading data (/data/load), retrieving the count of records (/data/count), and deleting all records (/data/delete).

- It handles exceptions gracefully and returns appropriate HTTP responses (200 OK for successful operations, 500 Internal Server Error for errors).

- Dependencies like DataLoadingService and
  JdbcTemplate are injected into the controller through
  constructor-based dependency injection (@Autowired).

This controller is designed to integrate PDF data loading functionality (DataLoadingService) with database operations (JdbcTemplate) through a RESTful API, making it suitable for applications where data extraction and persistence are required.

## 2.2 Prompt Handlers
### 2.2.1 QAController

*Listing 4-8.* QAController.java that exposes endpoints for question and answers against the LLM

```
import org.springframework.beans.factory.annotation.Autowired;
import org.springframework.web.bind.annotation.GetMapping;
import org.springframework.web.bind.annotation.RequestMapping;
import org.springframework.web.bind.annotation.RequestParam;
import org.springframework.web.bind.annotation.RestController;

import java.util.LinkedHashMap;
import java.util.Map;

@RestController
@RequestMapping("/qa")
public class QAController {

    private final QAService qaService;

    @Autowired
    public QAController(QAService qaService) {
        this.qaService = qaService;
    }

    @GetMapping
    public Map completion(
```

```
                @RequestParam(value = "question",
                defaultValue = "What is the purpose of CVS?")
                String question,
                @RequestParam(value = "stuffit", defaultValue
                = "true") boolean stuffit) {
        String answer = this.qaService.generate(question,
        stuffit);
        Map map = new LinkedHashMap();
        map.put("question", question);
        map.put("answer", answer);
        return map;
    }

}
```

This Java code defines a RESTful controller (QAController) that handles requests related to a question and answer (QA) service (QAService). Here's a breakdown of what each part of the code does:

1. **Imports**

    - Imports necessary classes from Spring Framework (org.springframework.beans.factory. annotation.Autowired, org.springframework. web.bind.annotation.*) for dependency injection, request mapping, and handling annotations

    - Imports java.util.LinkedHashMap and java. util.Map for constructing response data structures

2. **RestController Annotation** (@RestController)

    - Indicates that this class is a REST controller, which means it handles HTTP requests and automatically serializes responses as JSON/XML (typically JSON by default)

3. **RequestMapping Annotation** (@RequestMapping("/qa"))

   - Maps all HTTP requests with the base URL /qa to this controller

4. **Constructor**

   - Constructor injection (@Autowired) is used to inject QAService into the controller:

     - QAService qaService: An instance of QAService used to generate answers based on questions

5. **Method** completion()

   - HTTP GET endpoint (@GetMapping) mapped to /qa.

   - Accepts two request parameters:

     - question: Represents the question to be answered. Defaults to "What is the purpose of CVS?" if not provided

     - stuffit: Represents a boolean flag. Defaults to true if not provided

   - Calls qaService.generate(question, stuffit) to generate an answer based on the provided question and stuffit flag.

   - Constructs a LinkedHashMap named map, adds question and answer entries to it, and returns the map.

   - The response is automatically serialized to JSON format due to the @RestController annotation.

## Summary

The QAController class provides a simple REST API to retrieve answers for questions using a QAService:

- It has a single endpoint (/qa) that accepts parameters for question and stuffit.

- The completion() method handles GET requests, where:

  - question specifies the question to answer (defaulting to a predefined question)

  - stuffit is a boolean flag (defaulting to true)

- Upon receiving a request, it delegates the question and flag to qaService.generate(question, stuffit) to retrieve an answer.

- It constructs a JSON response containing the original question and the generated answer.

    This controller is suitable for applications where there is a need to provide a straightforward question and answer functionality over HTTP, leveraging Spring's REST capabilities and dependency injection for service integration.

### 2.2.2 QAService

*Listing 4-9.*  QAService.java that takes in the prompt and returns a response from the LLM

```
import org.slf4j.Logger;
import org.slf4j.LoggerFactory;
import org.springframework.ai.chat.ChatClient;
import org.springframework.ai.chat.ChatResponse;
import org.springframework.ai.chat.prompt.SystemPromptTemplate;
import org.springframework.ai.chat.messages.Message;
```

```
import org.springframework.ai.chat.messages.UserMessage;
import org.springframework.ai.chat.prompt.Prompt;
import org.springframework.ai.document.Document;
import org.springframework.ai.vectorstore.VectorStore;
import org.springframework.beans.factory.annotation.Autowired;
import org.springframework.beans.factory.annotation.Value;
import org.springframework.core.io.Resource;
import org.springframework.stereotype.Service;

import java.util.List;
import java.util.Map;
import java.util.stream.Collectors;

@Service
public class QAService {

    private static final Logger logger = LoggerFactory.
    getLogger(QAService.class);

    @Value("classpath:/prompts/system-qa.st")
    private Resource qaSystemPromptResource;

    @Value("classpath:/prompts/system-chatbot.st")
    private Resource chatbotSystemPromptResource;

    private final ChatClient chatClient;

    private final VectorStore vectorStore;

    @Autowired
    public QAService(ChatClient chatClient, VectorStore
    vectorStore) {
        this.chatClient = chatClient;
        this.vectorStore = vectorStore;
    }
```

```
public String generate(String message, boolean stuffit) {
    Message systemMessage = getSystemMessage(message,
    stuffit);
    UserMessage userMessage = new UserMessage(message);
    Prompt prompt = new Prompt(List.of(systemMessage,
    userMessage));

    logger.info("Asking AI model to reply to question.");
    ChatResponse chatResponse = chatClient.call(prompt);
    logger.info("AI responded.");
    return chatResponse.getResult().getOutput().getContent();
}

private Message getSystemMessage(String query, boolean
stuffit) {
    if (stuffit) {
        logger.info("Retrieving relevant documents");
        List<Document> similarDocuments = vectorStore.
        similaritySearch(query);
        logger.info(String.format("Found %s relevant
        documents.", similarDocuments.size()));
        String documents = similarDocuments.
        stream().map(entry -> entry.getContent()).
        collect(Collectors.joining("\n"));
        SystemPromptTemplate systemPromptTemplate = new
        SystemPromptTemplate(this.qaSystemPromptResource);
        return systemPromptTemplate.createMessage(Map.
        of("documents", documents));
    } else {
        logger.info("Not stuffing the prompt, using generic
        prompt");
```

```
        return new SystemPromptTemplate(this.
        chatbotSystemPromptResource).createMessage();
    }
  }
}
```

This Java code defines a service (QAService) that interacts with a chat client (ChatClient) and a vector store (VectorStore) to generate responses based on user messages. Let's break down what each part of the code does:

1. **Imports**

    - Imports necessary classes from Spring Framework (org.springframework.beans.factory. annotation.Autowired, org.springframework. beans.factory.annotation.Value, org. springframework.core.io.Resource, org. springframework.stereotype.Service) for dependency injection and service annotations

    - Imports various classes related to chat functionality (org.springframework.ai.chat.*, org. springframework.ai.document.Document, org. springframework.ai.vectorstore.VectorStore) for handling messages, prompts, and vector operations

    - Imports logging utilities (org.slf4j.Logger, org. slf4j.LoggerFactory) for logging messages

2. **Service Annotation** (@Service)

    - Marks the class QAService as a service component that should be automatically detected and registered as a Spring bean

3. **Logger Declaration**

- Defines a static logger (`private static final Logger logger`) using SLF4J for logging messages related to `QAService`

4. **Field Declarations**

- `qaSystemPromptResource` and `chatbotSystemPromptResource`: Resources (`Resource` type) for system prompts loaded from classpath files (`system-qa.st` and `system-chatbot.st`)

- `chatClient`: An instance of `ChatClient` used to interact with the AI model

- `vectorStore`: An instance of `VectorStore` used for vector operations, likely related to document similarity search

5. **Constructor**

- Constructor injection (`@Autowired`) is used to inject dependencies into the service:

    - `ChatClient chatClient`: An instance of `ChatClient` used for making chat-related calls

    - `VectorStore vectorStore`: An instance of `VectorStore` used for vector operations

6. **Method** `generate (String message, boolean stuffit)`

- Public method that generates a response based on a user message and a boolean flag `stuffit`

- Constructs a `Prompt` object using a `Message` from `getSystemMessage(message, stuffit)` and a `UserMessage` created from the user-provided message

- Logs an info message indicating the initiation of the AI model's response

- Calls `chatClient.call(prompt)` to retrieve a `ChatResponse`

- Logs an info message indicating the AI's response

- Returns the output content from `chatResponse.getResult().getOutput().getContent()` as a string

7. **Method** `getSystemMessage(String query, boolean stuffit)`

- Private method that generates a `Message` object based on the query and `stuffit` flag

- If `stuffit` is true:

  - Logs an info message indicating retrieval of relevant documents

  - Uses `vectorStore.similaritySearch(query)` to find similar documents

  - Converts the documents into a string (`documents`) joined by newline characters

  - Uses `SystemPromptTemplate` and `qaSystemPromptResource` to create a message with the documents as parameters

- If `stuffit` is false:

  - Logs an info message indicating a generic prompt usage

  - Uses `SystemPromptTemplate` and `chatbotSystemPromptResource` to create a generic message

  - Returns the generated `Message` object

171

**Summary**

The QAService class encapsulates logic to interact with a chat client and a vector store to handle user queries and generate responses:

- It provides a generate() method that takes a user message and a flag (stuffit) to determine how to formulate the response.

- Depending on the stuffit flag, it either searches for similar documents and uses them to formulate a response or uses a generic prompt template.

- Logging is used extensively to track the flow of operations within the service.

- This service is designed to integrate with an AI model (ChatClient) and a vector-based storage (VectorStore) to provide intelligent responses to user queries, potentially tailored based on document similarity.

**Summary**

In this section, we looked at ingesting a PDF document, which is unstructured data. Leveraging the Spring AI framework, we were able to query the document with relative ease. In the next section, we will explore how to ingest a structured document such as a JSON file.

# 4.7 Ingesting Structured Data with Spring AI

## 4.7.1 Introduction

In Section 4.5, we explored how to ingest a PDF, an example of unstructured data. In this section, we will examine how to train LLMs on structured data, such as JSON files.

The process of ingestion or ETL is similar to that of PDF ingestion, but the way embeddings are created is slightly different.

For our example, we will use `bikes.json`, which is available at `https://github.com/banup-kubeforce/health-rag/blob/main/src/main/resources/data/bikes.json`.

`bikes.json` includes the following fields: `name`, `shortDescription`, `description`, `price`, and `tags`.

## 4.7.2 Let's Code

We will build upon the code used in Section 4.5 with a few modifications:

1. Add a `loadJson` method to the `DataLoadingService` class (see Listing 4-10).

***Listing 4-10.*** loadJson() menthod to interact with JSON files

```
public void loadJson() {
    // read json file
    JsonReader jsonReader = new JsonReader(bikesResouce, new
    ProductMetadataGenerator(),
        "name","shortDescription", "description",
        "price","tags");

    // create document object
    List<Document> documents = jsonReader.get();

    // add to vectorstore
    vectorStore.add(documents);
}
```

Purpose of the Code

The loadJson method is designed to read data
from a JSON file, process it into a structured format,
and store it in a vector store for efficient retrieval.
Here's a step-by-step explanation of what this
method does:

1. *Initialize the JSON Reader*

   - The JsonReader is initialized with a resource
     pointing to the JSON file, a metadata generator
     (ProductMetadataGenerator), and a list of keys
     to extract from the JSON.

2. *Read and Process the JSON Data*

   - The get method of the JsonReader is
     called to read the JSON file and process it.
     The ProductMetadataGenerator is used
     to extract and format specific fields (name,
     shortDescription, description, price, and
     tags) from the JSON data.

3. *Store the Processed Data*

   - The processed data, now in the form of
     Document objects, is added to a vectorStore.
     This step stores the data in a way that it can be
     efficiently retrieved and queried later.

2. Introduce a new class, ProductMetadataGenerator
   (see Listing 4-11).

***Listing 4-11.*** ProductMedataGenerator.java that extracts specified metadata

```java
import org.springframework.ai.reader.JsonMetadataGenerator;

import java.util.Map;

public class ProductMetadataGenerator implements
JsonMetadataGenerator {

    @Override
    public Map<String, Object> generate(Map<String, Object>
    jsonMap) {
        return Map.of("name", jsonMap.get("name"),
                "shortDescription", jsonMap.
                get("shortDescription"));
    }

}
```

Purpose of the Code

The ProductMetadataGenerator class is designed to extract specific metadata from a JSON-like map structure. When the generate method is called with a map (representing a JSON object), it creates a new map containing only the nameand shortDescription entries from the original map. This is useful for scenarios where you need to extract and possibly transform certain fields from a JSON object for further processing or storage.

You can clone the repository from here https:// github.com/banup-kubeforce/health-rag. Run the project and call loadJson using Postman, as demonstrated below in Figure 4-11.

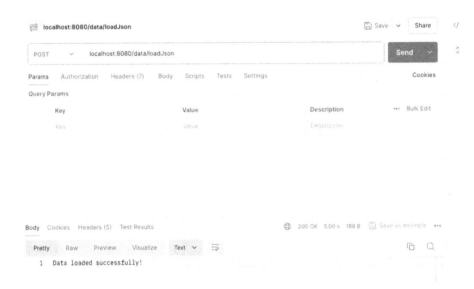

***Figure 4-11.*** *Postman UI showing the execution of loadJson*

3. Upon successful completion of the load, verify the vector table in Postgres. See Figure 4-12.

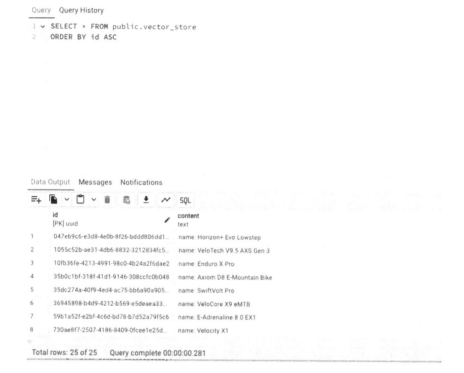

*Figure 4-12.*  *pgAdmin UI showing the contents of vector_store table after execution of jsonLoad()*

4.  With the data now in the vector database, you can begin your prompt session with the LLM as shown in Figure 4-13.

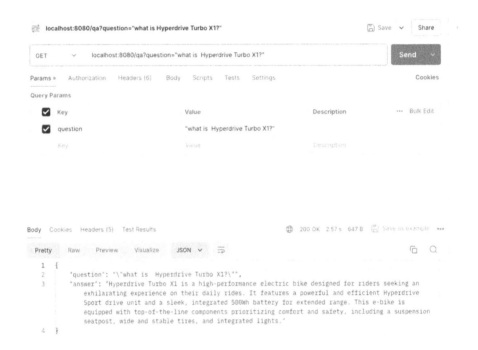

*Figure 4-13.* *Postman UI showing the results of the question posed*

# 4.8 Conclusion

In this chapter, we have thoroughly explored the intricacies of Spring
AI and Retrieval-Augmented Generation (RAG). We began with a
fundamental understanding of token limits and context windows in Large
Language Models (LLMs) and how these constraints impact the processing
and comprehension capabilities of these models.

We then delved into the concept of RAG, understanding its evolution
from Naive RAG to Advanced RAG and Modular RAG, highlighting the
enhancements and optimizations at each stage. The implementation of
RAG in the context of private enterprise data was discussed, emphasizing
the benefits such as enhanced information accuracy, improved decision-
making, scalability, personalization, and cost efficiency. We also addressed

the challenges related to accuracy, relevancy, and privacy, providing strategies to mitigate these issues.

Further, we outlined the structure and benefits of RAG pipelines, from simple to complex, showcasing their application in various scenarios. This included the development of basic, intermediate, and advanced RAG pipelines, each suited to different levels of complexity and specificity in information retrieval and response generation.

The practical implementation of RAG with Spring AI was demonstrated through the ETL (Extract, Transform, Load) and query processes. We covered the coding aspects, including setting up the project, configuring data sources, and modifying prompt templates to suit specific use cases. The example of ingesting unstructured data from a PDF document illustrated the ease of querying with Spring AI.

In the final section, we transitioned to the ingestion of structured data using a JSON file (`bikes.json`). We discussed the necessary modifications to the existing codebase, including adding a new method and class, and provided a practical example of loading and querying this data.

By the end of this chapter, you should have a comprehensive understanding of how to leverage Spring AI and RAG to enhance the capabilities of LLMs, enabling them to process and generate responses based on both unstructured and structured data efficiently. This knowledge is pivotal in harnessing the full potential of AI-driven solutions in various enterprise contexts, leading to more informed decision-making and optimized resource utilization.

# CHAPTER 5

# Conversational AI with Spring AI

## 5.1 Introduction

Many businesses and organizations rely on basic chatbots for customer interactions. However, these simple rule-based systems often fall short, frustrating users with their limited understanding and rigid responses. Traditional chatbots struggle to comprehend context, handle complex queries, or engage in nuanced dialogue, leaving customers feeling unheard and dissatisfied.

Conversational AI represents a significant leap forward, addressing many of these shortcomings. Unlike basic chatbots, advanced conversational AI systems can understand, process, and respond to human language in a natural and meaningful way. These technologies bring several key improvements:

1. **Contextual Understanding**: Conversational AI can grasp the nuances of language and maintain context throughout a conversation, leading to more coherent and relevant interactions.

2. **Adaptive Learning**: These systems can learn from interactions, continuously improving their responses and understanding over time.

© Banu Parasuraman 2024
B. Parasuraman, *Mastering Spring AI*, https://doi.org/10.1007/979-8-8688-1001-5_5

3. **Emotional Intelligence**: Advanced AI can detect sentiment and tone, allowing for more empathetic and appropriate responses.

4. **Multiturn Dialogue**: Conversational AI can engage in complex, multistep conversations, unlike simple chatbots that often struggle with follow-up questions.

5. **Personalization**: By analyzing user data and past interactions, these systems can provide tailored experiences and recommendations.

From more sophisticated virtual assistants to AI-powered customer service platforms, conversational AI is transforming the way we interact with technology, offering more natural, efficient, and satisfying experiences than traditional chatbots.

Spring AI, a robust framework for building AI applications, offers a powerful platform to develop and deploy conversational AI solutions. In this chapter, we will delve into the intricacies of creating conversational AI using Spring AI, with a particular focus on implementing Chain of Thought (CoT) prompting. CoT prompting allows for more nuanced and contextually aware interactions by mimicking the human thought process, leading to more accurate and satisfying responses.

We will also explore how to develop a custom chat interface to facilitate user interactions. By the end of this chapter, you will have a solid understanding of how to build and deploy a conversational AI system that can handle complex dialogues and provide meaningful user experiences.

Whether you are a developer looking to enhance your skill set, a business leader aiming to improve customer engagement, or an AI enthusiast eager to explore the latest advancements in the field, this chapter will provide you with the knowledge and tools to create cutting-edge conversational AI solutions.

# 5.2  Prompting Types in Conversational AI

Prompting is a fundamental aspect of conversational AI, enabling systems to guide user interactions, elicit specific responses, and maintain coherent dialogues. By understanding and implementing various prompting techniques, developers can create more engaging and effective conversational agents. In this section, we will explore the different types of prompting used in conversational AI, their benefits, and how they can be applied to build advanced conversational systems.

## 5.2.1  Types of Prompting in Conversational AI[1]

1. **Direct Prompting**

   Direct prompting involves asking users straightforward questions or providing clear instructions. This type of prompting is useful for obtaining specific information or guiding users through a predefined process. For example, a customer support bot might use direct prompting to gather details about a user's issue:

   - **Example**: "Can you please describe the issue you are facing with our product?"

     Direct prompting is effective for maintaining control over the conversation and ensuring that users provide the necessary information.

---

[1] The reference papers are listed at the end of the chapter

2. **Indirect Prompting**

   Indirect prompting is subtler and encourages
   users to share information or take action without
   explicitly asking for it. This technique can make
   the conversation feel more natural and less
   interrogative. Indirect prompts often take the form
   of statements or suggestions:

   - **Example**: "It sounds like you might be having
     trouble with your account settings. Let me know if
     you need any help with that."

   Indirect prompting helps create a more
   conversational tone and can make users feel
   more comfortable sharing information.

3. **Open-Ended Prompting**

   Open-ended prompting involves asking questions
   that require more elaborate responses, allowing
   users to provide detailed information and express
   themselves freely. This type of prompting is
   useful for gathering comprehensive data and
   understanding user needs more deeply:

   - **Example**: "How can we improve your experience
     with our service?"

   Open-ended prompts encourage users to share
   their thoughts and opinions, providing valuable
   insights that can inform the development of
   more personalized and effective solutions.

4. **Closed-Ended Prompting**

Closed-ended prompting asks questions that can be answered with a simple "yes" or "no" or with specific, limited choices. This type of prompting is useful for quickly confirming information or guiding users through binary decision-making processes:

- **Example**: "Did you receive the confirmation email? Yes or No."

    Closed-ended prompts help streamline the conversation and keep it focused on specific tasks or decisions.

5. **Contextual Prompting**

Contextual prompting leverages the context of previous interactions to generate relevant and coherent prompts. This type of prompting ensures that the conversation remains logical and consistent, improving the overall user experience:

- **Example**: If a user previously mentioned having trouble logging in, the system might prompt: "Earlier, you mentioned having trouble logging in. Have you been able to resolve that issue?"

    Contextual prompting enhances the system's ability to maintain context and provide responses that are tailored to the user's ongoing needs and concerns.

6. **Clarification Prompting**

Clarification prompting is used to resolve ambiguities or misunderstandings in the conversation. When the system is unsure about the user's intent or requires additional information, it can ask clarifying questions to ensure accurate understanding:

- **Example**: "I didn't quite understand that. Are you asking about our return policy or our exchange policy?"

   Clarification prompting helps prevent miscommunication and ensures that the system provides accurate and relevant responses.

7. **Chain of Thought (CoT) Prompting**

Chain of Thought (CoT) prompting is an advanced technique that involves breaking down complex queries into smaller, manageable steps. By guiding users through a series of questions and answers, CoT prompting mimics human-like reasoning and improves the accuracy and relevance of responses:

- **Example**: If a user asks, "What are the steps to reset my password?", the system might respond: "First, you need to go to the login page. Do you see the 'Forgot Password' link?"

   CoT prompting helps create a logical flow of conversation and enhances the system's ability to handle complex queries and multistep processes.

8. **ReAct Prompting**

ReAct (Reason and Act) prompting is a sophisticated technique that combines reasoning with action-oriented prompts to guide users through complex tasks. It involves first understanding the user's query, reasoning through the necessary steps, and then prompting the user to take specific actions:

- **Example**: If a user asks, "How do I set up a new email account?", the system might respond: "To set up a new email account, first open your email client. Do you see the 'Add Account' option in the settings menu?"

  ReAct prompting improves the system's ability to handle tasks that require both understanding and actionable guidance, making the interaction more effective and user-friendly.

9. **Few-Shot Prompting**

Few-shot prompting involves providing the AI with a few examples of the desired output along with the input. This helps the model understand the task better and generate appropriate responses based on the given examples:

- **Example**: To train the AI on how to respond to customer inquiries, you might provide a few examples: "Q: What is your return policy? A: You can return items within 30 days for a full refund."

  Few-shot prompting improves the AI's performance on specific tasks by leveraging a small set of training examples.

10. **Zero-Shot Prompting**

    Zero-shot prompting enables the AI to handle tasks
    without any prior examples. The system relies on its
    general knowledge and understanding of language
    to generate responses based on the input alone:

    - **Example**: A user asks a previously unencountered
      question: "Can you explain quantum computing?"
      The AI generates a response based on its built-
      in knowledge: "Quantum computing leverages
      the principles of quantum mechanics to perform
      calculations that would be infeasible for classical
      computers."

    Zero-shot prompting allows the AI to tackle a
    wide range of queries without needing specific
    training for each one.

11. **In-Context Learning Prompting**

    In-context learning prompting involves providing
    the AI with context within the prompt itself, helping
    it generate more relevant and accurate responses.
    This can include background information, specific
    instructions, or previous interactions:

    - **Example**: If a user asks about a topic that requires
      prior context: "Given that we discussed our new
      product features in the last meeting, can you
      summarize the key points?"

    In-context learning prompting ensures that
    the AI incorporates relevant context into its
    responses, enhancing the overall interaction
    quality.

12. **Persona-Based Prompting**

Persona-based prompting tailors the AI's responses to fit a specific personality or style, making the interaction more engaging and consistent with the desired persona:

- **Example**: A customer service bot is designed to be friendly and empathetic: "I'm really sorry to hear about your issue. Let's get that sorted out for you as quickly as possible!"

Persona-based prompting enhances user engagement by providing a consistent and relatable interaction style.

13. **Constrained Prompting**

Constrained prompting limits the AI's responses to a predefined set of options or rules, ensuring that the output stays within desired boundaries. This is useful for maintaining control over the conversation and ensuring compliance with specific guidelines:

- **Example**: When handling sensitive information, the AI is constrained to provide only general advice and avoid specific recommendations: "For detailed advice on this matter, please consult with a certified professional."

Constrained prompting ensures that the AI operates within safe and acceptable limits, particularly in regulated environments.

Table 5-1 summarizes the type of prompts with benefits and used cases with an example to help decide on the type that best suits the use case.

189

***Table 5-1.*** *Prompt types and use cases*

| Prompting Type | Description | Example | Key Benefit | Business Use Cases |
|---|---|---|---|---|
| **Direct Prompting** | Asks straightforward questions or provides clear instructions | Can you please describe the issue you are facing with our product? | Maintains conversation control and ensures necessary information is provided | Customer support ticketing, order processing, appointment scheduling |
| **Indirect Prompting** | Subtly encourages users to share information without explicitly asking | It sounds like you might be having trouble with your account settings. Let me know if you need any help with that. | Creates a more natural conversational tone | Customer feedback collection, upselling, customer retention strategies |
| **Open-Ended Prompting** | Asks questions requiring elaborate responses | How can we improve your experience with our service? | Gathers comprehensive data and deeper insights | Market research, product development feedback, employee satisfaction surveys |

(*continued*)

***Table 5-1.*** (*continued*)

| Prompting Type | Description | Example | Key Benefit | Business Use Cases |
|---|---|---|---|---|
| **Closed-Ended Prompting** | Asks questions with simple "yes/no" or limited choice answers | Did you receive the confirmation email? Yes or No. | Streamlines conversation and focuses on specific tasks | Lead qualification, customer segmentation, quick polls or surveys |
| **Contextual Prompting** | Uses previous interaction context to generate relevant prompts | Earlier, you mentioned having trouble logging in. Have you been able to resolve that issue? | Enhances context maintenance and tailor's responses to user needs | Personalized customer support, targeted marketing campaigns, ongoing customer engagement |
| **Clarification Prompting** | Resolves ambiguities or misunderstandings | I didn't quite understand that. Are you asking about our return policy or our exchange policy? | Prevents miscommunication and ensures accurate responses | Complex customer inquiries, technical support, legal or compliance-related queries |

(*continued*)

***Table 5-1.*** (*continued*)

| Prompting Type | Description | Example | Key Benefit | Business Use Cases |
|---|---|---|---|---|
| **Chain of Thought (CoT) Prompting** | Breaks down complex queries into smaller steps | First, you need to go to the login page. Do you see the 'Forgot Password' link? | Creates logical conversation flow and handles complex queries | Troubleshooting guides, product onboarding, complex financial advice |
| **ReAct Prompting** | Combines reasoning with action-oriented prompts for complex tasks | To set up a new email account, first open your email client. Do you see the 'Add Account' option in the settings menu? | Improves handling of tasks requiring understanding and actionable guidance | Interactive tutorials, guided product setup, complex customer service scenarios |
| **Few-Shot Prompting** | Provides the AI with a few examples of the desired input/ output pairs before asking it to perform a task | Here are two examples of summarizing news articles: [examples]. Now, summarize this article: [new article] | Improves AI performance on specific tasks with minimal examples | Content generation, data classification, sentiment analysis |

(*continued*)

*Table 5-1.* (*continued*)

| Prompting Type | Description | Example | Key Benefit | Business Use Cases |
|---|---|---|---|---|
| **Zero-Shot Prompting** | Asks the AI to perform a task without any specific examples relying on its pretrained knowledge | Translate the following English text to French: [text] | Leverages AI's broad knowledge for versatile task completion | Multilingual customer support, diverse content creation, ad hoc data analysis |
| **In-Context Learning Prompting** | Embeds learning examples within the prompt itself to guide the AI's response | Complete the pattern: 2, 4, 6, 8, [blank]. The pattern is adding 2 each time. Now complete this pattern: 3, 6, 9, [blank] | Enables quick adaptation to new tasks without fine-tuning | Customized responses, dynamic rule-based systems, adaptive chatbots |
| **Persona-Based Prompting** | Instructs the AI to adopt a specific persona or role when responding | You are a friendly knowledgeable tech support specialist. Help the user with their printer issue. | Creates consistent and appropriate tone for specific contexts | Role-specific customer service, brand-aligned communications, specialized virtual assistants |

(*continued*)

***Table 5-1.*** (*continued*)

| Prompting Type | Description | Example | Key Benefit | Business Use Cases |
|---|---|---|---|---|
| **Constrained Prompting** | Sets specific constraints or rules for the AI to follow in its responses | Explain quantum computing in exactly 50 words using only words with fewer than 3 syllables. | Ensures AI responses meet specific criteria or format requirements | Compliance-adherent responses, format-specific content generation, controlled information disclosure |

# 5.2.2  Benefits of Using Various Prompting Types

1. **Enhanced User Engagement**

   Using a variety of prompting types keeps the conversation dynamic and engaging. By mixing direct, indirect, open-ended, closed-ended, contextual, clarification, Chain of Thought, and ReAct prompts, the system can cater to different user preferences and interaction styles.

2. **Improved Data Collection**

   Different prompting types allow the system to gather a wide range of information from users. Open-ended prompts can elicit detailed responses, while closed-ended prompts can quickly confirm specific details.

3. **Increased Conversational Coherence**

   Contextual and clarification prompting ensure that
   the conversation remains coherent and relevant. By
   maintaining context and resolving ambiguities, the
   system can provide more accurate and meaningful
   responses.

4. **Enhanced Problem-Solving**

   Chain of Thought and ReAct prompting help the
   system guide users through complex queries and
   multistep processes. This improves the system's
   problem-solving capabilities and ensures that users
   receive comprehensive support.

5. **Personalized User Experience**

   By leveraging various prompting types, the system
   can tailor its responses to individual users' needs
   and preferences. This creates a more personalized
   and satisfying user experience.

# 5.3 Implementing a Simple Conversation AI with Spring AI

In this section, we will walk through the process of creating a basic
conversational AI application using Spring AI. This project will demonstrate
how to leverage the capabilities of Spring AI to build an interactive chatbot
that can respond to user queries in real time. We will cover everything
from setting up your environment and initializing the project to creating
the server, defining routes, and building a simple front-end interface. By
the end of this section, you'll have a functional AI chatbot running locally,
providing a solid foundation for more advanced AI-driven applications.

We'll start by setting up the necessary development environment, followed by coding the server-side logic in Node.js using Express. The chatbot will communicate with a back-end service powered by Spring AI, handling user questions and returning AI-generated responses. The front-end interface will be a simple web page that allows users to interact with the chatbot.

This section is designed to be accessible to developers with basic knowledge of JavaScript and web development, providing clear instructions and code listings to guide you through each step. Whether you're a beginner or looking to enhance your skills in AI application development, this hands-on project will help you understand how to implement and expand upon conversational AI solutions using Spring AI.

# 5.3.1  Let's Code

**Prerequisites**

1.  **Code Setup**: Download the code from Section 4.7.2. Run this code and note the port and URL.

2.  **Environment Setup**: Ensure the latest Node.js (20.x and above) is installed on your machine. You can download it from the Node.js official website.

**Set Up Your Environment**
Ensure you have Node.js and npm (Node Package Manager) installed on your machine. You can download and install them from Node.js official website.

**Initialize Your Project (see Listing 5-1).**

***Listing 5-1.*** Make folder conversation_ai and initialize

```
mkdir conversation_ai
cd conversation_ai
npm init -y
```

**Install Express.js**

***Listing 5-2.*** Command to install express

```
npm install express
```

**Set Up the Project Structure**

***Listing 5-3.*** Folder structure for the project

```
Conversation_ai/
├── public/
│   ├── index.html
└── app.js
```

**Create the Server and Routes**

Create a new file named app.js and add the following code.

***Listing 5-4.*** app.js with specified routes

```
const express = require('express');
const path = require('path');
const axios = require('axios');
const cors = require('cors');
const app = express();
const port = 9090;

app.use(cors());
app.use(express.static('public'));
```

```
async function callExternalAPI(question) {
    try {
        const response = await axios.get(`http://localhost:
        8080/qa?question=${encodeURIComponent(question)}`);
        return response.data.answer;
    } catch (error) {
        console.error('Error calling external API:', error);
        return 'Sorry, I encountered an error while processing
        your request.';
    }
}

app.get('/ask', async (req, res) => {
    const question = req.query.question;
    if (!question) {
        return res.status(400).json({ error: 'Question is
        required' });
    }
    const answer = await callExternalAPI(question);
    res.json({ answer });
});

app.get('/', (req, res) => {
    res.sendFile(path.join(__dirname, 'public', 'index.html'));
});

app.listen(port, () => {
    console.log(`Server running at http://localhost:${port}`);
});
```

### Create an HTML File for the Front End

Create public/index.html with the following code (see Listing 5-5).

***Listing 5-5.*** Chabot code in index.html

```
<!DOCTYPE html>
<html lang="en">
<head>
    <meta charset="UTF-8">
    <meta name="viewport" content="width=device-width, initial-
    scale=1.0">
    <title>AI Chatbot</title>
    <style>
        body { font-family: Arial, sans-serif; max-width:
        800px; margin: 0 auto; padding: 20px; }
        #chatbox { height: 300px; border: 1px solid #ccc;
        overflow-y: scroll; margin-bottom: 10px; padding: 10px; }
        #question { width: 70%; padding: 5px; }
        #submit { padding: 5px 10px; }
    </style>
</head>
<body>
<h1>AI Chatbot</h1>
<div id="chatbox"></div>
<input type="text" id="question" placeholder="Ask a
question...">
<button id="submit">Send</button>

<script>
    const chatbox = document.getElementById('chatbox');
    const questionInput = document.getElementById('question');
    const submitButton = document.getElementById('submit');

    function addMessage(sender, message) {
        const messageElement = document.createElement('p');
```

```
        messageElement.innerHTML = `<strong>${sender}:</strong>
        ${message}`;
        chatbox.appendChild(messageElement);
        chatbox.scrollTop = chatbox.scrollHeight;
    }

    async function askQuestion() {
        const question = questionInput.value.trim();
        if (!question) return;

        addMessage('You', question);
        questionInput.value = '';

        try {
            const response = await fetch(`/ask?question=${encod
            eURIComponent(question)}`);
            const data = await response.json();
            addMessage('AI', data.answer);
        } catch (error) {
            console.error('Error:', error);
            addMessage('System', 'An error occurred while
            fetching the response.');
        }
    }

    submitButton.addEventListener('click', askQuestion);
    questionInput.addEventListener('keypress', (e) => {
        if (e.key === 'Enter') askQuestion();
    });
</script>
</body>
</html>
```

**Run These Node Files with "node app.js" or Using Jet Brain's PyCharm** (see Listing 5-6)

***Listing 5-6.*** Package.json

```
{
"name": "conversation-ai",
"version": "1.0.0",
"main": "app.js",
"scripts": {
  "test": "echo \"Error: no test specified\" && exit 1"
},
"keywords": [],
"author": "",
"license": "ISC",
"description": "",
"dependencies": {
  "axios": "^1.7.2",
  "express": "^4.19.2",
  "socket.io": "^4.7.5"
}
}
```

Make sure that the entry point for this application is defined in package.json.

In a command, line run: node app.js from the conversation_ai directory as shown in Figure 5-1.

```
banup@banus-MBP-2 conversation-ai % node app.js
Server running at http://localhost:9090
```

***Figure 5-1.*** *Application running on port 9090*

Go to the console at http://localhost:9090, and start your conversation as shown in Figure 5-2.

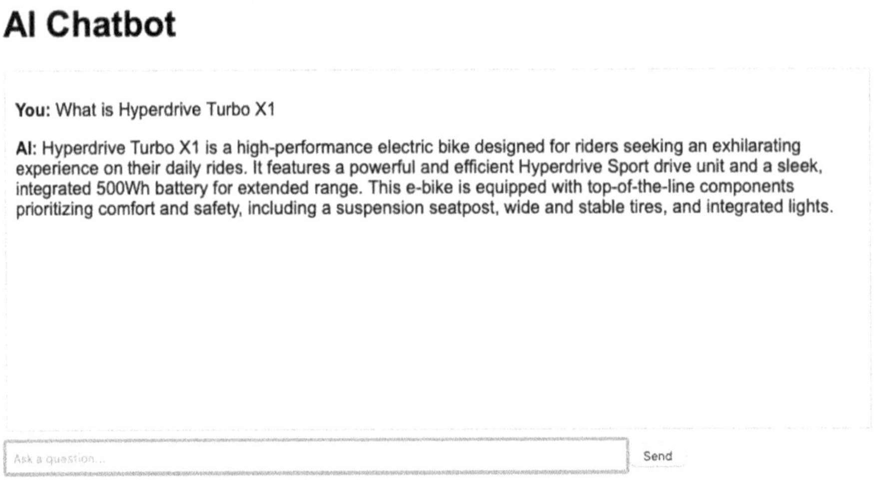

## AI Chatbot

**You:** What is Hyperdrive Turbo X1

**AI:** Hyperdrive Turbo X1 is a high-performance electric bike designed for riders seeking an exhilarating experience on their daily rides. It features a powerful and efficient Hyperdrive Sport drive unit and a sleek, integrated 500Wh battery for extended range. This e-bike is equipped with top-of-the-line components prioritizing comfort and safety, including a suspension seatpost, wide and stable tires, and integrated lights.

Ask a question...                                                                   Send

***Figure 5-2.***  *Conversation with AI*

This particular AI chat bot does not support conversational history. In order to enable conversational history, we will have to modify code both in Node.js and in Spring AI code.

# 5.4  Enabling Conversational History

## 5.4.1  Let's Code

**Prerequisites**

1. **Code Setup**: Download the code from Section 4.7.2. Run this code and note the port and URL.

2. **Environment Setup**: Ensure Node.js is installed on your machine. You can download it from the Node. js official website.

**Node.js**

In app.js, the post has to include a parameter history as shown in Listing 5-7.

*Listing 5-7.*  app.js with history

```
const express = require('express');
const path = require('path');
const axios = require('axios');
const cors = require('cors');
const app = express();
const port = 3000;

app.use(cors());
app.use(express.json());
app.use(express.static('public'));

async function callExternalAPI(question, history, stuffit
= true) {
    try {
        const response = await axios.post('http://
        localhost:8080/qahist', {
            question,
            stuffit,
            history
        });
        return response.data.answer;
    } catch (error) {
        console.error('Error calling external API:', error);
        return 'Sorry, I encountered an error while processing
        your request.';
    }
}
```

```
app.post('/ask', async (req, res) => {
    const { question, history } = req.body;
    if (!question) {
        return res.status(400).json({ error: 'Question is
        required' });
    }
    const answer = await callExternalAPI(question, history);
    res.json({ answer });
});

app.get('/', (req, res) => {
    res.sendFile(path.join(__dirname, 'public', 'index.html'));
```

**HTML File for Front End with History**

Update public/index.html as shown in Listing 5-8.

*Listing 5-8.* index.html with history

```
<!DOCTYPE html>
<html lang="en">
<head>
    <meta charset="UTF-8">
    <meta name="viewport" content="width=device-width, initial-
    scale=1.0">
    <title>AI Chatbot</title>
    <style>
        body { font-family: Arial, sans-serif; max-width:
        800px; margin: 0 auto; padding: 20px; }
        #chatbox { height: 300px; border: 1px solid
        #ccc; overflow-y: scroll; margin-bottom: 10px;
        padding: 10px; }
        #question { width: 70%; padding: 5px; }
        #submit { padding: 5px 10px; }
    </style>
```

```
</head>
<body>
<h1>AI Chatbot</h1>
<div id="chatbox"></div>
<input type="text" id="question" placeholder="Ask a
question...">
<button id="submit">Send</button>

<script>
    const chatbox = document.getElementById('chatbox');
    const questionInput = document.getElementById('question');
    const submitButton = document.getElementById('submit');
    let conversationHistory = [];

    function addMessage(sender, message) {
        const messageElement = document.createElement('p');
        messageElement.innerHTML = `<strong>${sender}:</strong>
        ${message}`;
        chatbox.appendChild(messageElement);
        chatbox.scrollTop = chatbox.scrollHeight;
    }

    async function askQuestion() {
        const question = questionInput.value.trim();
        if (!question) return;

        addMessage('You', question);
        questionInput.value = '';

        try {
            const response = await fetch('/ask', {
                method: 'POST',
                headers: {
                    'Content-Type': 'application/json',
```

```
        },
        body: JSON.stringify({ question, history:
        conversationHistory }),
    });
    const data = await response.json();
    addMessage('AI', data.answer);

    // Update conversation history
    conversationHistory.push({ user: question });
    conversationHistory.push({ assistant: data.
    answer });
} catch (error) {
    console.error('Error:', error);
    addMessage('System', 'An error occurred while
    fetching the response.');
}
    }
}

submitButton.addEventListener('click', askQuestion);
questionInput.addEventListener('keypress', (e) => {
    if (e.key === 'Enter') askQuestion();
});
</script>
</body>
</html>
```

**Spring AI Code**

Update QAHistController.java and QAHistService.java:

- QAHistController.java (see Listing 5-9).

CHAPTER 5    CONVERSATIONAL AI WITH SPRING AI

**Listing 5-9.** QAHistController.java that has @PostMapping to capture history

```
import org.springframework.beans.factory.annotation.Autowired;
import org.springframework.web.bind.annotation.*;

import java.util.LinkedHashMap;
import java.util.List;
import java.util.Map;

@RestController
@RequestMapping("/qahist")
public class QAHistController {

    private final QAHistService qaHistService;

    @Autowired
    public QAHistController(QAHistService qaHistService) {
        this.qaHistService = qaHistService;
    }

    @PostMapping
    public Map<String, String> completion(@RequestBody
    ConversationRequest request) {
        try{
        String answer = this.qaHistService.generate(
                request.getQuestion(),
                request.isStuffit(),
                request.getHistory()
        );

        Map<String, String> responseMap = new
        LinkedHashMap<>();
        responseMap.put("question", request.getQuestion());
        responseMap.put("answer", answer);
```

```
        return responseMap;
    } catch (Exception e) {
            throw e;
        }
    }

}
```

QAHistService.java

***Listing 5-10.*** QAHistService that handles history of chat

```
import org.slf4j.Logger;
import org.slf4j.LoggerFactory;
import org.springframework.ai.chat.ChatClient;
import org.springframework.ai.chat.ChatResponse;
import org.springframework.ai.chat.messages.AssistantMessage;
import org.springframework.ai.chat.messages.Message;
import org.springframework.ai.chat.messages.UserMessage;
import org.springframework.ai.chat.prompt.Prompt;
import org.springframework.ai.chat.prompt.SystemPromptTemplate;
import org.springframework.ai.document.Document;
import org.springframework.ai.vectorstore.VectorStore;
import org.springframework.beans.factory.annotation.Autowired;
import org.springframework.beans.factory.annotation.Value;
import org.springframework.core.io.Resource;
import org.springframework.stereotype.Service;

import java.util.ArrayList;
import java.util.List;
import java.util.Map;
import java.util.stream.Collectors;
@Service
public class QAHistService {
```

```java
private static final Logger logger = LoggerFactory.getLogger
(QAHistService.class);

@Value("classpath:/prompts/system-stuff.st")
private Resource qaSystemPromptResource;

@Value("classpath:/prompts/system-generic.st")
private Resource chatbotSystemPromptResource;

private final ChatClient chatClient;

@Autowired
VectorStore vectorStore;

@Autowired
public QAHistService(ChatClient chatClient, VectorStore
vectorStore) {
    this.chatClient = chatClient;
    this.vectorStore = vectorStore;
}

public String generate(String message, boolean
stuffit,List<Map<String, String>> history) {
    List<Message> messages = new ArrayList<>();

    // Add system message
    messages.add(getSystemMessage(message, stuffit));

    // Add conversation history
    for (Map<String, String> entry : history) {
        if (entry.containsKey("user")) {
            messages.add(new UserMessage(entry.
            get("user")));
        }
        if (entry.containsKey("assistant")) {
```

```java
            messages.add(new AssistantMessage(entry.
            get("assistant")));
        }
    }

    // Add the current user message
    messages.add(new UserMessage(message));

    // Create prompt with all messages
    Prompt prompt = new Prompt(messages);

    logger.info("Asking AI model to reply to question.");
    ChatResponse chatResponse = chatClient.call(prompt);
    logger.info("AI responded.");
    return chatResponse.getResult().getOutput().getContent();
}

private Message getSystemMessage(String query, boolean
stuffit) {
    if (stuffit) {
        logger.info("Retrieving relevant documents");
        List<Document> similarDocuments = vectorStore.
        similaritySearch(query);
        logger.info("Found {} relevant documents.",
        similarDocuments.size());

        String context = similarDocuments.stream()
                .map(entry -> entry.getContent())
                .collect(Collectors.joining("\n"));
        SystemPromptTemplate systemPromptTemplate = new
        SystemPromptTemplate(this.qaSystemPromptResource);
        return systemPromptTemplate.createMessage(Map.of("c
        ontext", context));
    }
```

```
else {
    logger.info("Not stuffing the prompt, using generic
    prompt");
    return new SystemPromptTemplate(this.
    chatbotSystemPromptResource).createMessage();
    }
}
```

Upon running the new code and going to the chat URL, you can now begin interacting with the LLM with chat history

### Sample Conversation

**You:** What is Hyperdrive Turbo X1

**AI:** Hyperdrive Turbo X1 is a high-performance electric bike designed for riders seeking an exhilarating experience on their daily rides. It features a powerful and efficient Hyperdrive Sport drive unit and a sleek, integrated 500Wh battery for extended range. This e-bike is equipped with top-of-the-line components prioritizing comfort and safety, including a suspension seatpost, wide and stable tires, and integrated lights.

**You:** What is it's price

**AI:** I'm sorry, but I don't have information on the price of the Hyperdrive Turbo X1.

**You:** What is the price of Hyperdrive Turbo X1

**AI:** The price of Hyperdrive Turbo X1 is 1999.99.

**You:** What is Hyperdrive Turbo X1

**AI:** Hyperdrive Turbo X1 is a high-performance electric bike designed for riders seeking an exhilarating experience on their daily rides. It features a powerful and efficient Hyperdrive Sport drive unit and a sleek, integrated 500Wh battery for extended range. This e-bike is equipped with top-of-the-line components prioritizing comfort and safety, including a suspension seatpost, wide and stable tires, and integrated lights.

**You:** What is it's price

**AI:** The price of the Hyperdrive Turbo X1 is $1999.99.

**Explanation of This Chat**

1. **Initial Lack of Specific Information:** In the first interaction, when asked about the Hyperdrive Turbo X1, the LLM provided general information about the product's features. However, the LLM didn't have specific price information in its initial response.

2. **Acknowledging Lack of Information**: When directly asked about the price immediately after, the LLM correctly acknowledged that it didn't have that specific information.

3. **Subsequent Provision of Price:** In a later interaction, when asked specifically about the price, the LLM provided the price of $1999.99. This might seem inconsistent with my earlier responses.

4. **Retention in Subsequent Interactions:** After providing the price once, it was able to include it in future responses about the product.

**Why This Behavior Occurs**

- AI models like ChatGPT don't have a persistent memory across conversations. Each response is generated based on the current prompt and the training data, not on previous interactions in the same conversation.

- The model might generate different responses to similar questions based on slight variations in how the question is asked or the context it's given.

- Once a piece of information (like the price) is introduced in the conversation, the model may incorporate it into subsequent responses within the same conversation context.

**To Improve Consistency and Accuracy**

1. Ensure that important details like price are included in the initial product description in your data.

2. Implement a knowledge base or database on your back end to store and retrieve consistent product information.

3. Use the conversation history feature more effectively to maintain context across multiple interactions.

# 5.5  Chain of Thought Prompting

This section delves into the concept of Chain of Thought prompting, exploring how it can be implemented in conversational AI systems to improve the interaction quality. We will examine the key benefits of CoT prompting, such as enhanced accuracy, improved user engagement, and better problem-solving capabilities. Furthermore, we'll explore practical examples and scenarios where CoT prompting can significantly enhance the effectiveness of AI-driven conversations.

By the end of this section, you'll have a thorough understanding of how Chain of Thought prompting works, why it is beneficial, and how you can implement it in your own AI projects using Spring AI. Whether you're building technical support systems, educational tools, or customer onboarding processes, CoT prompting will help you create more sophisticated, engaging, and context-aware AI applications.

## 5.5.1 What Is Chain of Thought (CoT) Prompting?

Chain of Thought (CoT) prompting is an advanced technique in conversational AI designed to enhance the interaction quality by mimicking human-like reasoning. It involves breaking down complex user queries into smaller, more manageable steps and guiding the user through a logical sequence of questions and responses. This approach helps maintain a coherent and structured dialogue, ensuring that each interaction builds upon the previous context, leading to more accurate and relevant outcomes.

In traditional conversational AI, responses are often generated based on the immediate user input, without much consideration of the broader context or logical flow of the conversation. CoT prompting, however, introduces a multistep reasoning process that enables the AI to handle intricate tasks and provide more thoughtful and comprehensive responses.

For instance, consider a user asking for advice on how to improve their website's SEO. A simple AI might provide a general list of tips, but an AI utilizing CoT prompting would first ask about the current state of the website, the user's goals, and any specific issues they are facing. This methodical approach ensures that the advice given is tailored to the user's unique situation, making the interaction much more valuable.

# 5.5.2 Benefits of CoT Prompting in Conversational AI

CoT prompting offers several key benefits that make it a powerful tool for enhancing conversational AI systems:

1. **Improved Accuracy and Relevance**

   By breaking down queries into smaller steps, CoT prompting ensures that each response is contextually accurate and relevant. The AI can validate assumptions, clarify ambiguities, and gather necessary information before providing a final response. This reduces the risk of misunderstandings and enhances the overall quality of the interaction.

2. **Enhanced User Engagement**

   CoT prompting keeps users engaged by creating a more interactive and dynamic conversation. Users are guided through a logical sequence of questions and responses, which makes the interaction feel more natural and human-like. This approach also helps maintain user interest, as they feel more understood and supported throughout the conversation.

3. **Better Problem-Solving Capabilities**

   Complex problems often require a step-by-step approach to solve effectively. CoT prompting equips conversational AI systems with the ability to handle such problems by breaking them down into manageable parts. This not only improves the

AI's problem-solving capabilities but also ensures that users receive comprehensive and actionable solutions.

4. **Increased Contextual Awareness**

   Maintaining context is crucial for meaningful interactions. CoT prompting allows conversational AI to retain and utilize context across multiple steps in the conversation. This ensures that the AI remembers relevant details and uses them to provide more coherent and consistent responses.

5. **Scalability and Flexibility**

   CoT prompting is highly scalable and can be applied to a wide range of applications, from customer support and virtual assistants to educational tools and beyond. Its logical and methodical approach makes it adaptable to various domains and user needs, enhancing the versatility of conversational AI systems.

## 5.5.3 Examples and Scenarios Where CoT Prompting Enhances Interactions

To illustrate the effectiveness of CoT prompting, let's explore a few examples and scenarios where this technique significantly enhances interactions:

1. **Technical Support**

   In a technical support scenario, users often present complex issues that require detailed troubleshooting. CoT prompting can guide users through a structured diagnostic process, asking relevant questions about their system configuration, recent changes, and specific error messages. By methodically gathering information, the AI can provide more accurate diagnoses and effective solutions.

- **Example**: A user reports that their application is crashing frequently. Instead of providing generic troubleshooting tips, the AI uses CoT prompting to ask about the operating system, recent software updates, specific actions that lead to the crash, and any error logs available. This detailed approach helps pinpoint the exact cause of the issue and offers targeted solutions.

2. **Customer Onboarding**

For businesses that offer complex products or services, onboarding new customers can be a challenging process. CoT prompting can streamline this process by guiding users through each step, ensuring they understand and complete all necessary tasks.

- **Example**: A new user is setting up a cloud storage service. The AI starts by asking about the user's storage needs, preferred devices, and any specific requirements. It then walks the user through account creation, setting up sync on devices, and understanding key features. This step-by-step guidance ensures a smooth onboarding experience.

3. **Health and Wellness Advice**

   In health and wellness applications, users may seek personalized advice based on their unique circumstances. CoT prompting can collect detailed information about the user's health status, lifestyle, and goals, providing tailored recommendations.

   - **Example**: A user asks for advice on starting a fitness routine. The AI begins by inquiring about the user's current fitness level, any health conditions, and their fitness goals. It then suggests a customized workout plan and dietary tips and tracks progress over time, ensuring that the advice is safe and effective.

4. **Financial Planning**

   Financial planning involves complex decision-making based on a variety of factors. CoT prompting can help users navigate these decisions by asking about their financial goals, current assets, liabilities, and risk tolerance.

   - **Example**: A user seeks advice on saving for retirement. The AI uses CoT prompting to gather information about the user's current income, savings, investment preferences, and retirement goals. It then provides a personalized savings plan, investment recommendations, and steps to optimize their financial strategy.

5.  **Educational Assistance**

    Educational tools can leverage CoT prompting to
    provide more interactive and effective learning
    experiences. By breaking down complex concepts
    into smaller, understandable steps, the AI can help
    students grasp difficult subjects more easily.

    - **Example**: A student is struggling with a math
      problem. The AI uses CoT prompting to walk the
      student through the problem-solving process,
      asking questions to ensure understanding of each
      step. This interactive approach helps the student
      learn and retain the material more effectively.

## 5.5.4  Conclusion

Chain of Thought prompting represents a significant advancement in
conversational AI, enabling systems to handle complex interactions with
greater accuracy, relevance, and user engagement. By breaking down
queries into smaller, manageable steps and guiding users through a logical
sequence of questions and responses, CoT prompting enhances the overall
quality of interactions and provides more meaningful and personalized
experiences. As we continue to develop and refine conversational AI
technologies, CoT prompting will play an increasingly important role in
creating sophisticated and effective dialogue systems.

## 5.5.5  Let's Code

- **Prerequisites**

    1.  **Code Setup**: Download the code from Section
        4.7.2. Run this code and note the port and URL.

2.  **Environment Setup**: Ensure Node.js is installed on your machine. You can download it from the Node.js official website.

- Modify App.js as shown in Listing 5-11.

***Listing 5-11.*** Modify App.js to handle ChainofThought processing

```
const cors = require('cors');
const app = express();
const port = 3000;

app.use(cors());
app.use(express.json());
app.use(express.static('public'));

async function callExternalAPI(question, history, stuffit
= true) {
    try {
        const response = await axios.post('http://
        localhost:8080/qacot', {
            question,
            stuffit,
            history
        });
        return {
            chainOfThought: response.data.chainOfThought,
            answer: response.data.answer
        };
    } catch (error) {
        console.error('Error calling external API:', error);
        return {
            chainOfThought: 'Error occurred',
```

```
            answer: 'Sorry, I encountered an error while
            processing your request.'
        };
    }
}

app.post('/ask', async (req, res) => {
    const { question, history } = req.body;
    if (!question) {
        return res.status(400).json({ error: 'Question is
        required' });
    }
    const response = await callExternalAPI(question, history);
    res.json(response);
});

app.listen(port, () => {
    console.log(`Server running at http://localhost:${port}`);
});
```

- Modify public/index.html

***Listing 5-12.*** Modify index.html to handle ChainofThought UI

```
<!DOCTYPE html>
<html lang="en">
<head>
    <meta charset="UTF-8">
    <meta name="viewport" content="width=device-width,
    initial-scale=1.0">
    <title>AI Bike Assistant</title>
    <style>
        body { font-family: Arial, sans-serif; max-width:
        800px; margin: 0 auto; padding: 20px; }
```

```
        #chatbox { height: 400px; border: 1px solid
        #ccc; overflow-y: scroll; margin-bottom: 10px;
        padding: 10px; }
        #question { width: 70%; padding: 5px; }
        #submit { padding: 5px 10px; }
        .chain-of-thought { font-style: italic; color: #666;
        margin-top: 5px; }
    </style>
</head>
<body>
<h1>AI Bike Assistant</h1>
<div id="chatbox"></div>
<input type="text" id="question" placeholder="Ask a question
about a bike...">
<button id="submit">Send</button>

<script>
    const chatbox = document.getElementById('chatbox');
    const questionInput = document.getElementById('question');
    const submitButton = document.getElementById('submit');
    let conversationHistory = [];

    function addMessage(sender, message, chainOfThought
    = null) {
        const messageElement = document.createElement('div');
        messageElement.innerHTML = `<strong>${sender}:</strong>
        ${message}`;
        if (chainOfThought) {
            messageElement.innerHTML += `<div class="chain-of-
            thought">Chain of Thought: ${chainOfThought}</div>`;
        }
        chatbox.appendChild(messageElement);
```

```
    chatbox.scrollTop = chatbox.scrollHeight;
}

async function askQuestion() {
    const question = questionInput.value.trim();
    if (!question) return;

    addMessage('You', question);
    questionInput.value = '';

    try {
        const response = await fetch('/ask', {
            method: 'POST',
            headers: {
                'Content-Type': 'application/json',
            },
            body: JSON.stringify({ question, history:
            conversationHistory }),
        });
        const data = await response.json();
        addMessage('AI', data.answer, data.chainOfThought);

        // Update conversation history
        conversationHistory.push({ user: question });
        conversationHistory.push({ assistant: data.
        answer });
    } catch (error) {
        console.error('Error:', error);
        addMessage('System', 'An error occurred while
        fetching the response.');
    }
}
```

```
    submitButton.addEventListener('click', askQuestion);
    questionInput.addEventListener('keypress', (e) => {
        if (e.key === 'Enter') askQuestion();
    });
</script>
</body>
</html>
```

- **Modify** QACOTController.java

  QACOTController.java must be modified also to handle
  CoT (see Listing 5-13).

***Listing 5-13.*** QACOTController.java with ChainOfThought
processing

```java
import org.springframework.beans.factory.annotation.Autowired;
import org.springframework.web.bind.annotation.*;

import java.util.LinkedHashMap;
import java.util.List;
import java.util.Map;

@RestController
@RequestMapping("/qacot")
public class QACOTController {

    private final QACOTService qaCOTService;

    @Autowired
    public QACOTController(QACOTService qaCOTService) {
        this.qaCOTService = qaCOTService;
    }
```

```java
@PostMapping
public Map<String, Object> completion(@RequestBody
ConversationRequest request) {
    String fullResponse = this.qaCOTService.generate(
            request.getQuestion(),
            request.isStuffit(),
            request.getHistory()
    );

    // Split the response into chain of thought and
    final answer
    String[] parts = fullResponse.split("6\\. Final answer:");
    String chainOfThought = parts[0].trim();
    String finalAnswer = parts.length > 1 ? parts[1].trim() :
    "No final answer provided.";

    Map<String, Object> responseMap = new LinkedHashMap<>();
    responseMap.put("question", request.getQuestion());
    responseMap.put("chainOfThought", chainOfThought);
    responseMap.put("answer", finalAnswer);
    return responseMap;
}

}
```

- Modify QACOTService.java as shown in Listing 5-14.

**Listing 5-14.** QACOTService.java with ChainOfThought processing

```java
import org.slf4j.Logger;
import org.slf4j.LoggerFactory;
import org.springframework.ai.chat.ChatClient;
import org.springframework.ai.chat.ChatResponse;
import org.springframework.ai.chat.messages.AssistantMessage;
```

```
import org.springframework.ai.chat.messages.Message;
import org.springframework.ai.chat.messages.UserMessage;
import org.springframework.ai.chat.prompt.Prompt;
import org.springframework.ai.chat.prompt.PromptTemplate;
import org.springframework.ai.chat.prompt.SystemPromptTemplate;
import org.springframework.ai.document.Document;
import org.springframework.ai.vectorstore.VectorStore;
import org.springframework.beans.factory.annotation.Autowired;
import org.springframework.beans.factory.annotation.Value;
import org.springframework.core.io.Resource;
import org.springframework.core.io.ResourceLoader;
import org.springframework.stereotype.Service;

import java.util.ArrayList;
import java.util.List;
import java.util.Map;
import java.util.regex.Matcher;
import java.util.regex.Pattern;
import java.util.stream.Collectors;

@Service
public class QACOTService {
    private static final Logger logger = LoggerFactory.getLogger
    (QACOTService.class);

    @Value("classpath:/prompts/system-stuff.st")
    private Resource qaSystemPromptResource;

    @Value("classpath:/prompts/system-generic.st")
    private Resource chatbotSystemPromptResource;

    @Value("classpath:/prompts/bike-prompts.st")
    private Resource bikePromptResource;
```

```java
private final ChatClient chatClient;
private final PromptTemplate bikePromptTemplate;

@Autowired
VectorStore vectorStore;

@Autowired
public QACOTService(ChatClient chatClient, VectorStore
vectorStore, @Value("classpath:/prompts/bike-prompts.st")
Resource bikePromptResource) {
    this.chatClient = chatClient;
    this.vectorStore = vectorStore;
    this.bikePromptTemplate = new PromptTemplate(bikePrompt
    Resource);
}

public String generate(String message, boolean stuffit,
List<Map<String, String>> history) {
    String bikeModel = extractBikeModel(message);
    List<Message> messages = new ArrayList<>();

    // Add system message
    messages.add(getSystemMessage(message, bikeModel,
    stuffit));

    // Add conversation history
    for (Map<String, String> entry : history) {
        if (entry.containsKey("user")) {
            messages.add(new UserMessage(entry.get("user")));
        }
        if (entry.containsKey("assistant")) {
            messages.add(new AssistantMessage(entry.
            get("assistant")));
        }
    }
```

```java
    // Add the current user message with a request for
    chain of thought
    messages.add(new UserMessage(message + " Please provide
    your chain of thought."));

    Prompt prompt = new Prompt(messages);

    logger.info("Asking AI model to reply with chain of
    thought for bike model: {}", bikeModel);
    ChatResponse chatResponse = chatClient.call(prompt);
    logger.info("AI responded with chain of thought for
    bike model: {}", bikeModel);
    return chatResponse.getResult().getOutput().
    getContent();
}

private Message getSystemMessage(String query, String
bikeModel, boolean stuffit) {
    String context = "";
    if (stuffit) {
        logger.info("Retrieving relevant documents for bike
        model: {}", bikeModel);
        List<Document> similarDocuments = vectorStore.
        similaritySearch(bikeModel + " " + query);
        logger.info("Found {} relevant documents.",
        similarDocuments.size());

        context = similarDocuments.stream()
                .map(Document::getContent)
                .collect(Collectors.joining("\n"));
    }

    logger.info("Creating prompt for bike model: {}",
    bikeModel);
```

```
      return bikePromptTemplate.createMessage(Map.of(
            "bikeModel", bikeModel,
            "context", context,
            "question", query
      ));
}

private String extractBikeModel(String message) {
    // This pattern looks for words that might be a
    bike model
    // It assumes the model is 2-3 words, possibly with
    numbers, before the word "bike" or "e-bike"
    Pattern pattern = Pattern.compile("(\\w+(?:\\s+\\w+)
    {0,2})\\s+(?:bike|e-bike)", Pattern.CASE_INSENSITIVE);
    Matcher matcher = pattern.matcher(message);

    if (matcher.find()) {
        return matcher.group(1).trim();
    } else {
        logger.warn("No bike model found in the message.
        Using a generic term.");
        return "electric bike";
    }
}
}
```

- Create a prompt template to handle bike-based queries. See Listing 5-15.

***Listing 5-15.*** bike-prompts.st to handle bike-based queries

You are an AI assistant specializing in electric bikes. When answering questions about bikes, please provide your chain of thought before giving the final answer. Your response should follow this structure:

1. Identify the key aspects of the question.
2. Recall relevant information about the {bikeModel}.
3. Consider any potential ambiguities or additional context needed.
4. Reason through the answer step by step.
5. Summarize your thoughts.
6. Provide a clear and concise final answer, starting with "Final answer:".

Here's some context about the {bikeModel}:
{context}

Now, please answer the following question about the {bikeModel}, providing your chain of thought before the final answer:

{question}

- The chat result is shown in Figure 5-3.

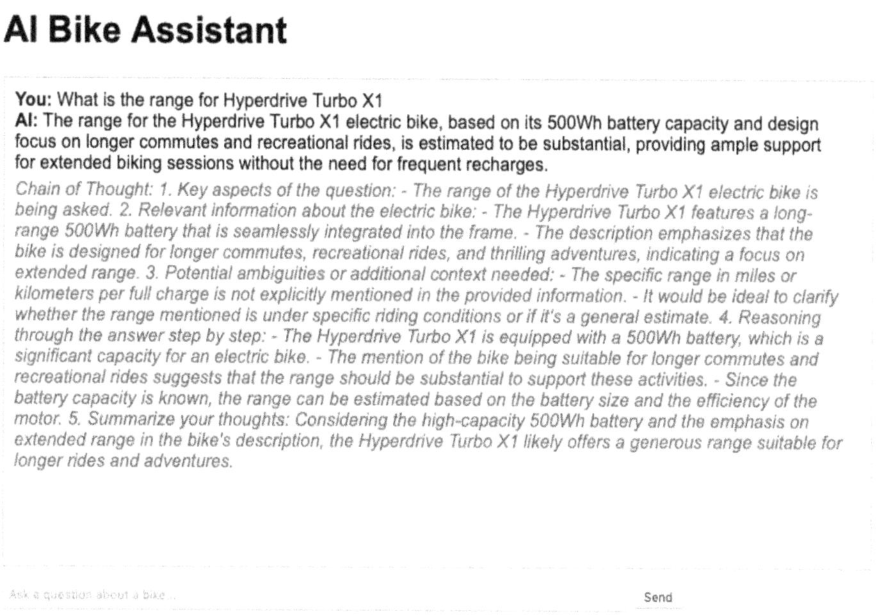

# AI Bike Assistant

**You:** What is the range for Hyperdrive Turbo X1
**AI:** The range for the Hyperdrive Turbo X1 electric bike, based on its 500Wh battery capacity and design focus on longer commutes and recreational rides, is estimated to be substantial, providing ample support for extended biking sessions without the need for frequent recharges.

*Chain of Thought: 1. Key aspects of the question: - The range of the Hyperdrive Turbo X1 electric bike is being asked. 2. Relevant information about the electric bike: - The Hyperdrive Turbo X1 features a long-range 500Wh battery that is seamlessly integrated into the frame. - The description emphasizes that the bike is designed for longer commutes, recreational rides, and thrilling adventures, indicating a focus on extended range. 3. Potential ambiguities or additional context needed: - The specific range in miles or kilometers per full charge is not explicitly mentioned in the provided information. - It would be ideal to clarify whether the range mentioned is under specific riding conditions or if it's a general estimate. 4. Reasoning through the answer step by step: - The Hyperdrive Turbo X1 is equipped with a 500Wh battery, which is a significant capacity for an electric bike. - The mention of the bike being suitable for longer commutes and recreational rides suggests that the range should be substantial to support these activities. - Since the battery capacity is known, the range can be estimated based on the battery size and the efficiency of the motor. 5. Summarize your thoughts: Considering the high-capacity 500Wh battery and the emphasis on extended range in the bike's description, the Hyperdrive Turbo X1 likely offers a generous range suitable for longer rides and adventures.*

Ask a question about a bike ...                                              Send

***Figure 5-3.*** *ChainOfThought output*

Analysis of the output shown in Figure 5-3.

- Based on the AI's response, it appears that the LLM (Language Learning Model) is primarily using the information provided in the context about the Hyperdrive Turbo X1. The response focuses on the known facts:

  1. The bike has a 500Wh battery capacity.

  2. It's designed for longer commutes and recreational rides.

  3. The battery is integrated into the frame.

  However, the AI doesn't provide a specific range in miles or kilometers, which is appropriate given that this information wasn't explicitly provided in the context.

231

- The LLM is using its general knowledge about electric bikes to make inferences, such as:

  1. A 500Wh battery is considered a "significant capacity" for an electric bike.

  2. The battery capacity and motor efficiency are factors in determining range.

  While the AI is making some logical inferences, it's not introducing any specific data that wasn't given (like exact mileage). Instead, it's using phrases like "estimated to be substantial" and "ample support for extended biking sessions" to describe the range without committing to specific numbers.

- This approach demonstrates that the AI is

  1. Staying within the bounds of the provided information.

  2. Using general knowledge about electric bikes to contextualize the information.

  3. Being cautious not to state specifics that weren't provided.

- If you want the AI to only use the exact information provided without any inferences or general knowledge application, you might need to adjust the prompt to be more restrictive. However, the current approach allows for a more natural and informative response while still maintaining accuracy to the given data.

# 5.6  ReACT Prompting

ReACT (Retrieval-Augmented Conversational Transformer) prompting is a robust technique, combining retrieval-based methods with generative models to enhance AI-driven conversations. This section introduces ReACT prompting, focusing on its mechanisms, benefits, and practical applications from a programmer's perspective.

## 5.6.1  What Is ReACT Prompting?

ReACT prompting is a state-of-the-art technique that fuses retrieval and generative models to create more dynamic and contextually accurate conversational AI. Unlike traditional models that depend solely on predefined responses or generic text generation, ReACT harnesses the power of retrieving relevant information from extensive datasets and generating coherent, context-aware replies.

## 5.6.2  The Mechanism Behind ReACT

The ReACT framework operates on a dual mechanism tailored for programmers:

1. **Retrieval Component**: This component utilizes algorithms to search through a database or knowledge base, retrieving the most relevant pieces of information related to the user's query. By integrating with tools like Elasticsearch or vector databases, the retrieval process ensures that conversations are grounded in accurate and pertinent data.

2. **Generative Component**: Leveraging Transformer-based models, the generative component constructs responses that are not only factually correct but also contextually and linguistically appropriate. This combination of retrieval and generation ensures the AI can handle both specific and open-ended queries effectively.

## 5.6.3  Benefits of ReACT Prompting

- **Enhanced Accuracy**: By incorporating a retrieval system, ReACT prompting significantly reduces the risk of generating incorrect or irrelevant responses.

- **Contextual Relevance**: The blend of retrieval and generative models ensures responses are tailored to the specific context of the conversation, resulting in more meaningful interactions.

- **Scalability**: ReACT prompting can be scaled across various domains and applications, making it a versatile tool for programmers working in different industries, from customer support to educational platforms.

- **Improved User Experience**: Users benefit from more accurate, relevant, and engaging conversations, enhancing their overall experience with AI-driven systems.

## 5.6.4  Practical Applications for Programmers

ReACT prompting is particularly valuable in scenarios where accurate information retrieval is crucial. Some of the prominent applications include

- **Customer Support**: Implementing ReACT prompting in customer support systems can provide precise and context-aware responses to customer queries, improving satisfaction and efficiency.

- **Healthcare**: Assisting healthcare professionals and patients with accurate medical information and guidance through well-implemented AI systems.

- **Education**: Developing educational platforms that offer students and educators tailored content and support based on specific queries and contexts.

- **Enterprise Solutions**: Enhancing internal communication and decision-making processes by integrating ReACT prompting to provide relevant information and insights on demand.

# 5.6.5  Let's code

To implement ReACT, we will have to modify both the Node.js and Spring AI code.

- **Prerequisites**

  1. **Code Setup**: Download the code from Section 4.7.2. Run this code and note the port and URL.

  2. **Environment Setup**: Ensure Node.js is installed on your machine. You can download it from the Node.js official website.

  - The App.js needs to be modified to handle ReACT prompting as shown in Listing 5-16.

***Listing 5-16.*** app,js with modifications to handle ReACT prompting

```
const express = require('express');
const path = require('path');
const axios = require('axios');
const cors = require('cors');
const app = express();
const port = 3000;

app.use(cors());
app.use(express.json());
app.use(express.static('public'));

async function callExternalAPI(question, history, stuffit
= true) {
    try {
        const response = await axios.post('http://
        localhost:8080/qareact', {
            question,
            stuffit,
            history
        });
        return parseReactResponse(response.data.answer);
    } catch (error) {
        console.error('Error calling external API:', error);
        return {
            thoughts: ['Error occurred'],
            actions: [],
            observations: [],
            conclusion: 'Sorry, I encountered an error while
            processing your request.'
        };
    }
}
```

```
function parseReactResponse(response) {
    const lines = response.split('\n');
    let result = {
        thoughts: [],
        actions: [],
        observations: [],
        conclusion: ''
    };
    let currentStep = '';

    for (const line of lines) {
        if (line.startsWith('Thought')) {
            currentStep = 'thought';
            result.thoughts.push(line);
        } else if (line.startsWith('Action')) {
            currentStep = 'action';
            result.actions.push(line);
        } else if (line.startsWith('Observation')) {
            currentStep = 'observation';
            result.observations.push(line);
        } else if (line.startsWith('Conclusion:')) {
            result.conclusion = line.replace('Conclusion:', '')
            .trim();
        } else if (line.trim() !== '') {
            // Append to the last item of the current step
            switch (currentStep) {
                case 'thought':
                    result.thoughts[result.thoughts.length - 1]
                    += ' ' + line.trim();
                    break;
                case 'action':
```

```
                        result.actions[result.actions.length - 1]
                        += ' ' + line.trim();
                        break;
                    case 'observation':
                        result.observations[result.observations.
                        length - 1] += ' ' + line.trim();
                        break;
                }
            }
        }

    return result;
}

app.post('/ask', async (req, res) => {
    const { question, history } = req.body;
    if (!question) {
        return res.status(400).json({ error: 'Question is
        required' });
    }
    const response = await callExternalAPI(question, history);
    res.json(response);
});

app.listen(port, () => {
    console.log(`Server running at http://localhost:${port}`);
});
```

- The public/index.html needs to be modified
  to handle ReACT at the UI level as shown in
  Listing 5-17.

***Listing 5-17.*** Index.html modified to handle ReACT

```html
<!DOCTYPE html>
<html lang="en">
<head>
    <meta charset="UTF-8">
    <meta name="viewport" content="width=device-width, initial-
    scale=1.0">
    <title>AI Bike Assistant (ReACT)</title>
    <style>
        body { font-family: Arial, sans-serif; max-width:
        800px; margin: 0 auto; padding: 20px; }
        #chatbox { height: 400px; border: 1px solid
        #ccc; overflow-y: scroll; margin-bottom: 10px;
        padding: 10px; }
        #question { width: 70%; padding: 5px; }
        #submit { padding: 5px 10px; }
        .thought { color: #0000FF; }
        .action { color: #008000; }
        .observation { color: #800080; }
        .conclusion { font-weight: bold; }
    </style>
</head>
<body>
<h1>AI Bike Assistant (ReACT)</h1>
<div id="chatbox"></div>
<input type="text" id="question" placeholder="Ask a question
about a bike...">
<button id="submit">Send</button>

<script>
    const chatbox = document.getElementById('chatbox');
    const questionInput = document.getElementById('question');
```

```javascript
const submitButton = document.getElementById('submit');
let conversationHistory = [];

function addMessage(sender, message) {
    const messageElement = document.createElement('div');
    messageElement.innerHTML = `<strong>${sender}:</strong>
    ${message}`;
    chatbox.appendChild(messageElement);
    chatbox.scrollTop = chatbox.scrollHeight;
}

function addReactResponse(response) {
    const responseElement = document.createElement('div');
    responseElement.innerHTML = '<strong>AI:</strong>';

    response.thoughts.forEach((thought, index) => {
        responseElement.innerHTML += `<p
        class="thought">Thought ${index + 1}:
        ${thought}</p>`;
        if (response.actions[index]) {
            responseElement.innerHTML += `<p
            class="action">Action ${index + 1}: ${response.
            actions[index]}</p>`;
        }
        if (response.observations[index]) {
            responseElement.innerHTML += `<p
            class="observation">Observation ${index + 1}:
            ${response.observations[index]}</p>`;
        }
    });

    responseElement.innerHTML +=
    `<p class="conclusion">Conclusion: ${response.
    conclusion}</p>`;
```

```
    chatbox.appendChild(responseElement);
    chatbox.scrollTop = chatbox.scrollHeight;
}

async function askQuestion() {
    const question = questionInput.value.trim();
    if (!question) return;

    addMessage('You', question);
    questionInput.value = '';

    try {
        const response = await fetch('/ask', {
            method: 'POST',
            headers: {
                'Content-Type': 'application/json',
            },
            body: JSON.stringify({ question, history:
            conversationHistory }),
        });
        const data = await response.json();
        addReactResponse(data);

        // Update conversation history
        conversationHistory.push({ user: question });
        conversationHistory.push({ assistant: data.
        conclusion });
    } catch (error) {
        console.error('Error:', error);
        addMessage('System', 'An error occurred while
        fetching the response.');
    }
}
```

```
    submitButton.addEventListener('click', askQuestion);
    questionInput.addEventListener('keypress', (e) => {
        if (e.key === 'Enter') askQuestion();
    });
</script>
</body>
</html>
```

- Add a prompt template react-prompt.st as shown in Listing 5-18.

***Listing 5-18.*** Prompt template with ReACT styling

```
You are an AI assistant specialized in answering questions
about bikes. Follow this format:

Thought: Analyze the question and consider what information
is needed.
Action: Decide what to do next. Options are:
- Search: Look up information in the provided context.
- Calculate: Perform a calculation if needed.
- Conclude: If you have enough information to answer the
question.
Observation: The result of your action.

Repeat the Thought/Action/Observation steps as necessary.

After your final observation, always provide a separate
conclusion:

Conclusion: Summarize your findings and answer the original
question directly in a concise manner.

Context:
{context}
```

Remember, your conclusion must always be separate from your observations and clearly marked with "Conclusion:".

- Modify QAReACTController.java to handle react type prompts.

***Listing 5-19.*** QAReACTController.java

```
import org.springframework.beans.factory.annotation.Autowired;
import org.springframework.stereotype.Service;
import org.springframework.web.bind.annotation.*;

import java.util.LinkedHashMap;
import java.util.Map;

@RestController
@RequestMapping("/qareact")

public class QAReACTController {

    private final QAReACTService qaReactService;

    @Autowired
    public QAReACTController(QAReACTService qaReactService) {
        this.qaReactService = qaReactService;
    }

    @PostMapping
    public Map<String, Object> completion(@RequestBody
    ConversationRequest request) {
        String fullResponse = this.qaReactService.generate(
                request.getQuestion(),
                request.isStuffit(),
                request.getHistory()
        );
```

```
        Map<String, Object> responseMap = new
        LinkedHashMap<>();
        responseMap.put("question", request.getQuestion());
        responseMap.put("answer", fullResponse);
        return responseMap;
    }
}
```

- Modify QAReACTService.java to handle ReACT as shown.

***Listing 5-20.*** QAReACTService.java

```
import org.springframework.ai.chat.ChatClient;
import org.springframework.ai.chat.prompt.Prompt;
import org.springframework.ai.chat.prompt.SystemPromptTemplate;
import org.springframework.ai.chat.messages.Message;
import org.springframework.ai.chat.messages.UserMessage;
import org.springframework.ai.chat.messages.AssistantMessage;
import org.springframework.ai.document.Document;
import org.springframework.ai.vectorstore.VectorStore;
import org.springframework.stereotype.Service;
import org.springframework.beans.factory.annotation.Value;
import org.springframework.core.io.Resource;

import java.util.ArrayList;
import java.util.List;
import java.util.Map;
import java.util.stream.Collectors;

@Service
public class QAReACTService {
    @Value("classpath:/prompts/react-prompt.st")
    private Resource reactPromptResource;
```

```java
private final ChatClient chatClient;
private final VectorStore vectorStore;

public QAReACTService(ChatClient chatClient, VectorStore
vectorStore) {
    this.chatClient = chatClient;
    this.vectorStore = vectorStore;
}

public String generate(String question, boolean stuffit,
List<Map<String, String>> history) {
    SystemPromptTemplate systemPromptTemplate = new SystemP
    romptTemplate(reactPromptResource);
    Message systemMessage = systemPromptTemplate.createMess
    age(Map.of("context", getContext(question, stuffit)));

    List<Message> messages = new ArrayList<>();
    messages.add(systemMessage);

    // Add conversation history
    for (Map<String, String> entry : history) {
        if (entry.containsKey("user")) {
            messages.add(new UserMessage(entry.
            get("user")));
        }
        if (entry.containsKey("assistant")) {
            messages.add(new AssistantMessage(entry.
            get("assistant")));
        }
    }
```

```java
        messages.add(new UserMessage(question + " Please
        structure your response as follows:\n" +
                "Thought 1: [Your thought process]\n" +
                "Action 1: [Your action]\n" +
                "Observation 1: [Your observation]\n" +
                "Thought 2: [Your thought process]\n" +
                "Action 2: [Your action]\n" +
                "Observation 2: [Your observation]\n" +
                "... (continue as needed)\n" +
                "Conclusion: [Your final conclusion]"));

    Prompt prompt = new Prompt(messages);
    String response = chatClient.call(prompt).getResult().
    getOutput().getContent();

    // Ensure there's a conclusion
    return ensureConclusion(response);
}

private String getContext(String query, boolean stuffit) {
    if (stuffit) {
        List<Document> similarDocuments = vectorStore.
        similaritySearch(query);
        return similarDocuments.stream()
                .map(Document::getContent)
                .collect(Collectors.joining("\n"));
    }
    return "";
}

private String ensureConclusion(String response) {
    if (!response.contains("Conclusion:")) {
        String[] parts = response.split("Observation ");
```

```
    if (parts.length > 1) {
        String lastObservation = parts[parts.length -
        1].trim();
        response += "\nConclusion: Based on the above
        analysis, " + lastObservation;
    } else {
        response += "\nConclusion: Based on the
        available information, a specific conclusion
        couldn't be drawn.";
    }
}
return response;
    }
}
```

- **Output**

  Upon asking the "Can Hyperdrive Turbo X1 be used in
  city?", the output is as shown in Figure 5-4.

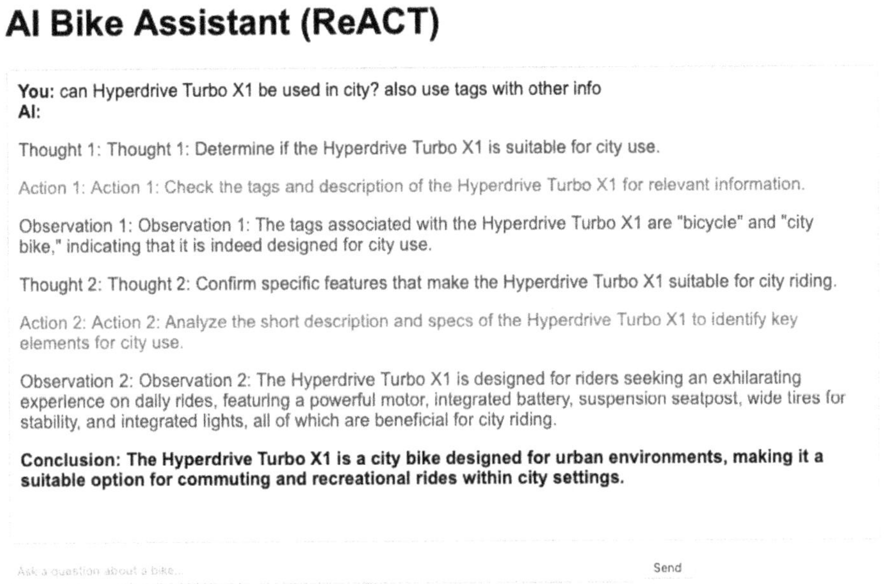

## AI Bike Assistant (ReACT)

**You:** can Hyperdrive Turbo X1 be used in city? also use tags with other info
**AI:**

Thought 1: Thought 1: Determine if the Hyperdrive Turbo X1 is suitable for city use.

Action 1: Action 1: Check the tags and description of the Hyperdrive Turbo X1 for relevant information.

Observation 1: Observation 1: The tags associated with the Hyperdrive Turbo X1 are "bicycle" and "city bike," indicating that it is indeed designed for city use.

Thought 2: Thought 2: Confirm specific features that make the Hyperdrive Turbo X1 suitable for city riding.

Action 2: Action 2: Analyze the short description and specs of the Hyperdrive Turbo X1 to identify key elements for city use.

Observation 2: Observation 2: The Hyperdrive Turbo X1 is designed for riders seeking an exhilarating experience on daily rides, featuring a powerful motor, integrated battery, suspension seatpost, wide tires for stability, and integrated lights, all of which are beneficial for city riding.

**Conclusion: The Hyperdrive Turbo X1 is a city bike designed for urban environments, making it a suitable option for commuting and recreational rides within city settings.**

Ask a question about a bike...                                    Send

***Figure 5-4.*** *Output of the ReACT interaction*

# 5.7 Conclusion

In this chapter, we explored the implementation of a conversational AI system using Spring AI. We started with an introduction to the various types of prompting in conversational AI, highlighting their benefits and applications. These included direct, indirect, open-ended, closed-ended, contextual, and clarification prompting, among others.

We then delved into the technical aspects of setting up a simple conversational AI system. The step-by-step guide provided detailed instructions on setting up the environment, initializing the project, and creating the server and front-end components. The example code listings and explanations were aimed at making the setup process clear and straightforward.

A significant focus was on enabling conversational history, which is crucial for maintaining context across interactions. This involved modifications to both the Node.js and Spring AI code to handle and store conversation history. By capturing and utilizing conversation history, the AI system can provide more coherent and contextually relevant responses.

The chapter also introduced advanced prompting techniques such as Chain of Thought (CoT) prompting and ReACT prompting. CoT prompting enhances the AI's ability to handle complex queries by breaking them down into manageable steps, while ReACT prompting combines retrieval and generative models to provide accurate and contextually relevant responses.

The implementation of these advanced techniques demonstrated how to create a more interactive and dynamic conversation flow. The examples provided illustrated how these techniques can be applied in real-world scenarios, such as technical support, customer onboarding, health and wellness advice, financial planning, and educational assistance.

In conclusion, this chapter provided a comprehensive guide to building and enhancing conversational AI systems using Spring AI. By leveraging various prompting techniques and enabling conversational history, developers can create sophisticated AI systems that offer more natural, efficient, and satisfying user interactions.

The next chapter will delve into the topic of function calling within conversational AI systems. We will explore how to implement and utilize function calling to extend the capabilities of AI interactions, allowing the system to perform specific actions and retrieve information dynamically during the conversation. Stay tuned for a deeper understanding of how function calling can enhance the functionality and responsiveness of your AI applications.

# CHAPTER 6

# Function Calling with Spring AI

## 6.1 Introduction

Building on our exploration of RAG and conversational AI in the previous chapters, we now turn our attention to a powerful capability in modern AI systems: function calling. This chapter will focus on implementing function calling using Spring AI, a framework that simplifies the integration of AI capabilities into Spring-based applications.

Function calling allows AI models to interact with external systems and perform specific tasks by invoking predefined functions. This capability bridges the gap between natural language processing and concrete actions in software systems. With Spring AI, developers can leverage this functionality to create more dynamic and capable AI-powered applications.

In this chapter, we'll cover

1. The concept of function calling in AI models

2. How Spring AI implements and facilitates function calling

3. Setting up a Spring AI project for function calling

© Banu Parasuraman 2024
B. Parasuraman, *Mastering Spring AI*, https://doi.org/10.1007/979-8-8688-1001-5_6

4. Defining and implementing custom functions

5. Integrating function calls with AI-generated responses

6. Best practices and common use cases for function calling

7. Handling errors and edge cases in function calling scenarios

By the end of this chapter, you'll have a solid understanding of how to implement function calling in your Spring AI projects, enabling your applications to perform a wide range of tasks based on natural language inputs.

# 6.2  The Concept of Function Calling in AI Models

Function calling is an emerging capability in artificial intelligence (AI) that bridges the gap between natural language understanding and executable actions. This concept involves AI models invoking predefined functions or methods to perform specific tasks based on user inputs or internal logic. By integrating function calling into AI systems, we enable models to go beyond passive information processing, allowing them to interact with external systems and perform real-world tasks.

1. **Understanding Function Calling in AI**

   At its core, function calling allows AI models to execute specific blocks of code—referred to as functions—in response to triggers. These triggers can be user commands, internal logic conditions, or external events. This ability transforms AI from a purely analytical tool into an active participant in software ecosystems, capable of carrying out tasks such as data retrieval, processing, and system control.

For instance, consider a customer support chatbot. Traditionally, the chatbot can answer frequently asked questions by retrieving information from a database. With function calling, the same chatbot can execute functions to reset a user's password, check the status of an order, or schedule a service appointment, thereby providing a more interactive and practical user experience.

2. **Historical Context and Evolution**

The idea of function calling in programming is not new. It has been a fundamental concept in software development since the inception of procedural and object-oriented programming languages. However, integrating this concept into AI models represents a significant evolution. Initially, AI systems were designed to mimic human cognitive processes—such as learning, reasoning, and perception—without direct interaction capabilities. The integration of function calling marks a shift toward operational AI, where models can perform specific actions based on their understanding and reasoning.

3. **Technical Overview of Function Calling**

From a technical perspective, function calling in AI involves several components:

- **Function Definitions**: These are blocks of code written to perform specific tasks. Functions can be simple (e.g., calculating a sum) or complex (e.g., processing a series of transactions).

- **Triggers**: These are conditions or events that prompt the AI to call a function. Triggers can be based on user inputs, time-based conditions, or other criteria defined within the AI model.

- **Function Execution Environment**: This is the context within which functions are executed. It includes the necessary resources, permissions, and dependencies required for the function to run successfully.

- **Response Handling**: After a function is called and executed, the AI model must handle the response appropriately. This involves interpreting the result and potentially taking further actions based on the outcome.

4. **Integrating Function Calling into AI Models**

Integrating function calling into AI models involves several steps:

1. **Defining Functions**: Developers must define the functions that the AI model will call. These functions should be modular, reusable, and designed to perform specific tasks efficiently.

2. **Mapping Triggers to Functions**: This involves identifying the conditions under which each function should be called. Triggers can be defined based on natural language inputs, internal logic, or external events.

3. **Implementing the Execution Logic**: The AI model must include logic to call the appropriate functions when the triggers are met. This requires integrating the function calling mechanism into the model's architecture.

4. **Testing and Validation**: Ensuring that function calls are triggered correctly and that the functions execute as expected is crucial. This involves rigorous testing and validation processes.

5. **Benefits of Function Calling in AI**

The integration of function calling into AI models offers several benefits:

- **Enhanced Capabilities**: AI models can perform a wider range of tasks, making them more useful in practical applications.

- **Increased Efficiency**: By automating routine tasks, function calling can significantly improve the efficiency of AI systems.

- **Improved User Experience**: Function calling allows AI models to provide more interactive and dynamic responses, enhancing user satisfaction.

- **Scalability**: Function calling enables AI models to scale their capabilities by leveraging external systems and resources.

6. **Challenges and Considerations**

While function calling offers many benefits, it also introduces several challenges:

- **Security**: Ensuring that function calls are secure and do not expose the system to vulnerabilities is crucial. This involves implementing robust authentication and authorization mechanisms.

- **Performance**: Function calls can introduce latency, especially if they involve external systems. Optimizing the performance of function calls is essential to maintain a responsive user experience.

- **Complexity**: Integrating function calling adds complexity to AI models, requiring careful design and implementation.

- **Error Handling**: Properly handling errors and exceptions that may occur during function execution is vital to ensure the reliability of the AI system.

7. **Real-World Applications**

Function calling is being leveraged in various real-world applications:

- **Customer Support**: AI chatbots can call functions to perform tasks such as resetting passwords, scheduling appointments, and processing refunds.

- **Automation**: AI models can automate routine tasks in business processes, such as generating reports, sending notifications, and updating records.

- **IoT Integration**: AI models can interact with Internet of Things (IoT) devices to control home automation systems, monitor environmental conditions, and manage smart appliances.

- **Healthcare**: AI systems can assist in healthcare by calling functions to schedule appointments, retrieve patient information, and process insurance claims.

8. **Future Directions**

The concept of function calling in AI is still evolving. Future directions may include

- **Advanced Orchestration**: Developing more sophisticated orchestration mechanisms to manage complex sequences of function calls.

- **Contextual Function Calling**: Enhancing AI models to call functions based on deeper contextual understanding and multiturn conversations.

- **Interoperability**: Improving interoperability between AI models and diverse external systems to expand the range of possible function calls.

- **Machine Learning Integration**: Leveraging machine learning techniques to optimize function calling strategies and improve decision-making processes.

# 6.2.1 Function Calling Illustrated

This section describes an algorithmic approach to handling user queries in a retail use case, emphasizing the role of function calling based on the user's intent. The process is divided into several key functions that work together to interpret the user's request, determine the required actions, and generate an appropriate response.

The code outlines a systematic approach to processing user queries by recognizing their intent and, if necessary, calling specific functions to generate an appropriate response.

***Listing 6-1.*** An algorithm for function calling in GenAI

```
FUNCTION process_user_query(user_input):
    // Process input and recognize intent
    intent = analyze_intent(user_input)

    IF intent requires_function_call THEN
        function_name, parameters = extract_function_
        info(intent, user_input)
        result = execute_function(function_name, parameters)
        response = generate_response(intent, result)
    ELSE
        response = generate_direct_response(intent, user_input)
    END IF

    RETURN response

FUNCTION analyze_intent(user_input):
    // NLP processing to determine user's intent
    tokens = tokenize(user_input)
    intent = classify_intent(tokens)
    RETURN intent

FUNCTION extract_function_info(intent, user_input):
    function_name = map_intent_to_function(intent)
    parameters = extract_parameters(user_input, function_name)
    RETURN function_name, parameters
```

```
FUNCTION execute_function(function_name, parameters):
    // Call appropriate function based on function_name
    IF function_name == "checkProductAvailability" THEN
        RETURN checkProductAvailability(parameters["product"],
        parameters["location"])
    ELSE IF function_name == "other_function" THEN
        // Handle other functions
    END IF

FUNCTION checkProductAvailability(product, location):
    // Actual implementation would query a database or
    inventory system
    // This is a simplified example
    inventory_data = query_inventory_system(product, location)
    RETURN inventory_data

FUNCTION generate_response(intent, result):
    // Use NLG techniques to create a human-readable response
    response = format_response_template(intent, result)
    RETURN response

// Main execution
user_input = "Is the iPhone 14 Pro in stock at the
downtown store?"
response = process_user_query(user_input)
output(response)
```

# 6.3 How Spring AI Implements and Facilitates Function Calling

Spring AI lets you integrate custom Java functions with Large Language Models (like Claude-3 series, GPT Series, Mistral, etc.). This allows the AI to call your functions and leverage external data/services. Here's the breakdown:

- **What You Can Do**

  - Register Java functions with Spring AI.

  - Functions can take arguments and return results.

  - Functions can access external data/APIs.

- **How It Works**

  - Train the AI model to recognize situations where it needs your function.

  - Spring AI handles communication between the model and your function.

  - The model sends a JSON request with arguments for your function.

  - Your function processes the request and returns a response.

- **Benefits**

  - Extend AI capabilities with custom logic.

  - Access external data sources within your AI interactions.

  - Build more dynamic and advanced AI applications.

- **How to Develop**

  - Implement a Java function with a clear name and description.

  - Define the function arguments (like a JSON schema).

  - Use @Bean annotation to register your function as a bean.

  - Reference the bean name in your prompt options when interacting with the model.

Spring AI simplifies development by handling communication and boilerplate code. This allows you to focus on building powerful custom functions that enhance your AI applications.

Figure 6-1 shows the flow which is as follows:

1. A chat prompt is received by Spring AI.

2. The Function Registry determines which functions are relevant to the prompt. Functions can be sourced from Spring beans or java.util.Function implementations.

3. The AI model processes the input, potentially using functions from the registry as needed.

4. The AI model generates a response, which is then output as the chat output.

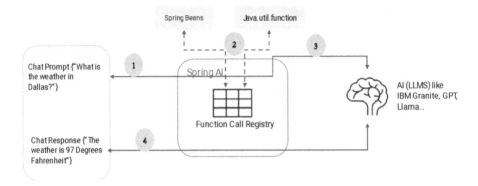

**Figure 6-1.** *Function calling with SpringAI*

# 6.4 Implementing a Spring AI Function Call Application

We will leverage a use case to implement function calling with Spring AI.

## 6.4.1 Use Case: Facilities Management

### Introduction to Facilities Management Use Case

Facilities management is a critical function for large organizations, particularly government agencies like the US General Services Administration (GSA), which oversees a vast portfolio of federal buildings. This use case focuses on creating a robust, accessible system for managing and querying information about these facilities.

For this use case, we demonstrate that we can

1.  Build an API using data stored in Postgres and hosted locally and use in a function call. This will mimic data available in a datacenter.

2. We will scrape a GSA website to get the contact information. This will demonstrate web scraping as a function call.

3. We will call an external weather API. This will demonstrate a function call to an external API.

4. We will then register these function calls in Spring and have the LLM figure out which function it needs to call.

# GSA Facilities API

This project creates a REST API for accessing information about buildings leased and owned by the US General Services Administration (GSA). The API provides detailed facility data, making it easier for developers and researchers to access and analyze this information programmatically.

- **Data Source**

  The dataset used for this API is sourced directly from the GSA's Inventory of Owned and Leased Properties (IOLP). The raw data can be found at: `https://inventory.data.gov/dataset/9a9e946e-124e-46f5-a934-e458a6c1c2b2/resource/f42e1db9-50a6-4011-a683-2dbd03263490/download/2024-7-19-iolp-buildings.xlsx`.

  This dataset is regularly updated by the GSA and contains comprehensive information about federal buildings across the United States.

  Technology Stack

  **API Framework**: Spring Data REST

  **Database**: PostgreSQL

  **Language**: Java

- **Data Structure**
  - The API exposes the following fields for each building:
    1. Location code (primary key)
    2. Real property asset name
    3. Installation name
    4. Owned or leased
    5. GSA region
    6. Street address
    7. City
    8. State
    9. Zip code
    10. Latitude
    11. Longitude
    12. Building rentable square feet
    13. Available square feet
    14. Construction date
    15. Congressional district
    16. Congressional district representative name
    17. Building status
    18. Real property asset type

- **API Usage**

  The API follows REST principles and provides endpoints for querying building information. Here's an example of how to retrieve data for a specific building: GET `http://localhost:8081/buildings/search/byCity?city=anchorage`.

  Listing 6-2 shows the sample output.

*Listing 6-2.* Sample output in json

```json
{
  "_embedded" : {
    "buildings" : [ {
      "realPropertyAssetName" : "3000 C STREET",
      "installationName" : "NA",
      "ownedOrLeased" : "L",
      "gsaRegion" : "10",
      "streetAddress" : "3000 C ST",
      "city" : "ANCHORAGE",
      "state" : "AK",
      "zipcode" : "99503      ",
      "latitude" : 61.1930468,
      "longitude" : -149.88742,
      "buildingRentableSquareFeet" : 14805.0,
      "availableSquareFeet" : 0.0,
      "constructionDate" : 2000,
      "congressionalDistrict" : "0200",
      "congressionalDistrictRepresentativeName" : "Mary
      Peltola",
      "buildingStatus" : "Active               ",
      "realPropertyAssetType" : "BUILDING  ",
```

```
    "_links" : {
      "self" : {
        "href" : "http://localhost:8081/buildings/AK3414"
      },
      "building" : {
        "href" : "http://localhost:8081/buildings/AK3414"
      }
    }
  }
 }
}
```

- **Getting Started**

  - To set up and run this project locally:

    1. Clone the repository from GitHub
       (https://github.com/banup-kubeforce/
       functioncallinginspringai.git).

    2. Ensure you have Java and PostgreSQL
       installed on your system.

    3. Configure the database connection in the
       application properties.

    4. Run the application using your preferred
       IDE or via command line.

# Spring AI Code

We will create three functions to demonstrate the Spring AI's capabilities
with function calling. These functions will be in the theme of facilities
management with a Leasing Service, Contact Service, and Weather
Service. These services will be called in the FunctionCalling service and
exposed as API using the FunctionCallingController.

**Prerequisites**

1) Code from GitHub (`https://github.com/banup-kubeforce/functioncallinginspringai.git`)

   a. Data service

   b. Code for this project

2) OpenAI API key (`https://openai.com/index/openai-api/`)

1. **LeasingService.java**

   **Overview**

   The Leasing Service is designed to facilitate facilities management by providing building leasing information based on city queries. The service interacts with an external API to fetch and process data related to available buildings in a specified city. It is implemented as a Spring Boot service, utilizing RESTful communication to achieve its functionality. See Listing 6-3 for the implementation.

*Listing 6-3.* LeasingService.java

```
import org.slf4j.Logger;
import org.slf4j.LoggerFactory;
import org.springframework.stereotype.Service;
import org.springframework.web.client.RestClient;

import java.util.List;
import java.util.function.Function;
@Service
public class LeasingService implements Function<LeasingService.
Request, LeasingService.Response> {
```

```java
private static final Logger log = LoggerFactory.
getLogger(LeasingService.class);
private final RestClient restClient;

public LeasingService() {
    this.restClient = RestClient.create("http://
    localhost:8081/buildings");
}

@Override
public Response apply( LeasingService.Request request) {
    log.info("Building Request: {}",request);
    LeasingService.Response response = restClient.get()
            .uri("/search/byCity?city={question}",
            request.city)
            .retrieve()
            .body(Response.class);

    log.info("Building API Response: {}", response);
    return response;

}
```

Key Components of LeasingService.java

- **Logging**: The Logger is used to log the incoming requests and responses for better traceability and debugging.

- **RestClient**: This is configured to interact with the external leasing API hosted at http://localhost:8081/ buildings.

- **apply Method**: This method processes the incoming request, makes a REST call to fetch the building data, and returns the response.

2. **ContactInfoService.java**

**Overview**

The Contact Info Service is another key component in demonstrating Spring AI's function calling capabilities within the facilities management theme. This service is designed to scrape and retrieve contact information related to inventory of owned and leased properties from an external website. The service extracts relevant contact details, such as names, phone numbers, email addresses, and regions, and provides this data in a structured format.

The ContactInfoService class is a Spring Service that implements the Function interface. It uses the Jsoup library to connect to a specified URL, scrape the required contact information from a web page, and return the data as a structured response.

Listing 6-4 is the implementation of ContactInfoService.java.

***Listing 6-4.*** ContactInfoService.java

```
import java.io.IOException;
import java.util.ArrayList;
import java.util.List;
import java.util.function.Function;

@Service
public class ContactInfoService implements
Function<ContactInfoService.Request, ContactInfoService.
Response> {
```

```
private static final Logger log = LoggerFactory.
getLogger(ContactInfoService.class);
private static final String URL = "https://www.gsa.gov/
about-us/contact-us/contact-information-for-inventory-of-
owned-and-lea";

@Override
public Response apply(Request request) {
    log.info("Contact Info Request: {}", request);

    try {
        Document doc = Jsoup.connect(URL).get();

        Elements rows = doc.select("table[summary='Contact
        information for Inventory of Owned and Leased
        Properties'] tbody tr");
        List<ContactInfo> contacts = new ArrayList<>();

        for (Element row : rows) {
            Elements columns = row.select("td");
            if (columns.size() == 4) {
                String region = columns.get(0).text();
                String name = columns.get(1).text();
                Element contactInfoColumn = columns.get(2);
                String states = columns.get(3).text();

                String phone = contactInfoColumn.
                select("a[href^=tel]").first() != null
                        ? contactInfoColumn.
                        select("a[href^=tel]").
                        first().text()
                        : "";
                String email = contactInfoColumn.
                select("a[href^=mailto]").text();
```

```
                ContactInfo contact = new
                ContactInfo(region, name, phone, email,
                states);
                contacts.add(contact);
            }
        }

        Response response = new Response(contacts);
        log.info("Contact Info Response: {}", response);
        return response;
    } catch (IOException e) {
        log.error("Error scraping webpage", e);
        return new Response(new ArrayList<>());
    }
}

public record Request(String dummy) {} // You might not
need any input for this function
public record Response(List<ContactInfo> contacts) {}
public record ContactInfo(String region, String name,
String phone, String email, String states) {}
}
```

Key Components of ContactInfoService.java

- **Logging**: The Logger is used to log the incoming requests and responses as well as any errors encountered during the scraping process.

- **Jsoup**: This library is used to connect to the external URL and parse the HTML content to extract contact information.

- **Scraping Logic**: The apply method connects to the URL, selects the relevant table rows, and iterates through them to extract and store the contact details in a list.

- **Response Structure**: The response contains a list of ContactInfo records, each holding the region, name, phone, email, and state information.

3. **WeatherService.java**

   **Overview**

   The Weather Service is the third key component in our demonstration of Spring AI's function calling capabilities within the facilities management theme. This service is designed to fetch and provide current weather information for a specified city. By integrating with a third-party weather API, it showcases how external data sources can be leveraged within a Spring Boot application.

   The WeatherService class is a Spring Service that implements the Function interface. It interacts with an external weather API to retrieve weather data for a given city and returns the information in a structured format.

   Listing 6-5 is the implementation of WeatherService.java.

***Listing 6-5.*** WeatherService.java

```
import org.slf4j.Logger;
import org.slf4j.LoggerFactory;
import org.springframework.stereotype.Service;
```

```
import org.springframework.web.client.RestClient;

import java.util.function.Function;

/*
   Weather API
   https://www.weatherapi.com/api-explorer.aspx
 */
@Service
public class WeatherService implements Function<WeatherService.
Request, WeatherService.Response> {

    private static final Logger log = LoggerFactory.
getLogger(WeatherService.class);
    private final RestClient restClient;
    private final WeatherConfigProperties weatherProps;

    public WeatherService(WeatherConfigProperties props) {
        this.weatherProps = props;
        log.debug("Weather API URL: {}", weatherProps.
        apiUrl());
        log.debug("Weather API Key: {}", weatherProps.
        apiKey());
        this.restClient = RestClient.create(weatherProps.
        apiUrl());
    }

    @Override
    public Response apply(WeatherService.Request
    weatherRequest) {
        log.info("Weather Request: {}",weatherRequest);
        Response response = restClient.get()
                .uri("/current.json?key={key}&q={q}",
                weatherProps.apiKey(), weatherRequest.city())
```

```
            .retrieve()
            .body(Response.class);
      log.info("Weather API Response: {}", response);
      return response;
    }

    // mapping the response of the Weather API to records. I
    only mapped the information I was interested in.
    public record Request(String city) {}
    public record Response(Location location,Current
    current) {}
    public record Location(String name, String region, String
    country, Long lat, Long lon){}
    public record Current(String temp_f, Condition condition,
    String wind_mph, String humidity) {}
    public record Condition(String text){}

}
```

### Key Components of WeatherService.java

- **Logging**: The Logger is used to log the incoming requests and responses as well as debug information such as API URL and key.

- **RestClient**: This is configured to interact with the external weather API using the base URL and API key provided by WeatherConfigProperties.

- **apply Method**: This method processes the incoming request, makes a REST call to fetch the current weather data, and returns the response.

- **WeatherConfigProperties**: This configuration class holds the API URL and key, which are necessary for authenticating and interacting with the weather API.

**Response Structure**

The response contains detailed weather information structured into records:

- **Location**: Information about the city, region, country, and geographical coordinates

- **Current**: Current weather conditions, including temperature, wind speed, humidity, and a textual description of the weather

4. **FunctionCallingService.java**

   **Overview**

   The Function Calling Service is the central component that demonstrates the integration and orchestration of multiple services using Spring AI's function calling capabilities. This service coordinates the interaction between the Leasing Service, Contact Info Service, and Weather Service, exposing their functionalities as APIs through the FunctionCallingController.

   The FunctionCallingService class is a Spring Service that utilizes the ChatClient to interact with OpenAI's chat models, enabling the invocation of specific functions based on user messages. It integrates the LeasingService, ContactInfoService, and WeatherService to provide a cohesive API for facilities management tasks.

   See Listing 6-6 for the implementation of FunctionCallingService.java.

***Listing 6-6.*** FunctionCallingService.java

```java
import org.springframework.ai.chat.client.ChatClient;
import org.springframework.ai.chat.messages.UserMessage;
import org.springframework.ai.chat.model.ChatResponse;
import org.springframework.ai.chat.prompt.Prompt;
import org.springframework.ai.model.function.
FunctionCallbackWrapper;
import org.springframework.ai.openai.OpenAiChatModel;
import org.springframework.ai.openai.OpenAiChatOptions;
import org.springframework.stereotype.Service;
import org.springframework.web.reactive.function.client.
WebClient;
import java.util.List;

@Service
public class FunctionCallingService {
    private final ChatClient chatClient;
    private final LeasingService leasingService; ;
    private final WeatherService weatherService;
    private final ContactInfoService contactInfoService;
    private final OpenAiChatModel chatModel;

    public FunctionCallingService(ChatClient chatClient,
LeasingService leasingService, WeatherService weatherService,
ContactInfoService contactInfoService, OpenAiChatModel
chatModel) {
        this.chatClient = chatClient;
        this.leasingService = leasingService;
        this.weatherService = weatherService;
        this.contactInfoService = contactInfoService;

        this.chatModel = chatModel;
    }
```

```java
public String generate(String message){
    UserMessage userMessage = new UserMessage(message);
    // ChatResponse response = chatClient.call(new
    Prompt(List.of(userMessage),OpenAiChatOptions.builder().
    withFunction("rectangleAreaFunction").build()));

/*

    var promptOptions = OpenAiChatOptions.builder()
            .withFunctionCallbacks(List.
            of(FunctionCallbackWrapper.builder(new
            MockWeatherService())
                    .withName("CurrentWeatherService")
                    .withDescription("Get the Weather
                    in location")
                    .withResponseConverter((response) -> ""
                    + response.temp())
                    .build()))
            .build();

*/

    var promptOptions = OpenAiChatOptions.builder()
            .withFunctionCallbacks(List.of(
                    FunctionCallbackWrapper.
                    builder(leasingService)
                            .withName("LeasingService")
                            .withDescription("Get the
                            buildings in a city")
                            .withResponseConverter((re
                            sponse) -> "" + response._
                            embedded().buildings())
                            .build(),
                    FunctionCallbackWrapper.
                    builder(contactInfoService)
```

```
                    .withName("ContactInfoService")
                    .withDescription("Get contact
                    information for GSA regions")
                    .withResponseConverter((respo
                    nse) -> {
                        StringBuilder result = new
                        StringBuilder();
                        for (ContactInfoService.
                        ContactInfo contact :
                        response.contacts()) {
                            result.append(String.
                            format("Region: %s\nName:
                            %s\nPhone: %s\nEmail:
                            %s\nStates: %s\n\n",
                                    contact.region(),
                                    contact.
                                    name(), contact.
                                    phone(), contact.
                                    email(), contact.
                                    states())));
                        }
                        return result.toString();
                    })
                    .build(),
            FunctionCallbackWrapper.
            builder(weatherService)
                    .withName("WeatherService")
                    .withDescription("Get the weather
                    for a city")
                    .withResponseConverter((response)
                    -> "" + response.current())
```

```
                    .build()
        ))
        .build();
    ChatResponse response = chatModel.call(new Prompt
    (List.of(userMessage), promptOptions));
    return response.getResult().getOutput().getContent().
    toString();
  }
}
```

**Key Components of FunctionCallingService.java**

- **ChatClient**: This client interacts with the OpenAI chat models, sending user messages and receiving responses.

- **Service Integration**: The LeasingService, ContactInfoService, and WeatherService are injected into this service, allowing their functionalities to be accessed and coordinated.

- **PromptOptions**: Configured with FunctionCallbackWrapper for each service, specifying the service name, description, and response converter logic.

- **generate Method**: This method processes the incoming user message, constructs the prompt options, and invokes the chat model to get the appropriate service response.

## Response Conversion

**LeasingService**: Converts the response to a string representation of the list of buildings

**ContactInfoService**: Converts the response to a formatted string containing contact information for each region

**WeatherService**: Converts the response to a string representation of the current weather information

5. **FunctionCallingController.java**

### Overview

The Function Calling Controller is an integral part of our demonstration of Spring AI's function calling capabilities within the facilities management theme. This controller serves as the web layer, exposing the functionalities of the Leasing Service, Contact Info Service, and Weather Service through RESTful APIs. By acting as an interface between the clients and the underlying services, the controller facilitates seamless interaction and data retrieval based on user queries.

The FunctionCallingController class is a Spring REST Controller that exposes endpoints for interacting with the FunctionCallingService. It processes user messages, invokes the corresponding services, and returns the responses in a structured format.

Listing 6-7 is the implementation of FunctionCallingController.java.

***Listing 6-7.*** FunctionCallingController.java

```java
import org.springframework.beans.factory.annotation.Autowired;
import org.springframework.web.bind.annotation.GetMapping;
import org.springframework.web.bind.annotation.RequestMapping;
import org.springframework.web.bind.annotation.RequestParam;
import org.springframework.web.bind.annotation.RestController;

import java.util.LinkedHashMap;
import java.util.Map;

@RestController
@RequestMapping("/fc")
public class FunctionCallingController {
    private final FunctionCallingService
functionCallingService;

    @Autowired
    public FunctionCallingController(FunctionCallingService
    functionCallingService) {
        this.functionCallingService = functionCallingService;
    }

    @GetMapping
    public Map completion(
            @RequestParam(value = "question", defaultValue =
            "What are the buildings available in the city")
            String question) {
        String answer = this.functionCallingService.
        generate(question);
        Map map = new LinkedHashMap();
        map.put("question", question);
        map.put("answer", answer);
```

```
        return map;
    }
}
```

### Key Components of FunctionCallingController.java

- **FunctionCallingService**: This service is injected into the controller to handle the business logic of processing user messages and invoking the appropriate integrated services.

- **REST Endpoint**: The @GetMapping("/generate") annotation exposes the /generate endpoint, which accepts a message parameter from the HTTP request and passes it to the FunctionCallingService.

- **RequestParam**: The @RequestParam annotation is used to extract the message parameter from the query string of the HTTP request.

### Endpoint Description

- **/generate**: This endpoint accepts a GET request with a message parameter. The message is processed by the FunctionCallingService, which determines the appropriate function to call (e.g., Leasing Service, Contact Info Service, Weather Service) based on the message content. The response from the service is then returned to the client.

### Integration with FunctionCallingService

The FunctionCallingController relies on the FunctionCallingService to orchestrate the interactions between the various services. When a request is received at the /generate endpoint, the controller forwards the message to the FunctionCallingService, which handles the logic of invoking the correct service and processing the response.

# AI Chat UI

## Introduction to AI Chat UI

The AI Chat UI is designed to provide an interactive interface for users to communicate with the AI-driven services integrated within our facilities management system. This user interface (UI) consists of an HTML structure, client-side JavaScript for handling user interactions, and an app script to manage the communication with the back-end services.

1. **index.html**

   The index.html file defines the basic structure of the chat interface, including the chatbox for displaying messages and input elements for user interaction.

   Listing 6-8 shows the content of index.html.

*Listing 6-8.* Index.html

```
<!DOCTYPE html>
<html lang="en">
<head>
    <meta charset="UTF-8">
    <meta name="viewport" content="width=device-width, initial-
    scale=1.0">
    <title>AI Chatbot</title>
    <style>
        #chatbox {
            height: 400px;
            overflow-y: auto;
            border: 1px solid #ccc;
            padding: 10px;
            margin-bottom: 10px;
        }
```

```
        table {
            border-collapse: collapse;
            width: 100%;
        }
        th, td {
            border: 1px solid #ddd;
            padding: 8px;
            text-align: left;
        }
        th {
            background-color: #f2f2f2;
        }
    </style>
</head>
<body>
<div id="chatbox"></div>
<input type="text" id="userInput" placeholder="Type your
message...">
<button onclick="sendMessage()">Send</button>

<script src="https://cdnjs.cloudflare.com/ajax/libs/
marked/2.0.3/marked.min.js"></script>
<script src="client.js"></script>
</body>
</html>
```

Key Components of index.html

- **Chatbox**: A div element with the ID chatbox where chat
  messages will be displayed. It is styled to have a fixed
  height, scrollable content, and a bordered box.

- **User Input**: An input field with the ID userInput for
  users to type their messages.

- **Send Button**: A button that triggers the sendMessage() function to send the user's message.

- **External Scripts**: Includes the marked library for Markdown parsing and the client.js script for client-side functionality.

2. **client.js**

   The client.js file handles the client-side interactions, sending user messages to the back end and updating the chatbox with responses.

   Listing 6-9 shows the code for client.js.

*Listing 6-9.* client.js

```
function sendMessage() {
    const userInput = document.getElementById('userInput');
    const chatbox = document.getElementById('chatbox');
    const question = userInput.value.trim();

    if (question) {
        // Display user message
        chatbox.innerHTML += `<p><strong>You:</strong>
        ${question}</p>`;

        // Call the API
        fetch(`/ask?question=${encodeURIComponent(question)}`)
            .then(response => response.json())
            .then(data => {
                // Use marked library to render Markdown,
                including tables
                const renderedAnswer = marked(data.answer);
                chatbox.innerHTML += `<p><strong>AI:</strong>
                ${renderedAnswer}</p>`;
```

285

```
                chatbox.scrollTop = chatbox.scrollHeight;
        })
        .catch(error => {
            console.error('Error:', error);
            chatbox.innerHTML += '<p><strong>AI:</strong>
            Sorry, I encountered an error.</p>';
        });

    userInput.value = '';
    }
}
// Add event listener for Enter key
document.getElementById('userInput').
addEventListener('keypress', function(event) {
    if (event.key === 'Enter') {
        sendMessage();
    }
});
```

Key Components of client.js

- **sendMessage Function**: Retrieves the user's input,
  updates the chatbox with the user's message, and sends
  the message to the back end using a fetch request

- **Fetch Request**: Sends the user's message to the /
  generate endpoint and processes the response to
  display in the chatbox

- **Chatbox Updates**: Dynamically adds user and bot
  messages to the chatbox

3. **App.js**

The app.js file is responsible for setting up the back-end server, handling incoming requests, and invoking the appropriate services.

Listing 6-10 shows the modified app.js.

***Listing 6-10.*** App.js

```
const express = require('express');
const path = require('path');
const axios = require('axios');
const cors = require('cors');
const app = express();
const port = 9090;

app.use(cors());
app.use(express.static('public'));

async function callExternalAPI(question) {
    try {
        const response = await axios.get(`http://localhost:
        8080/fc?question=${encodeURIComponent(question)}`);
        return response.data.answer;
    } catch (error) {
        console.error('Error calling external API:', error);
        return 'Sorry, I encountered an error while processing
        your request.';
    }
}

app.get('/ask', async (req, res) => {
    const question = req.query.question;
    if (!question) {
```

```
        return res.status(400).json({ error: 'Question is
        required' });
    }
    const answer = await callExternalAPI(question);
    res.json({ answer });
});

app.get('/', (req, res) => {
    res.sendFile(path.join(__dirname, 'public', 'index.html'));
});

app.listen(port, () => {
    console.log(`Server running at http://localhost:${port}`);
});
```

Key Components of app.js

- **Express Setup**: Sets up an Express server to handle HTTP requests

- **/generate Endpoint**: Handles GET requests to the /generate endpoint, forwards the message to the back-end service, and returns the response to the client

- **Axios**: Used to make HTTP requests to the back-end service

4. **Integration and Workflow**

   1. **User Interaction**: The user types a message into the input field and clicks the send button.

   2. **Client-Side Processing**: The sendMessage function in client.js handles the user input and sends it to the back end via a fetch request.

3. **Server-Side Handling**: The app.js file processes the request, forwards it to the back-end service, and returns the response.

4. **Response Display**: The client-side script updates the chatbox with the bot's response.

# Output

The following is the UI and sample output (see Figure 6-2).

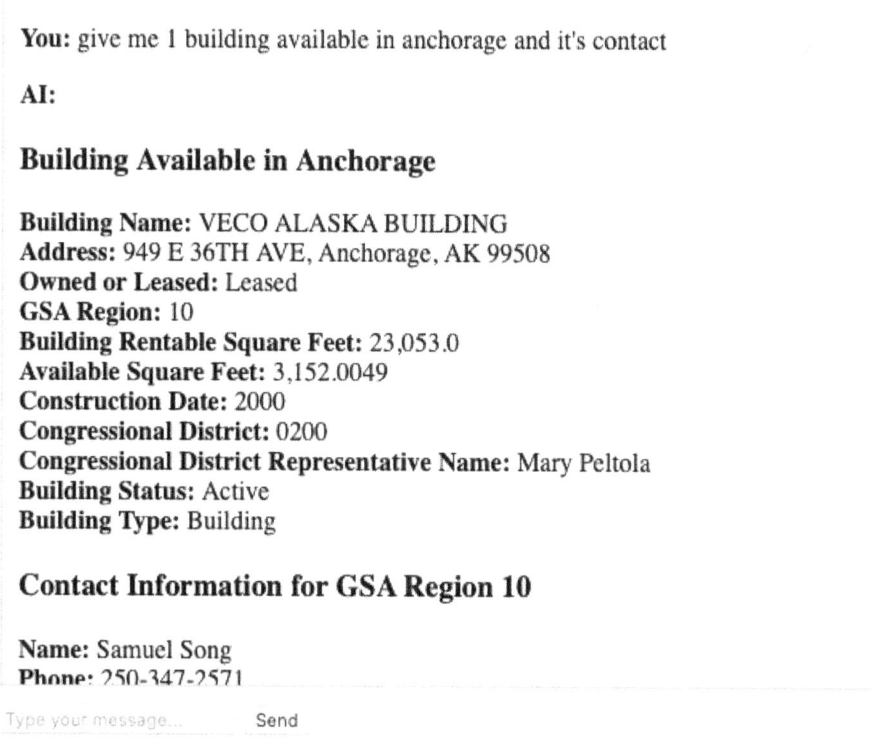

**You:** give me 1 building available in anchorage and it's contact

**AI:**

### Building Available in Anchorage

**Building Name:** VECO ALASKA BUILDING
**Address:** 949 E 36TH AVE, Anchorage, AK 99508
**Owned or Leased:** Leased
**GSA Region:** 10
**Building Rentable Square Feet:** 23,053.0
**Available Square Feet:** 3,152.0049
**Construction Date:** 2000
**Congressional District:** 0200
**Congressional District Representative Name:** Mary Peltola
**Building Status:** Active
**Building Type:** Building

### Contact Information for GSA Region 10

**Name:** Samuel Song
**Phone:** 250-347-2571

Type your message...        Send

***Figure 6-2.*** *Output*

Sample conversation output is as shown below in Figure 6-3.

**You:** in Tabular form give me 2 building with available square feet in anchorage and it's contact along with the weather

**AI:**

Here is the requested information in tabular form:

| Building Name | Address | Available Square Feet | Contact Name | Contact Phone | Contact Email | Weather Condition | Temperature (°F) | Wind (mph) | |
|---|---|---|---|---|---|---|---|---|---|
| PROSPECTUS WAREHOUSE | 319 E SHIP CREEK AVE, Anchorage, AK 99501 | 10,000 | Samuel Song | 250-347-2571 | Samuel.Song@gsa.gov | Light rain shower | 48.9 | 4.5 | |
| ANCHORAGE FEDERAL BUILDING US COURTHOUSE ANNEX | 222 W 8TH AVE, Anchorage, AK 99513 | 27,689.02 | Samuel Song | 250-347-2571 | Samuel.Song@gsa.gov | Light rain shower | 48.9 | 4.5 | |

## Additional Contact Information for GSA Regions

- **Region 10 Contact**: Samuel Song
  - **Phone**: 250-347-2571
  - **Email**: Samuel.Song@gsa.gov
  - **States**: AK, ID, OR, WA

## Weather in Anchorage

- **Condition**: Light rain shower
- **Temperature**: 48.9°F
- **Wind**: 4.5 mph
- **Humidity**: 90%

***Figure 6-3.*** *Sample output*

# CHAPTER 7

# Productionizing Spring AI

## 7.1 Introduction

As AI models transition from development to production, ensuring their robustness, scalability, and ethical deployment becomes paramount. This chapter will delve into the critical aspects of productionizing AI, focusing on governance frameworks and best practices that ensure AI systems are reliable, fair, and compliant with regulatory standards.

- **AI Governance**

  AI governance refers to the framework of policies, processes, and controls that oversee the development and deployment of AI systems. It aims to ensure that AI is used responsibly and ethically and in compliance with laws and regulations.

  **Key Components of AI Governance**

  - **Ethical Guidelines:** Establishing ethical principles to guide AI development and usage

  - **Regulatory Compliance:** Ensuring AI systems comply with relevant laws and regulations, such as GDPR for data privacy

- **Risk Management:** Identifying and mitigating risks associated with AI deployment, including biases, data security, and unintended consequences

- **Transparency and Accountability:** Ensuring AI decisions can be explained and attributed to responsible parties

- **Continuous Monitoring:** Regularly auditing AI systems to ensure ongoing compliance and performance standards

- **Prompt Governance (Testing and Evaluation)**

  Prompt governance focuses on the management and oversight of AI prompts used in generative models, ensuring their reliability, accuracy, and ethical use.

  **Key Aspects of Prompt Governance**

  - **Prompt Testing:** Rigorous testing of prompts to ensure they produce the desired and accurate outputs

  - **Evaluation Metrics:** Defining and using appropriate metrics to evaluate prompt performance, such as precision, recall, and F1 score

  - **Bias and Fairness:** Ensuring prompts do not produce biased or harmful outputs and adhere to fairness standards

  - **Version Control:** Maintaining version control for prompts to track changes and improvements over time

- **User Feedback Integration:** Collecting and integrating feedback from end users to refine and improve prompts

- **Scaling AI Systems**

  Scaling AI systems involves optimizing them to handle increased workloads and data volumes efficiently while maintaining performance and reliability.

  **Strategies for Scaling AI**

  - **Infrastructure Optimization:** Utilizing cloud resources, Kubernetes, and containerization to manage and scale AI workloads

  - **Model Optimization:** Techniques such as model pruning, quantization, and distillation to reduce model size and improve efficiency

  - **Data Management:** Implementing efficient data pipelines and storage solutions to handle large datasets

  - **Load Balancing:** Distributing workloads evenly across servers to prevent bottlenecks and ensure high availability

  - **Monitoring and Alerting:** Setting up monitoring tools to track system performance and alert on any issues

- **Security and Privacy**

  Ensuring the security and privacy of AI systems is crucial to protect sensitive data and maintain user trust.

### Key Considerations

- **Data Encryption:** Encrypting data at rest and in transit to prevent unauthorized access

- **Access Controls:** Implementing strict access controls and authentication mechanisms

- **Data Anonymization:** Anonymizing data to protect user privacy, especially in compliance with regulations like GDPR

- **Threat Detection:** Using AI-driven security tools to detect and respond to threats in real time

- **Regular Audits:** Conducting regular security audits to identify and address vulnerabilities

- **Conclusion**

  Productionizing Spring AI involves a comprehensive approach that encompasses governance, scaling, security, and continuous improvement. By adhering to best practices and implementing robust frameworks, organizations can ensure their AI systems are reliable, ethical, and scalable, driving significant value and innovation.

# 7.2  AI Governance

AI governance is essential is making sure that the Generative AI app you are creating works within a bounded context and does not hallucinate. It is also important to meet regulations.

# 7.2.1 Common Regulatory Themes

1. **Explainability and Interpretability**: These concepts refer to the ability to understand and explain how an AI system makes decisions. An explainable AI system should be able to provide clear reasons for its outputs in a way that humans can comprehend.

2. **Justifiability and Conceptual Soundness**: This theme focuses on ensuring that AI systems are built on sound principles and that their decisions can be justified logically and ethically. The underlying concepts and methodologies should be valid and well-founded.

3. **Fairness and No Unjust Bias**: This principle aims to ensure that AI systems do not discriminate against individuals or groups based on protected characteristics such as race, gender, age, or religion. The goal is to create systems that make fair and equitable decisions.

4. **Customer Transparency and Recourse**: This theme emphasizes the importance of being open with customers about how AI systems are used in decision-making processes that affect them. It also involves providing mechanisms for customers to challenge decisions or seek remedies if they believe they've been unfairly treated.

5. **Robustness, Reliability, and Stability**: These concepts relate to the consistent and dependable performance of AI systems. A robust system should maintain its accuracy and effectiveness across various conditions and over time, without unexpected failures or significant deviations in output.

6. **Accountability**: This principle focuses on establishing clear lines of responsibility for AI systems' decisions and actions. It involves determining who is answerable for the system's outputs and ensuring there are mechanisms in place to address issues or mistakes.

These themes are interconnected and collectively aim to ensure that AI systems are developed and used in ways that are ethical, transparent, and beneficial to society. They form a framework for responsible AI governance and are increasingly important as AI becomes more prevalent in various sectors.

## 7.2.2  Action Plan for the Enterprise

Creating an action plan for an enterprise to execute according to these regulatory themes is a comprehensive process. Here's a step-by-step approach to develop such a plan:

1. **Assessment and Gap Analysis**

   - Evaluate current AI systems and practices against each theme.

   - Identify gaps and areas for improvement.

2. **Establish Governance Structure**

- Create an AI ethics committee or designate responsible teams.

- Define roles and responsibilities for AI governance.

3. **Develop Policies and Guidelines**

- Draft clear policies aligned with each regulatory theme.

- Create guidelines for AI development, deployment, and use.

4. **Implementation Strategy**: For each theme, develop specific actions. For example:

a) **Explainability and Interpretability**

- Implement tools for visualizing AI decision processes.

- Train developers in explainable AI techniques.

- Tools

    1. LIME (Local Interpretable Model-Agnostic Explanations) `https://www.mdpi.com/2504-4990/3/3/27`

    2. SHAP (SHapley Additive exPlanations) `https://www.sciencedirect.com/science/article/abs/pii/S0169260721006581`

    3. ELI5 (Explain Like I'm 5) `https://arxiv.org/abs/1907.09190`

    4. InterpretML `https://interpret.ml/`

    5. IBM's AI Explainability 360 `https://aix360.res.ibm.com/`

b) **Justifiability and Conceptual Soundness**

- Establish review processes for AI models and methodologies.

- Document the rationale behind model choices.

- Tools

    1. Model Cards (documentation framework) `https://huggingface.co/blog/model-cards`

    2. Deon (ethics checklist for data scientists) `https://deon.drivendata.org/`

    3. Datasheets for Datasets `https://arxiv.org/abs/1803.09010`

c) **Fairness and No Unjust Bias**

- Implement bias detection tools in the AI pipeline.

- Conduct regular fairness audits on AI systems.

- Tools

    1. Fairlearn (Microsoft's fairness assessment tool) `https://fairlearn.org`

    2. AI Fairness 360 (IBM's bias detection and mitigation toolkit) `https://aif360.res.ibm.com`

    3. Aequitas (bias audit toolkit) `http://aequitas.dssg.io`

    4. What-If Tool (Google's fairness visualization tool) `https://research.google/pubs/the-what-if-tool-interactive-probing-of-machine-learning-models/#:~:text=The%20What%2DIf%20Tool%20lets,to%20multiple%20ML%20fairness%20metrics.`

d) **Customer Transparency and Recourse**

- Develop clear communication materials about AI use.

- Establish a process for customers to challenge AI decisions.

- Tools

    1. GDPR compliance tools (e.g., OneTrust, TrustArc)

    2. Customer feedback management systems

    3. Automated decision explanation generators

e) **Robustness, Reliability, and Stability**

- Implement rigorous testing protocols.

- Establish monitoring systems for AI performance.

- Tools

    1. MLflow (for model lifecycle management)

    2. Kubeflow (for deploying ML workflows)

    3. Seldon Core (for model deployment and monitoring)

    4. Prometheus (for monitoring and alerting)

f) **Accountability**

- Create a chain of responsibility for AI systems.

- Implement logging and auditing mechanisms.

- Tools

    1. GitLab or GitHub (for version control and collaboration)

    2. Jira (for project management and issue tracking)

    3. Datadog (for logging and monitoring)

    4. Splunk (for data monitoring and analytics)

5. **Training and Education**

   - Develop training programs for employees on these themes.

   - Conduct workshops and seminars to build awareness.

6. **Continuous Monitoring and Improvement**

   - Establish KPIs for each theme.

   - Regularly review and update practices.

7. **Stakeholder Engagement**

   - Engage with customers, regulators, and industry peers.

   - Participate in AI ethics forums and discussions.

8. **Documentation and Reporting**

   - Maintain comprehensive documentation of AI systems.

   - Prepare regular reports on compliance with these themes.

9. **Risk Management**

   - Conduct risk assessments for AI systems.

   - Develop mitigation strategies for identified risks.

10. **External Validation**

    - Consider third-party audits or certifications.

    - Engage with external experts for review and guidance.

This action plan provides a framework for systematically addressing these regulatory themes. The specific details and priorities would need to be tailored to the enterprise's size, industry, and current AI maturity level.

## 7.2.3  Regulations Across the Globe

Table 7-1 shows the various regulations adopted by different countries over the years.

***Table 7-1.***  *Global regulations impacting GenAI and LLMs*

| 2018 | 2019 | 2020 | 2021 | 2022 | 2023 | 2024 |
|------|------|------|------|------|------|------|
| •European Union (GPDR fine imposed for 20Million Euros or 4% of company turnover) - https://gdpr-info.eu/issues/fines-penalties/ | •Columbia – National Policy for Digital Transformation and AI https://fair1ac.iadb.org/en/hub/colombia | •Norway – National AI Strategy - https://www.regjeringen.no/contentassets/1febbbb2c4f d4b7d92c67ddd353b6ae8/en-gb/pdfs/ki-strategi_en.pdf | •United States – National Artificial Intelligence Initiative https://www.uspto.gov/sites/default/files/documents/National-Artificial-Intelligence-Initiative-Overview.pdf | •United Kingdom – AI Regulation Policy - https://www.mayerbrown.com/fr/insights/publications/2022/08/uk-government-proposes-a-new-approach-to-regulating-artificial-intelligence-ai | •New York City – AI hiring law - https://www.nytimes.com/2023/05/25/technology/ai-hiring-law-new-york.html | •European Union – EU AI Act endorsed and begins rolling out in 2024 - https://kpmg.com/dk/en/home/insights/2024/06/the-eu-ai-act-are-you-ready-for-the-new-legislation.html#:~:text=The%20EU%20Parliament%20has%20already,the%20associated%20requirements%20and%20obligations. |
| •Germany – AI Strategy report released https://ai-watch.ec.europa.eu/countries/germany/germany-ai-strategy-report_en | •Australia – AI Ethics Framework - https://www.industry.gov.au/publications/australias-artificial-intelligence-ethics-framework | •Serbia – Strategy for the development of AI - https://www.srbija.gov.rs/tekst/en/149169/strategy-for-the-development-of-artificial-intelligence-in-the-republic-of-serbia-for-the-period-2020-2025.php | •European Union – The AI Act (Fine of 30Million Euros or 6% of company's global revenue) - https://www.loc.gov/item/global-legal-monitor/2021-05-26/european-union-commission-publishes-proposal-to-regulate-artificial-intelligence/#:~:text=For%20using%20prohibited%20AI%2 0practices,4%25%20of%20t he%20total%20worldwide | •China – Internet Information Service Algorithmic Management (IISARM) regulations - https://digichina.stanford.edu/work/translation-internet-information-service-algorithmic-recommendation-management-provisions-effective-march-1-2022/ | | |
| •South Korea – AI Strategy https://www.msit.go.kr/eng/bbs/view.do?sCode=eng&mId=4&mPid=2&pageIndex=&bbsSeqNo=42&nttSeqN o=509&searchOpt=ALL&searchTxt\:~:text=The%20strategy%20has%20the%20vision,ethics'%20and%2010%20action%20plans. | | | | •Canada – Bill C27, AI and Data Act (Fine of S25 Million or 5% of company's gross revenue) - https://www.gmundlabs.com/blog/what-you-need-to-know-about-canada-bill-c-27/#:~:text=Business%20could%20receive%20fines%20of,collecting%20or%20using%20personal%20information. | | |

# 7.3  LLM Ops

This section, **LLMOps (Large Language Model Operations)**, explores the unique set of practices and technologies designed specifically for handling the complexities associated with LLMs in production environments.

# 7.3.1  What Is LLMOps

LLMOps (Large Language Model Operations) is a set of practices and technologies specifically designed for the deployment, management, and optimization of Large Language Models in production environments. It encompasses the entire lifecycle of LLMs, from development and training to deployment, monitoring, and continuous improvement, with a focus on the unique challenges and requirements of working with these complex, data-intensive models.

# 7.3.2  LLMOps vs. MLOps

LLMOps and MLOps are both operations frameworks, but they cater to different aspects of machine learning and AI systems. Here are the key differences between LLMOps (Large Language Model Operations) and MLOps (Machine Learning Operations):

1. **Scope and Focus**

   - **LLMOps (Large Language Model Operations)**

     - **Focus**: Primarily on the deployment, management, and optimization of Large Language Models (LLMs) like GPT, BERT, etc.

     - **Scope**: Handles specific challenges related to Large Language Models, such as fine-tuning, prompt management, and serving large-scale inference requests

     - **Specialized Practices**: Includes prompt engineering, handling context windows, managing model versions and variants for specific use cases, and ensuring the ethical use of LLMs

- **MLOps (Machine Learning Operations)**

  - **Focus**: Broader focus on the deployment, management, and scaling of machine learning models in general

  - **Scope**: Encompasses the entire ML lifecycle, including data preprocessing, model training, validation, deployment, monitoring, and continuous integration/continuous deployment (CI/CD) practices for ML models

  - **General Practices**: Involves data versioning, model versioning, automated retraining, monitoring for model drift, and ensuring reproducibility

2. **Lifecycle Management**

    1. **LLMOps**

       - **Model Deployment**: Focused on deploying Large Language Models with considerations for high computational requirements and efficient inference

       - **Prompt Management**: Involves designing and managing prompts to optimize the performance and relevance of LLM responses

       - **Fine-Tuning**: Deals with fine-tuning pretrained language models for specific tasks or domains

       - **Inference Optimization**: Techniques to optimize inference speed and cost, such as model distillation or quantization

- **Ethical and Responsible AI**: Ensures the models are used ethically, addressing concerns like bias and inappropriate content generation

2. **MLOps**

- **Data Management**: Involves data collection, preprocessing, and versioning to ensure high-quality input for models

- **Model Training**: Covers the training process, including hyperparameter tuning and resource management

- **Model Deployment**: Manages the deployment of models into production environments, ensuring scalability and reliability

- **Monitoring and Maintenance**: Continuously monitors models for performance degradation, drift, and anomalies and maintains them accordingly

- **Automation and CI/CD**: Integrates ML workflows with CI/CD pipelines for automated testing, deployment, and updates

3. **Tools and Technologies**

   1. **LLMOps**

      - **Specialized Tools**: Tools specifically designed for Large Language Models, such as Transformer libraries, distributed training frameworks, and LLM-specific serving infrastructure

      - **Prompt Engineering Tools**: Platforms that assist in designing, testing, and managing prompts for optimal LLM performance

2.  **MLOps**

- **General ML Tools**: A wide array of tools for various stages of the ML lifecycle, including data versioning tools (e.g., DVC), training frameworks (e.g., TensorFlow, PyTorch), and deployment tools (e.g., Kubeflow, MLflow)

- **Monitoring and Logging**: Tools for monitoring model performance, logging predictions, and tracking metrics (e.g., Prometheus, Grafana)

4.  **Challenges and Considerations**

1.  **LLMOps**

- **Resource Intensive**: Managing the high computational demands of training and serving Large Language Models

- **Ethical Use**: Ensuring responsible use of LLMs to mitigate risks associated with biases and inappropriate content

- **Scalability**: Optimizing inference for scalability without compromising performance

2.  **MLOps**

- **Data Quality**: Ensuring high-quality and relevant data for training models

- **Reproducibility**: Maintaining reproducibility across different environments and over time

- **Model Drift**: Monitoring and addressing model drift to ensure long-term performance and accuracy

5. **Fine-Tuning**

   - **LLMOps**: Focuses on starting with a pretrained foundation model (e.g., GPT) and fine-tuning it with new, domain-specific data to achieve high performance with relatively less data and computational resources.

   - **MLOps**: While also involving fine-tuning, MLOps deals with a broader range of models and may require more extensive data preprocessing and feature engineering.

6. **Human Feedback**

   - **LLMOps**: Uses Reinforcement Learning from Human Feedback (RLHF) to improve the performance of LLMs, essential for tasks that are open-ended and subjective

   - **MLOps**: May involve human feedback but typically focuses on more structured forms of feedback, such as labeled datasets for supervised learning

7. **Hyperparameter Tuning**

   - **LLMOps**: Involves tuning specific hyperparameters that significantly impact the performance and cost of LLMs, such as batch sizes, learning rates, and model architectures.

   - **MLOps**: Hyperparameter tuning is also crucial but spans a wider variety of models and algorithms, each with its own set of hyperparameters.

8. **Performance Metrics**

   - **LLMOps**: Evaluates models using metrics like BLEU and ROUGE, which are specific to natural language processing tasks, and requires careful interpretation to ensure meaningful evaluations

   - **MLOps**: Uses a broader range of performance metrics depending on the model and application, such as accuracy, precision, recall, F1 score, and area under the ROC curve

9. **Prompt Engineering**

   - **LLMOps**: Heavily relies on designing effective prompt templates to elicit accurate and relevant responses from LLMs, addressing challenges like model hallucination and data leakage.

   - **MLOps**: Prompt engineering is less relevant; instead, it focuses on feature engineering and model selection to optimize performance.

10. **LLM Chains or Pipelines**

    - **LLMOps**: Involves creating pipelines that chain multiple LLM calls or integrate with external systems to perform complex tasks, often facilitated by frameworks like LangChain

    - **MLOps**: Builds end-to-end pipelines for various ML tasks, including data ingestion, preprocessing, model training, evaluation, and deployment, using tools like Kubeflow and MLflow

11.  **Computational Resource Management**

- **LLMOps**: Manages extensive computational requirements for training and deploying LLMs, often utilizing GPUs for efficient data-parallel operations and employing techniques like model compression and distillation to reduce inference costs

- **MLOps**: Also focuses on resource management but typically deals with a wider range of model sizes and complexities, balancing CPU, GPU, and memory usage for optimal performance and cost efficiency

# 7.3.3 Metrics to Consider When Working with LLMs

Core Performance Metrics

1.  **Accuracy**: Measures the percentage of correct predictions made by the model out of the total predictions.

2.  **BLEU (Bilingual Evaluation Understudy)**: Evaluates the quality of text which has been machine-translated from one language to another.

3.  **ROUGE (Recall-Oriented Understudy for Gisting Evaluation)**: Measures the overlap between the model's output and reference output, commonly used for summarization tasks.

4.  **Perplexity**: Measures how well a probability model predicts a sample. Lower perplexity indicates better performance.

5. **F1 Score**: Combines precision and recall into a single metric, especially useful for imbalanced datasets.

6. **Precision and Recall**: Precision measures the accuracy of the positive predictions, while recall measures the ability of the model to find all relevant instances in the dataset.

Resource Utilization

1. **Inference Latency**: Measures the time taken by the model to generate a response

2. **Throughput**: Number of inferences the model can handle per second

3. **Memory Usage**: Amount of memory consumed during training and inference

4. **Compute Utilization**: Utilization of computational resources such as GPUs or TPUs

Model Training and Tuning

1. **Training Time**: Total time taken to train the model

2. **Hyperparameters**: Key hyperparameters such as learning rate, batch size, and number of epochs

3. **Loss Function**: Tracks the loss value during training to monitor convergence

4. **Gradient Norms**: Helps in diagnosing issues like vanishing or exploding gradients

Data Quality and Distribution

1. **Input Data Quality**: Ensures the quality and cleanliness of the data fed into the model

2. **Distribution Shifts**: Monitors for shifts in data distribution which might affect model performance

3. **Outliers and Anomalies**: Identifies unusual data points that might impact model performance

User Interaction and Feedback

1. **User Feedback**: Collects qualitative feedback from users interacting with the model

2. **Engagement Metrics**: Measures user engagement and satisfaction with the model outputs

3. **Error Analysis**: Analyzes errors made by the model to identify areas for improvement

Ethical and Bias Considerations

1. **Fairness Metrics**: Monitors for biases in the model's predictions across different demographic groups

2. **Content Safety**: Ensures the model does not generate harmful or inappropriate content

3. **Transparency**: Tracks how transparent and interpretable the model's decisions are

Operational Metrics

1. **Deployment Stability**: Measures the stability and reliability of the model in production

2. **Scalability**: Monitors the model's ability to scale with increasing loads

3. **Cost Efficiency**: Tracks the cost associated with training and deploying the model

Example Metrics Specific to LLMs

1. **Token-Level Accuracy**: Accuracy at the token level, useful for tasks like translation and text generation.

2. **Context Window Utilization**: Monitors how effectively the model uses the context window for generating responses

3. **Prompt Effectiveness**: Evaluates how well different prompts elicit desired responses from the model

# 7.3.4 Tools for LLMOps

Table 7-2 shows the tools that can used in the LLMOps process.

***Table 7-2.*** *Tools that be leveraged to implement an LLMOps process within an enterprise*

| Category | Tool | Description |
|---|---|---|
| **Model Training and Fine-Tuning** | Hugging Face Transformers | Provides pretrained models and tools for fine-tuning and deploying LLMs |
| | OpenAI API | Access to GPT-3 and GPT-4 via API for integration and fine-tuning |
| | Google Cloud AI Platform | Supports training and deploying large models with robust infrastructure |
| | Amazon SageMaker | Comprehensive suite for training, deploying, and managing ML models, including LLMs |
| | IBM Watsonx | Enterprise AI platform for scaling AI workloads, including tools for LLMs |
| | TensorFlow | An open source machine learning framework for training and fine-tuning LLMs |
| | PyTorch | Another popular open source machine learning framework for training and fine-tuning LLMs |

*(continued)*

*Table 7-2.* (*continued*)

| Category | Tool | Description |
|---|---|---|
| **Deployment and Inference** | Microsoft Azure Machine Learning | Tools for deploying LLMs, including model management and monitoring |
| | Ray Serve | High scalability and low latency serving for ML models, including LLMs |
| | TorchServe | Flexible and easy-to-use tool for serving PyTorch models |
| | AWS SageMaker Inference | Provides scalable and secure deployment options for LLMs |
| | Google Cloud AI Platform Prediction | Supports deploying and serving LLMs |
| **Prompt Engineering and Management** | LangChain | Facilitates the creation of pipelines that chain together multiple LLM calls |
| | PromptLayer | Tools for managing, optimizing, and versioning prompts |
| | Microsoft Prompt Flow | Tool for managing and optimizing prompts for LLMs |
| | LangSmith | Advanced tools for prompt engineering, management, and optimization |
| | OpenAI's Prompt Library | Offers a collection of prebuilt prompts for various tasks and domains |
| **Monitoring and Optimization** | Weights & Biases | Tracks experiments, visualizes model performance, and collaborates on ML projects |

(*continued*)

*Table 7-2.* (*continued*)

| Category | Tool | Description |
|---|---|---|
| | Neptune.ai | Tracks and visualizes metrics and hyperparameters for LLM performance monitoring |
| | Fiddler AI | Model monitoring and explainability tools |
| | Evidently AI | Provides monitoring and analytics tools for LLM performance and data quality |
| | Hugging Face's Model Evaluation | Offers tools for evaluating and comparing LLM performance |
| **Data Management** | DVC (Data Version Control) | Manages data, models, and experiments for reproducibility and efficient handling |
| | Pachyderm | Data versioning and lineage tracking for managing large datasets |
| | Apache Hudi | Manages data lakes and provides data versioning and governance |
| | Delta Lake | Offers data versioning, governance, and reliability for large datasets |
| **Ethical and Bias Considerations** | IBM Watson OpenScale | Monitors AI models for fairness, bias detection, and explainability |
| | Aequitas | Open source bias and fairness audit toolkit |
| | AI Fairness 360 | Open source toolkit for detecting and mitigating bias in AI models |

(*continued*)

***Table 7-2.*** *(continued)*

| Category | Tool | Description |
|---|---|---|
| | Fairlearn | Python package for fairness metrics and bias mitigation |
| **Resource Management** | KubeFlow | Platform for deploying, scaling, and managing ML workflows on Kubernetes |
| | Apache Spark | Distributed computing for training large models and managing datasets |
| | Ray | High-performance computing framework for scaling LLM training and deployment |
| | Dask | Parallel computing library for scaling data processing and model training |
| **Collaboration and Experimentation** | Google Colab | Cloud-based notebook environment for collaborative development and experimentation |
| | Jupyter Notebooks | Widely used for developing and sharing code, data analysis, and visualizations |
| | GitHub Codespaces | Cloud-based development environment for collaborative coding and experimentation |
| | Replit | Cloud-based platform for collaborative coding, experimentation, and deployment |

*(continued)*

*Table 7-2.* (*continued*)

| Category | Tool | Description |
|---|---|---|
| **Integration and Automation** | Airflow | Author, schedule, and monitor workflows to automate LLM training and deployment pipelines |
| | MLflow | Manages the ML lifecycle, including experimentation, reproducibility, and deployment |
| | Zapier | Automates workflows by integrating various tools and platforms |
| | MLOps | Set of practices and tools for automating the ML lifecycle, including LLM training and deployment |

# 7.4 Prompt Governance (Testing and Evaluation)

Prompt governance focuses on the management and oversight of AI prompts used in generative models, ensuring their reliability, accuracy, and ethical use.

**Key Aspects of Prompt Governance**

- **Prompt Testing:** Rigorous testing of prompts to ensure they produce the desired and accurate outputs

- **Evaluation Metrics:** Defining and using appropriate metrics to evaluate prompt performance, such as precision, recall, and F1 score

- **Bias and Fairness:** Ensuring prompts do not produce biased or harmful outputs and adhere to fairness standards

- **Version Control:** Maintaining version control for prompts to track changes and improvements over time

- **User Feedback Integration:** Collecting and integrating feedback from end users to refine and improve prompts

# 7.4.1  Prompt Governance in Spring AI

Spring AI allows you to govern your prompts through an RelevancyEvaluator interface.

Here is a brief on that interface.

It is available at org.springframework.ai.evaluation.

1. **Evaluator Interface:** The Evaluator interface is defined in Evaluator.java. It's a functional interface with a single method:

```
public interface Evaluator {
        EvaluationResponse evaluate(EvaluationRequest
        evaluationRequest);
}
```

This interface is implemented by the RelevancyEvaluator class.

2. **RelevancyEvaluator:** The RelevancyEvaluator class implements the Evaluator interface. Its main purpose is to evaluate if a response to a query is relevant based on the provided context. Here are the key components:

a. Constructor

```
public RelevancyEvaluator(ChatClient.Builder
chatClientBuilder)
```

> It takes a ChatClient.Builder as a parameter,
> which is used to create a chat client for evaluation.

b.  evaluate() method

> This method takes an EvaluationRequest and returns an
> EvaluationResponse. It does the following:

- Extracts the response and context from the
  evaluation request

- Uses a predefined prompt template to create a
  query for the chat client

- Sends the query to the chat client and receives
  an evaluation response

- Interprets the response (looking for "yes"
  or "no")

> Creates and returns an EvaluationResponse object

c.  doGetSupportingData() method

> This protected method extracts the supporting data (context)
> from the EvaluationRequest.

3. **EvaluationRequest:** This class represents the input
   for evaluation, containing

- userText: The original query

- dataList: A list of Content objects (context)

- responseContent: The response to be evaluated

4. **EvaluationResponse:** This class represents the output of the evaluation, containing

- pass: A boolean indicating if the evaluation passed

- score: A float value (0 or 1 in this implementation)

- feedback: A string for additional feedback (empty in this implementation)

- metadata: A map for additional metadata (empty in this implementation)

The RelevancyEvaluator uses a chat client to determine if a given response is relevant to the query based on the provided context. It formats a prompt using a template, sends it to the chat client, and interprets the response as either passing (yes) or failing (no) the relevancy check.

## 7.4.2 Let's Code

**Prerequisites**

1) OpenAI API key.

2) Download code from GitHub (https://github.com/banup-kubeforce/ragwithevaluator.git).

3) Pgvector with bikes.json as shown in Chapter 4.

4) Postgres db.

1. Configuring pom.xml (see Listing 7-1)

***Listing 7-1.*** POM.xml

```
<?xml version="1.0" encoding="UTF-8"?>
<project xmlns="http://maven.apache.org/POM/4.0.0"
xmlns:xsi="http://www.w3.org/2001/XMLSchema-instance"
```

```xml
xsi:schemaLocation="http://maven.apache.org/POM/4.0.0
https://maven.apache.org/xsd/maven-4.0.0.xsd">
<modelVersion>4.0.0</modelVersion>
<parent>
    <groupId>org.springframework.boot</groupId>
    <artifactId>spring-boot-starter-parent</artifactId>
    <version>3.2.3</version>
    <relativePath/> <!-- lookup parent from repository -->
</parent>
<groupId>com.example</groupId>
<artifactId>spring-ai-rag</artifactId>
<version>0.0.1-SNAPSHOT</version>
<name>spring-ai-rag</name>
<description>Simple AI Application using OpenAPI Service
for RAG</description>
<properties>
    <java.version>17</java.version>
</properties>
<dependencyManagement>
    <dependencies>
        <dependency>
            <groupId>org.springframework.ai</groupId>
            <artifactId>spring-ai-bom</artifactId>
            <version>1.0.0-SNAPSHOT</version>
            <type>pom</type>
            <scope>import</scope>
        </dependency>
    </dependencies>
</dependencyManagement>
<dependencies>
    <dependency>
```

```xml
            <groupId>org.springframework.boot</groupId>
            <artifactId>spring-boot-starter-web</artifactId>
        </dependency>

        <dependency>
            <groupId>org.springframework.boot</groupId>
            <artifactId>spring-boot-starter-actuator</artifactId>
        </dependency>
        <dependency>
            <groupId>org.springframework.ai</groupId>
            <artifactId>spring-ai-openai-spring-boot-starter</
            artifactId>
        </dependency>
        <dependency>
            <groupId>org.springframework.ai</groupId>
            <artifactId>spring-ai-pgvector-store-spring-boot-
            starter</artifactId>
        </dependency>
        <dependency>
            <groupId>org.springframework.ai</groupId>
            <artifactId>spring-ai-pdf-document-reader</artifactId>
        </dependency>

        <dependency>
            <groupId>org.springframework.boot</groupId>
            <artifactId>spring-boot-starter-test</artifactId>
            <scope>test</scope>
        </dependency>
    </dependencies>

    <build>
        <plugins>
            <plugin>
```

```
      <groupId>org.springframework.boot</groupId>
      <artifactId>spring-boot-maven-plugin</artifactId>
    </plugin>
  </plugins>
</build>
<repositories>
  <repository>
    <id>spring-milestones</id>
    <name>Spring Milestones</name>
    <url>https://repo.spring.io/milestone</url>
    <snapshots>
      <enabled>false</enabled>
    </snapshots>
  </repository>
  <repository>
    <id>spring-snapshots</id>
    <name>Spring Snapshots</name>
    <url>https://repo.spring.io/snapshot</url>
    <releases>
      <enabled>false</enabled>
    </releases>
  </repository>
</repositories>

</project>
```

2.  Using junit to test and evaluate

    a.  ChatbotTests.java (see Listing 7-2)

***Listing 7-2.*** ChatbotTests.java with junit framework

```
import com.example.rag.data.DataController;
import org.junit.jupiter.api.Disabled;
import org.junit.jupiter.api.Test;
import org.springframework.ai.chat.client.ChatClient;
import org.springframework.ai.chat.client.advisor.
QuestionAnswerAdvisor;
import org.springframework.ai.chat.model.ChatModel;
import org.springframework.ai.chat.model.ChatResponse;
import org.springframework.ai.evaluation.EvaluationRequest;
import org.springframework.ai.evaluation.EvaluationResponse;
import org.springframework.ai.evaluation.RelevancyEvaluator;
import org.springframework.ai.model.Content;
import org.springframework.ai.vectorstore.SearchRequest;
import org.springframework.ai.vectorstore.VectorStore;
import org.springframework.beans.factory.annotation.Autowired;
import org.springframework.boot.test.context.SpringBootTest;

import java.util.List;

import static org.junit.jupiter.api.Assertions.assertTrue;

@SpringBootTest
public class ChatbotTests {

    @Autowired
    private ChatModel chatModel;

    @Autowired
    private DataController dataController;

    @Autowired
    private VectorStore vectorStore;
```

```
@Test
//@Disabled("Run test manually when you add your API KEY to
application.yml")
void testEvaluation() {

    //dataController.delete();
    //dataController.load();

    String userText = "What is CVS's annual turover?";

    ChatResponse response = ChatClient.builder(chatModel)
            .build().prompt()
            .advisors(new QuestionAnswerAdvisor(vectorStore,
            SearchRequest.defaults()))
            .user(userText)
            .call()
            .chatResponse();

    var relevancyEvaluator = new
    RelevancyEvaluator(ChatClient.builder(chatModel));
    EvaluationRequest evaluationRequest = new
    EvaluationRequest(userText,
            (List<Content>) response.getMetadata().
            get(QuestionAnswerAdvisor.RETRIEVED_DOCUMENTS),
            response.toString());
    EvaluationResponse evaluationResponse =
    relevancyEvaluator.evaluate(evaluationRequest);

    System.out.println("Response " + evaluationResponse);
    System.out.println("Score: " + evaluationResponse.
    getScore());
```

```
System.out.println("Feedback:"+ evaluationResponse.
getFeedback());
assertTrue(evaluationResponse.isPass(), "Response is
not relevant to the question");

    }
}
```

b.  Running unit tests manually

    Make sure that the following is commented out:

    //@Disabled("Run test manually when you add
    your API KEY to application.yml")

    **In an IDE (e.g., IntelliJ IDEA, Eclipse)**

    - Run the test.

    - Right-click the test class (ChatbotTests) or the
      specific test method (testEvaluation) and select
      Run or Debug.

    - View the results.

        - After the test runs, look at the test results
          pane, usually at the bottom or side of
          the IDE.

        - This pane will show the status of the test
          (e.g., passed, failed) and any assertion errors
          or exceptions that occurred during the test.

c.  Here is an example run with positive results for

    prompt: "What is the cheapest bike?" (see
    Figure 7-1)

***Figure 7-1.*** *Output of a positive prompt valuation result*

Note that we have loaded our vector database with bikes.json.

d. Here is the example run with a negative result using the following prompt.

Prompt: "What is CVS's annual turnover"
***See Figure 7-2.***

***Figure 7-2.*** *Output of a negative prompt valuation result*

3. Testing through a URL

You can also expose the testing and evaluation through a URL. This will require addition of two pieces of code QAController and QAService.

a. QAController.java (see Listing 7-3)

**Listing 7-3.** QAController.java

```java
import org.springframework.ai.chat.client.ChatClient;
import org.springframework.beans.factory.annotation.Autowired;
import org.springframework.web.bind.annotation.*;
import org.springframework.ai.chat.model.ChatResponse;
import org.springframework.ai.chat.client.advisor.
QuestionAnswerAdvisor;
import org.springframework.ai.evaluation.EvaluationRequest;
import org.springframework.ai.evaluation.EvaluationResponse;
import org.springframework.ai.evaluation.RelevancyEvaluator;
import org.springframework.ai.model.Content;
import org.springframework.ai.chat.model.ChatModel;

import java.util.LinkedHashMap;
import java.util.List;
import java.util.Map;

@RestController
@RequestMapping("/qa")
public class QAController {

    private final QAService qaService;
    private final ChatModel chatModel;

    @Autowired
    public QAController(QAService qaService, ChatModel
    chatModel) {
        this.qaService = qaService;
        this.chatModel = chatModel;
    }

    @GetMapping
    public Map completion(
```

```java
        @RequestParam(value = "question", defaultValue =
        "What is the cheapest bike?") String question,
        @RequestParam(value = "stuffit", defaultValue =
        "true") boolean stuffit) {
    String answer = this.qaService.generate(question,
    stuffit);
    Map map = new LinkedHashMap();
    map.put("question", question);
    map.put("answer", answer);
    return map;
}

@GetMapping("/test")
public ChatResponse testResponse(
        @RequestParam(value = "question", defaultValue = "
        What is the cheapest bike?") String question,
        @RequestParam(value = "stuffit", defaultValue =
        "true") boolean stuffit) {
    return qaService.generateTestResponse(question,
    stuffit);
}

@GetMapping("/evaluate")
public Map<String, Object> evaluateResponse(
        @RequestParam(value = "question", defaultValue = "
        What is the cheapest bike?") String question,
        @RequestParam(value = "stuffit", defaultValue =
        "true") boolean stuffit) {
    ChatResponse response = qaService.
    generateTestResponse(question, stuffit);

    var relevancyEvaluator = new
    RelevancyEvaluator(ChatClient.builder(chatModel));
```

```
EvaluationRequest evaluationRequest = new
EvaluationRequest(question,
        (List<Content>) response.getMetadata().
        get(QuestionAnswerAdvisor.RETRIEVED_DOCUMENTS),
        response.toString());
EvaluationResponse evaluationResponse =
relevancyEvaluator.evaluate(evaluationRequest);

Map<String, Object> result = new LinkedHashMap<>();
result.put("question", question);
result.put("answer", response.getResult().getOutput().
getContent());
result.put("isRelevant", evaluationResponse.isPass());
result.put("evaluationScore", evaluationResponse.
getScore());
result.put("evaluationFeedback", evaluationResponse.
getFeedback());

    return result;
    }
}
```

Description of Code

- **Imports**: The code imports various Spring and AI-related classes, including those for chat models, evaluators, and web controllers.

- **Class Definition**: QAController is defined as a REST controller with the base path "/qa".

- **Dependencies**

  - QAService: A service class for generating answers

  - ChatModel: A model for chat-based interactions

- **Endpoints**

  i.  GET "/qa"

      - Accepts a question and a boolean parameter "stuffit"

      - Returns a map with the question and generated answer

  ii. GET "/qa/test"

      - Similar to the first endpoint, but returns a ChatResponse object

  iii. GET "/qa/evaluate"

      - Generates a response to the question

      - Evaluates the relevance of the response using a RelevancyEvaluator

      - Returns a map with the question, answer, relevance score, and evaluation feedback

  iv. Evaluation Process

      - Uses RelevancyEvaluator to assess the quality of the generated answer

      - Constructs an EvaluationRequest with the question, retrieved documents, and the response

      - Returns various evaluation metrics like relevance, score, and feedback

  v.  Data Structures

      - Uses LinkedHashMap to maintain the order of inserted key/value pairs in the response

      vi.   AI Integration

- Utilizes Spring AI's chat and evaluation capabilities

- Implements a question-answering system with relevance evaluation

    b.   QAService.java (see Listing 7-4)

*Listing 7-4.* QAService.java

```java
import org.springframework.ai.chat.client.ChatClient;
import org.springframework.ai.chat.model.ChatResponse;
import org.springframework.ai.chat.model.ChatModel;
import org.springframework.ai.chat.client.advisor.
QuestionAnswerAdvisor;
import org.springframework.ai.vectorstore.SearchRequest;
import org.springframework.ai.vectorstore.VectorStore;
import org.springframework.beans.factory.annotation.Autowired;
import org.springframework.stereotype.Service;

@Service
public class QAService {

    private final ChatModel chatModel;
    private final VectorStore vectorStore;

    @Autowired
    public QAService(ChatModel chatModel, VectorStore vectorStore) {
        this.chatModel = chatModel;
        this.vectorStore = vectorStore;
    }

    public String generate(String message, boolean stuffit) {
        ChatResponse response = generateTestResponse(message,
        stuffit);
```

```
    return response.getResult().getOutput().getContent();
}

public ChatResponse generateTestResponse(String message,
boolean stuffit) {
    ChatClient chatClient = ChatClient.builder(chatModel).
    build();

    if (stuffit) {
        return chatClient.prompt()
                .advisors(new QuestionAnswerAdvisor(vectorSto
                re, SearchRequest.defaults()))
                .user(message)
                .call()
                .chatResponse();
    } else {
        return chatClient.prompt()
                .user(message)
                .call()
                .chatResponse();
    }
}
}
```

Description of Code

- **Imports**: The code imports various Spring AI classes
  related to chat models, vector stores, and advisors.

- **Class Definition**: QAService is annotated with
  @Service, indicating it's a Spring service component.

- **Dependencies**:

  ChatModel: A model for chat-based interactions

VectorStore: A storage system for vector representations, likely used for semantic search

Constructor:

Autowired constructor that injects ChatModel and VectorStore

- **Methods**

  - generate(String message, boolean stuffit): Calls generateTestResponse and extracts the content from the response

  - generateTestResponse(String message, boolean stuffit): Creates a ChatClient using the provided ChatModel

    Handles two scenarios based on the stuffit boolean:

    If stuffit is true:

    Uses a QuestionAnswerAdvisor with the VectorStore

    This likely enhances the response with relevant information from the vector store.

    If stuffit is false:

    Directly sends the user message to the chat model without additional context

- **AI Integration**

  Utilizes Spring AI's chat capabilities

  Integrates with a vector store for potential Retrieval-Augmented Generation

Flexibility

The stuffit parameter allows toggling between a simple chat response and a more context-aware response using the vector store.

c.   Run the tests in postman (see Figure 7-3 for a positive valuation and Figure 7-4 for a negative valuation)

***Figure 7-3.*** *Output of a positive valuation of response through an API*

***Figure 7-4.*** *Output of a negative prompt valuation of response through an API*

# 7.5 Scaling Spring AI

Spring AI is based on the framework of Spring Boot, and as such, it adopts its characteristics.

But there are additional components that need to scale along with Spring AI.

1. **Vector Databases**

   - **Purpose**: Store and query high-dimensional vector representations of data, crucial for semantic search and similarity matching.

   - **Scaling Considerations**

     - **Horizontal Scaling**: Distribute vectors across multiple nodes.

     - **Indexing Strategies**: Implement efficient indexing (e.g., HNSW, IVF) for fast retrieval.

- **Caching**: Implement in-memory caching for frequently accessed vectors.

- **Batch Operations**: Optimize for bulk inserts and updates.

- **Examples**: Pinecone, Weaviate, Milvus, Qdrant

2. **Databases (If Used in Function Calls)**

- **Purpose:** Store structured data that may be queried or updated during AI operations.

- **Scaling Considerations**

  - **Read Replicas**: Implement read replicas for distributing query load.

  - **Sharding**: Partition data across multiple databases for improved performance.

  - **Connection Pooling**: Optimize database connections to handle high concurrency.

  - **Query Optimization**: Regular performance tuning of queries and indexes.

- **Examples**: PostgreSQL, MySQL, MongoDB

3. **Document Stores (If Used in RAG or Function Calls)**

- **Purpose**: Store and retrieve unstructured or semistructured documents for context augmentation.

- **Scaling Considerations**

  - **Distributed Storage**: Implement a distributed file system for large-scale document storage.

- **Caching**: Implement document caching to reduce retrieval latency.

- **Indexing**: Use full-text search engines for efficient document retrieval.

- **Compression**: Implement document compression to optimize storage and transfer.

- **Examples**: Elasticsearch, Apache Solr, MongoDB

4. **LLMs (Large Language Models)**

- **Purpose**: Core AI models that power natural language understanding and generation

- **Scaling Considerations**

  - **Model Parallelism**: Distribute large models across multiple GPUs or TPUs.

  - **Inference Optimization**: Use techniques like quantization and pruning for faster inference.

  - **Caching**: Implement response caching for common queries.

  - **Load Balancing**: Distribute requests across multiple model instances.

- **Examples**: OpenAI's GPT models, Google's PaLM, Anthropic's Claude

5. **APIs**

- **Purpose**: Provide interfaces for external systems to interact with the AI application.

- **Scaling Considerations**

  - **Rate Limiting**: Implement rate limiting to prevent abuse and ensure fair usage.

  - **API Gateways**: Use API gateways for traffic management, security, and monitoring.

  - **Versioning**: Implement API versioning to manage changes and updates.

  - **Caching**: Implement response caching for frequently requested data.

  - **Asynchronous Processing**: Use message queues for handling long-running operations.

When scaling these components alongside Spring AI, consider the following general strategies:

1. **Microservice Architecture**: Decompose the application into smaller, independently scalable services.

2. **Containerization**: Use Docker for consistent deployment across environments.

3. **Orchestration**: Implement Kubernetes for automated scaling and management of containers.

4. **Monitoring and Observability**: Implement comprehensive monitoring for all components to identify bottlenecks and issues.

5. **Global Distribution**: Use content delivery networks (CDNs) and geographically distributed instances for lower latency.

6. **Fault Tolerance**: Implement circuit breakers, retries, and fallback mechanisms for resilience.

7. **Continuous Integration and Deployment (CI/CD)**: Automate testing and deployment processes for frequent, reliable updates.

By carefully considering the scaling needs of each of these components in conjunction with Spring AI, you can build a robust, high-performance AI system capable of handling large-scale production workloads.

# 7.6  Security in Spring AI

Security is a critical aspect of deploying Spring AI applications, especially when dealing with sensitive data and powerful AI models. Here's a comprehensive look at security considerations in Spring AI:

1. **Authentication and Authorization**

   - Implement Spring Security for robust authentication mechanisms.

   - Use OAuth 2.0 and OpenID Connect for secure token-based authentication.

   - Implement role-based access control (RBAC) for fine-grained authorization.

   - Consider using JSON Web Tokens (JWT) for stateless authentication.

2. **API Security**

   - Use HTTPS/TLS for all communications.

   - Implement API keys or client certificates for API access.

- Use API gateways (e.g., Spring Cloud Gateway) for centralized security enforcement.

- Implement rate limiting to prevent abuse and DDoS attacks.

3. **Input Validation and Sanitization**

   - Validate and sanitize all user inputs to prevent injection attacks.

   - Use Spring's @Valid annotation for automatic bean validation.

   - Implement custom validators for AI-specific input requirements.

4. **Secure Configuration Management**

   - Use Spring Cloud Config for centralized, encrypted configuration management.

   - Avoid hardcoding sensitive information (e.g., API keys, passwords) in the code.

   - Use environment variables or secure vaults (e.g., HashiCorp Vault) for storing secrets.

5. **Data Protection**

   - Implement encryption for data at rest and in transit.

   - Use Spring Data's auditing capabilities to track data access and modifications.

   - Implement data masking for sensitive information in logs and outputs.

6. **Model Security**

- Protect AI models from unauthorized access or theft.

- Implement model versioning and access controls.

- Consider using model encryption techniques for highly sensitive models.

7. **Prompt Injection Prevention**

- Implement strict input validation for prompts sent to AI models.

- Use sandboxing techniques to isolate potentially malicious prompts.

- Implement content filtering to prevent generation of harmful content.

8. **Audit Logging**

- Implement comprehensive logging of all security-relevant events.

- Use Spring AOP for aspect-oriented logging.

- Consider using a centralized log management system (e.g., ELK stack).

9. **Secure Communication with External Services**

- Use mutual TLS (mTLS) for secure service-to-service communication.

- Implement circuit breakers (e.g., Spring Cloud Circuit Breaker) to handle external service failures securely.

10. **Container Security**

- Use minimal base images to reduce attack surface.

- Implement container scanning in CI/CD pipelines.

- Use Kubernetes security features like Pod Security Policies.

11. **Dependency Management**

- Regularly update dependencies to patch known vulnerabilities.

- Use tools like OWASP Dependency-Check in your build pipeline.

- Implement a software bill of materials (SBOM) for transparency.

12. **Privacy Compliance**

- Implement data anonymization techniques where appropriate.

- Ensure compliance with regulations like GDPR, CCPA, etc.

- Provide mechanisms for data subject access requests and right to be forgotten.

13. **Secure Development Practices**

- Implement secure coding guidelines.

- Conduct regular security code reviews.

- Use static code analysis tools integrated into your CI/CD pipeline.

14. **AI-Specific Security Considerations**

    - Implement safeguards against model inversion attacks.

    - Consider differential privacy techniques for training data protection.

    - Implement monitoring for abnormal model behavior or outputs.

15. **Access Control for AI Capabilities**

    - Implement fine-grained access controls for different AI functionalities.

    - Use Spring Security's method-level security for controlling access to specific AI operations.

16. **Secure Model Deployment**

    - Implement secure channels for model updates and deployments.

    - Use integrity checks to ensure deployed models haven't been tampered with.

17. **Error Handling and Information Disclosure**

    - Implement custom error handling to prevent information leakage.

    - Use Spring's @ControllerAdvice for global exception handling.

18. **Security Headers**

    - Implement security headers (e.g., Content Security Policy, X-Frame-Options).

    - Use Spring Security's header configuration options.

19. **Monitoring and Incident Response**

- Implement real-time security monitoring and alerting.

- Develop and regularly test an incident response plan.

20. **Regular Security Assessments**

- Conduct periodic penetration testing and vulnerability assessments.

- Perform regular security audits of your Spring AI application.

To implement these security measures in Spring AI:

1. Leverage Spring Security's integration with Spring Boot for easy setup of security features.

2. Use Spring Security's OAuth2 support for implementing OAuth 2.0 and OpenID Connect.

3. Utilize Spring Cloud Security for distributed system security patterns.

4. Implement custom SecurityConfigurer classes to define application-specific security rules.

5. Use Spring AOP for cross-cutting security concerns like audit logging.

Remember, security is an ongoing process. Regularly review and update your security measures to address new threats and vulnerabilities in the rapidly evolving AI landscape.

# 7.7 Performance Optimization in Spring AI

Performance optimization is crucial for Spring AI applications to ensure efficient and responsive AI-driven systems. Here's a comprehensive look at performance optimization strategies for Spring AI:

1. **AI Model Optimization**

   - **Model Quantization**: Reduce model precision (e.g., FP32 to INT8) for faster inference.

   - **Model Pruning**: Remove less important weights to reduce model size.

   - **Model Distillation**: Create smaller, faster models that approximate larger ones.

   - **Caching**: Implement response caching for frequent queries.

   - **Batching**: Process multiple inputs simultaneously for increased throughput.

2. **Database Optimization**

   - **Indexing**: Properly index frequently queried fields.

   - **Query Optimization**: Use Spring Data JPA's query optimization features.

   - **Connection Pooling**: Configure HikariCP for optimal database connections.

   - **Caching**: Implement second-level caching with Hibernate.

   - **Pagination**: Use Spring Data's Pageable interface for large result sets.

3. **Vector Store Optimization**

- **Efficient Indexing**: Use approximate nearest neighbor algorithms (e.g., HNSW, IVF).

- **Caching**: Implement in-memory caching for frequently accessed vectors.

- **Batch Operations**: Optimize for bulk inserts and updates.

- **Distributed Storage**: Consider distributed vector databases for large-scale applications.

4. **JVM Tuning**

- **Garbage Collection**: Choose and configure the appropriate GC algorithm (e.g., G1GC).

- **Memory Allocation**: Optimize heap size and other memory-related JVM parameters.

- **JIT Compilation**: Use -XX:+TieredCompilation for improved performance.

5. **Asynchronous Processing**

- Use Spring's @Async annotation for nonblocking operations.

- Implement CompletableFuture for parallel processing.

- Use reactive programming with Spring WebFlux for highly concurrent applications.

6. **Caching Strategies**

- Implement Spring Cache abstraction with distributed caches like Redis.

- Use Caffeine for high-performance local caching.

- Implement cache warming strategies for critical data.

7. **Load Balancing and Clustering**

- Use Spring Cloud Load Balancer for client-side load balancing.

- Implement session replication or sticky sessions for stateful applications.

- Use Spring Session for distributed session management.

8. **Connection Pooling**

- Configure connection pools for external services (e.g., AI model servers, APIs).

- Use WebClient with connection pooling for efficient HTTP requests.

9. **Optimized Data Serialization**

- Use efficient serialization formats like Protocol Buffers or MessagePack.

- Implement JSON views to limit serialized data to what's necessary.

10. **Compression**

- Enable GZIP compression for HTTP responses.

- Implement compression for large data transfers between services.

11. **Lazy Loading**

- Use Spring Data JPA's lazy loading features for entity relationships.

- Implement lazy initialization for resource-intensive beans.

12. **Profiling and Monitoring**

- Use Spring Boot Actuator for application metrics.

- Implement distributed tracing with Spring Cloud Sleuth and Zipkin.

- Use Java profilers (e.g., YourKit, JProfiler) to identify bottlenecks.

13. **API Optimization**

- Implement GraphQL with Spring for flexible and efficient data fetching.

- Use projections in Spring Data to fetch only required data.

- Implement API pagination for large datasets.

14. **In-Memory Data Grids**

- Use Hazelcast or Apache Ignite for distributed caching and computing.

15. **Optimized Logging**

- Use asynchronous appenders for logging.

- Implement log levels appropriately to reduce I/O overhead.

16. **Thread Pool Optimization**

    - Configure and optimize thread pools for specific use cases.

    - Use virtual threads (Project Loom) for high-concurrency scenarios.

17. **Resource Management**

    - Implement proper resource closing with try-with-resources.

    - Use connection pooling for resource-intensive external services.

18. **Content Delivery Networks (CDNs)**

    - Use CDNs for static assets and potentially for API caching.

19. **Database Query Optimization**

    - Use database-specific optimizations (e.g., PostgreSQL's JSONB for semistructured data).

    - Implement database partitioning for large datasets.

20. **AI-Specific Optimizations**

    - Implement efficient tokenization and preprocessing pipelines.

    - Use optimized libraries for numerical computations (e.g., BLAS, cuDNN).

Implementation in Spring AI

1. Use Spring Boot's auto-configuration for optimal out-of-the-box performance.

2.  Leverage Spring Cloud for distributed system patterns that enhance performance.

3.  Utilize Spring Data repositories for efficient database operations.

4.  Implement caching with Spring Cache and distribute with Spring Cloud.

5.  Use Spring WebFlux for reactive programming in high-concurrency scenarios.

6.  Leverage Spring Boot Actuator for performance monitoring and metrics.

# 7.8  Let's Code (Scaling, Security, and Performance)

Here is a sample implementation of the two class QAController and QAService that addresses scalability, security and performance

a.  QAController.java (Listing 7-5)

***Listing 7-5.*** QAController.java with scaling, security, and performance

```
import org.springframework.ai.chat.model.ChatResponse;
import org.springframework.ai.chat.model.ChatModel;
import org.springframework.beans.factory.annotation.Autowired;
import org.springframework.web.bind.annotation.*;
import org.springframework.security.access.prepost.
PreAuthorize;
import org.springframework.cache.annotation.Cacheable;
import org.springframework.scheduling.annotation.Async;
```

```java
import org.springframework.http.ResponseEntity;
import org.springframework.validation.annotation.Validated;

import javax.validation.constraints.NotBlank;
import java.util.concurrent.CompletableFuture;
import java.util.Map;

@RestController
@RequestMapping("/api/v1/qa")
@Validated
public class QAController {

    private final QAService qaService;

    @Autowired
    public QAController(QAService qaService) {
        this.qaService = qaService;
    }

    @GetMapping
    @PreAuthorize("hasRole('USER')")
    @Cacheable(value = "qaResponses", key = "#question +
    #stuffit")
    public ResponseEntity<Map<String, String>> completion(
            @RequestParam @NotBlank String question,
            @RequestParam(defaultValue = "true") boolean
            stuffit) {
        String answer = this.qaService.generate(question,
        stuffit);
        return ResponseEntity.ok(Map.of("question", question,
        "answer", answer));
    }
}
```

```
@GetMapping("/test")
@PreAuthorize("hasRole('ADMIN')")
public ResponseEntity<ChatResponse> testResponse(
        @RequestParam @NotBlank String question,
        @RequestParam(defaultValue = "true") boolean
        stuffit) {
    return ResponseEntity.ok(qaService.
    generateTestResponse(question, stuffit));
}

@GetMapping("/evaluate")
@PreAuthorize("hasRole('ADMIN')")
@Async
public CompletableFuture<ResponseEntity<Map<String,
Object>>> evaluateResponse(
        @RequestParam @NotBlank String question,
        @RequestParam(defaultValue = "true") boolean
        stuffit) {
    return CompletableFuture.supplyAsync(() -> {
        Map<String, Object> result = qaService.
        evaluateResponse(question, stuffit);
        return ResponseEntity.ok(result);
    });
}
}
```

b.    QAService.java (Listing 7-6)

***Listing 7-6.*** QAService.java with scaling, security, and performance

```
import org.springframework.ai.chat.client.ChatClient;
import org.springframework.ai.chat.model.ChatResponse;
import org.springframework.ai.chat.model.ChatModel;
```

```
import org.springframework.ai.chat.client.advisor.
QuestionAnswerAdvisor;
import org.springframework.ai.vectorstore.SearchRequest;
import org.springframework.ai.vectorstore.VectorStore;
import org.springframework.beans.factory.annotation.Autowired;
import org.springframework.stereotype.Service;
import org.springframework.cache.annotation.Cacheable;
import org.springframework.transaction.annotation.
Transactional;
import org.springframework.retry.annotation.Retryable;
import org.springframework.ai.evaluation.EvaluationRequest;
import org.springframework.ai.evaluation.EvaluationResponse;
import org.springframework.ai.evaluation.RelevancyEvaluator;
import org.springframework.ai.model.Content;

import java.util.List;
import java.util.Map;
import java.util.concurrent.TimeUnit;

@Service
public class QAService {

    private final ChatModel chatModel;
    private final VectorStore vectorStore;

    @Autowired
    public QAService(ChatModel chatModel, VectorStore
    vectorStore) {
        this.chatModel = chatModel;
        this.vectorStore = vectorStore;
    }

    @Cacheable(value = "qaResponses", key = "#message +
    #stuffit")
```

```
@Transactional(readOnly = true)
@Retryable(maxAttempts = 3, backoff = @Backoff(delay
= 1000))
public String generate(String message, boolean stuffit) {
    ChatResponse response = generateTestResponse(message,
    stuffit);
    return response.getResult().getOutput().getContent();
}

@Transactional(readOnly = true)
@Retryable(maxAttempts = 3, backoff = @Backoff(delay
= 1000))
public ChatResponse generateTestResponse(String message,
boolean stuffit) {
    ChatClient chatClient = ChatClient.builder(chatModel)
            .withTimeout(30, TimeUnit.SECONDS)
            .build();

    if (stuffit) {
        return chatClient.prompt()
                .advisors(new QuestionAnswerAdvisor(vectorS
                tore, SearchRequest.defaults()))
                .user(message)
                .call()
                .chatResponse();
    } else {
        return chatClient.prompt()
                .user(message)
                .call()
                .chatResponse();
    }
}
```

```java
@Transactional(readOnly = true)
public Map<String, Object> evaluateResponse(String
question, boolean stuffit) {
    ChatResponse response = generateTestResponse(question,
    stuffit);

    var relevancyEvaluator = new
    RelevancyEvaluator(ChatClient.builder(chatModel));
    EvaluationRequest evaluationRequest = new
    EvaluationRequest(question,
            (List<Content>) response.getMetadata().
            get(QuestionAnswerAdvisor.RETRIEVED_DOCUMENTS),
            response.toString());
    EvaluationResponse evaluationResponse =
    relevancyEvaluator.evaluate(evaluationRequest);

    return Map.of(
            "question", question,
            "answer", response.getResult().getOutput().
            getContent(),
            "isRelevant", evaluationResponse.isPass(),
            "evaluationScore", evaluationResponse.
            getScore(),
            "evaluationFeedback", evaluationResponse.
            getFeedback()
    );
    }
}
```

**Key Changes and Improvements**

1. **Scaling**

   - Added @Async for asynchronous processing in the evaluate endpoint

   - Used CompletableFuture for nonblocking operations

   - Implemented caching with @Cacheable to reduce load on the AI model

2. **Security**

   - Added @PreAuthorize annotations for role-based access control

   - Implemented input validation with @Validated and @NotBlank

   - Updated the API path to include versioning (/api/v1/qa)

3. **Performance**

   - Implemented caching for responses

   - Added @Transactional(readOnly = true) for read-only operations

   - Implemented retry logic with @Retryable for resilience

   - Set a timeout for the ChatClient to prevent long-running requests

4. **General Improvements**

- Used ResponseEntity for more control over HTTP responses

- Improved error handling and input validation

- Used Map.of() for creating immutable maps

- Removed redundant ChatModel injection in the controller

To fully implement these changes, you'll need to add the following dependencies and configurations to your project:

1. Spring Security for @PreAuthorize

2. Spring Cache for @Cacheable

3. Spring Retry for @Retryable

4. Spring Async for @Async

Also, ensure that you have the appropriate security configuration, caching configuration, and async executor configuration in your application.

These modifications enhance the scalability, security, and performance of your Spring AI application. Remember to test thoroughly and adjust based on your specific requirements and infrastructure.

# CHAPTER 8

# Use Cases

## 8.1 Introduction

In the previous chapters, we explored how to leverage Spring Boot and Spring AI for building Generative AI (GenAI) interactions. We've delved into the technical aspects of integrating GenAI within the Spring ecosystem, focusing on enabling seamless, scalable, and robust AI-driven applications.

In this chapter, we will shift our focus to practical applications— exploring the diverse use cases where GenAI can be harnessed within the Spring AI framework. From enhancing customer experiences to streamlining operations, we'll examine how Spring AI's capabilities can be applied across various domains, driving innovation and adding tangible value. By the end of this chapter, you'll have a comprehensive understanding of the potential GenAI holds when paired with the power and flexibility of Spring AI.

We will look at the following use cases:

1) Conversational AI as a singular interface for your enterprise applications

2) **Enhanced Decision Support Systems**: Using GenAI to provide advanced analytics and decision-making support, helping enterprises make informed choices based on real-time data and predictive insights.

B. Parasuraman, *Mastering Spring AI*, https://doi.org/10.1007/979-8-8688-1001-5_8

3) **Content Generation and Personalization**: Leveraging GenAI to create and customize content—whether it's marketing material, documentation, or customer communications—tailored to specific audiences or needs.

4) **AI-Driven Anomaly Detection**: Implementing GenAI for identifying unusual patterns or anomalies in data, which can be crucial for cybersecurity, fraud detection, and system monitoring.

5) **Intelligent Document Processing**: Automating the extraction, classification, and processing of information from structured and unstructured documents, reducing manual efforts and increasing accuracy.

6) **Customer Journey Optimization**: Utilizing GenAI to map and enhance customer journeys, providing personalized recommendations and insights that lead to higher engagement and satisfaction.

As we venture into these use cases, you'll see how GenAI, when integrated with Spring AI, can transform traditional enterprise operations, bringing intelligence, automation, and efficiency to the forefront. This chapter aims to not only demonstrate the practical applications of these technologies but also to inspire new possibilities for innovation within your own projects. By the end, you'll have a clearer vision of how to harness the full potential of GenAI with Spring AI, driving meaningful impact across your organization.

# 8.2 Conversational AI As a Singular Interface for Your Enterprise Applications

Imagine working in an enterprise where your day involves navigating through a multitude of applications—each designed to serve a specific function. You might use Salesforce for managing marketing campaigns and tracking sales leads, Tririga for scheduling and booking meeting rooms, Outlook for sending and receiving emails, Slack or Microsoft Teams for holding meetings and team collaborations, and specialized HR systems for managing employee records and benefits. Each of these systems has its own unique interface, requiring specialized knowledge to effectively update, retrieve, and maintain data.

For a sales employee, this can mean juggling multiple applications to accomplish daily tasks: pulling customer data from Salesforce, checking room availability in Tririga, scheduling meetings via Outlook, collaborating with colleagues on Slack, and ensuring all this activity aligns with your quarterly sales quota. The fragmented nature of these systems often leads to inefficiencies, as you need to constantly switch between platforms, each with its own learning curve and operational quirks. This not only consumes valuable time but also increases the risk of errors, as you might miss critical information or fail to update records accurately across all platforms.

Now, imagine a different scenario—a more streamlined, efficient way of working. What if, instead of interacting with each of these systems individually, you had a single interface that seamlessly integrates all these diverse applications? This is where Generative AI (GenAI) can revolutionize enterprise operations. Picture a GenAI-powered chatbot as your singular interface, capable of interacting with all your enterprise applications on your behalf.

With such a chatbot, your daily workflow could be significantly simplified. Need to check the status of a customer or update a sales record? Just ask the chatbot, and it will retrieve the information from Salesforce. Want to schedule a team meeting? The chatbot can automatically check room availability in Tririga, align schedules in Outlook, and send out invites via Slack or Teams—all in one go. Curious if you've met your quarterly quota? The chatbot can instantly pull that data and give you an update, along with insights on how you're tracking toward your goals.

This kind of unified interface not only saves time but also reduces the cognitive load on employees. Instead of remembering how to navigate through each system, employees can focus on what they do best: selling, strategizing, and engaging with customers. The chatbot becomes an intelligent assistant, streamlining workflows, improving data accuracy, and allowing employees to interact with complex enterprise systems using simple, natural language commands.

Moreover, this approach can democratize access to information and tools within an organization. You no longer need to be a specialist in Salesforce, Tririga, or Outlook to effectively do your job; the GenAI-powered chatbot acts as the intermediary, translating your needs into actionable commands across all platforms. This can lead to greater productivity, as employees spend less time on administrative tasks and more time on activities that drive business value.

How can we use Spring AI to create a solution

We will need the following:

1) An LLM that is multimodal

2) Conversation AI with history as described in Chapter 5

3) Integrations with the systems through function calling as described in Chapter 6

4) JavaScript or other UI generating tools

# 8.2.1  An LLM That Is Multimodal

**Objective:** Leverage a multimodal LLM that can process and generate responses across different modalities, such as text, images, and potentially other forms of data like audio or video.

### Implementation

- **Model Selection:** Choose a multimodal LLM that suits your application needs. For instance, you might select GPT-4 with multimodal capabilities or a similar model that can handle text, images, and more. This LLM will serve as the core engine of your solution, handling complex interactions that require understanding and generating responses across different types of data.

- **Spring AI Integration:** Integrate the multimodal LLM with Spring AI using APIs or SDKs provided by the model's platform. Spring AI can be configured to route different types of input (text, images, etc.) to the appropriate endpoints or services that handle multimodal processing.

- **Custom Pipelines:** Build custom processing pipelines within Spring AI to handle different modalities. For example, a pipeline might first analyze an image for content and then generate a text response based on that analysis. You can use Spring's flexible framework to orchestrate these pipelines, ensuring that all parts of the multimodal interaction work together seamlessly.

# 8.2.2 Conversational AI with History (As Described in Chapter 5)

**Objective:** Implement a conversational AI system that maintains conversation history, allowing for contextually relevant and continuous interactions.

### Implementation

- **Session Management:** Utilize the techniques discussed in Chapter 5 to manage session data and maintain conversation history within Spring AI. This involves storing the context of previous interactions, which can be retrieved and referenced in future conversations to provide more coherent and relevant responses.

- **Stateful Interactions:** Implement stateful conversation handling, where the AI can remember past user queries, preferences, and decisions. This can be achieved using session-scoped beans or external storage solutions, such as Redis or a relational database, integrated with Spring AI.

- **Context-Aware Responses:** Enhance the LLM's ability to generate context-aware responses by feeding it the relevant conversation history along with each new input. This ensures that the AI doesn't treat each interaction in isolation but rather as part of an ongoing dialogue.

# 8.2.3 Integrations with Systems Through Function Calling (As Described in Chapter 6)

**Objective:** Enable the AI to interact with various enterprise systems through function calls, allowing it to perform tasks like retrieving data, executing commands, and updating records.

### Implementation

- **Function Call Interfaces:** Implement function calling as described in Chapter 6, where Spring AI acts as an intermediary between the LLM and your enterprise systems. Define clear interfaces and endpoints for each function, ensuring that the LLM can trigger these functions based on user inputs.

- **API Gateway:** Use Spring Cloud Gateway or a similar API gateway solution to manage and route function calls to the appropriate back-end services. This allows for secure, scalable, and efficient communication between the AI and your enterprise systems.

- **Function Call Orchestration:** Implement orchestration logic within Spring AI to handle complex workflows involving multiple function calls. For example, scheduling a meeting might involve checking room availability, participant schedules, and then sending invitations—all of which can be coordinated through Spring AI.

# 8.2.4 JavaScript or Other UI Generating Tools

**Objective:** Create a user-friendly interface that allows users to interact with the AI system seamlessly.

### Implementation

- **Front-End Framework:** Use a modern front-end framework like React, Angular, or Vue.js to build the user interface. These frameworks work well with Spring Boot, allowing for smooth integration between the front end and back end.

- **Dynamic UI Components:** Implement dynamic UI components that can adapt based on the AI's responses. For instance, if the AI generates a text response, the UI might display it in a chat bubble, while an image response could be shown in a gallery format. Use JavaScript libraries or frameworks to manage these dynamic elements.

- **API Integration:** Connect the front end to your Spring AI back end via RESTful APIs or WebSockets. This will allow for real-time communication between the user interface and the AI system, ensuring a responsive and interactive experience.

- **User Experience (UX) Design:** Focus on creating an intuitive and engaging UX. This includes designing for accessibility, ensuring that the interface is easy to use, and providing clear feedback to users during their interactions with the AI.

# 8.3  Enhanced Decision Support Systems

Enterprises are inundated with vast amounts of data, making it challenging for decision-makers to sift through information, analyze it, and arrive at informed conclusions. This is where Large Language Models (LLMs) like GPT-4, Llama, or IBM Granite can play a transformative role in enhancing decision support systems within an enterprise.

## 8.3.1  The Role of LLMs in Decision Support Systems

LLMs are designed to process, understand, and generate human-like text, but their capabilities extend far beyond simple text generation. When integrated into decision support systems, LLMs can

1. **Analyze Large Datasets:** LLMs can quickly analyze vast amounts of structured and unstructured data, extracting insights that might not be immediately apparent to human analysts. This includes recognizing patterns, identifying trends, and even predicting future outcomes based on historical data.

2. **Natural Language Querying:** One of the most significant advantages of using LLMs in decision support is their ability to understand and respond to natural language queries. Decision-makers can ask questions in plain language, and the LLM can process these queries, retrieve relevant data, and present it in a comprehensible format. This eliminates the need for specialized knowledge in querying languages or database management.

3. **Contextual Recommendations:** LLMs can provide contextual recommendations by considering the broader context of a decision. For example, if a sales manager is evaluating a potential market expansion, the LLM can take into account not only the current sales data but also market trends, economic indicators, and competitive analysis to provide a well-rounded recommendation.

4. **Scenario Simulation:** LLMs can assist in simulating different decision-making scenarios. By adjusting various parameters and predicting the outcomes of different strategies, LLMs help decision-makers evaluate the potential impact of their choices before committing to a particular course of action.

5. **Automated Report Generation:** LLMs can automate the generation of reports and summaries based on the analysis of data. This includes creating executive summaries, detailed analytical reports, and even visual presentations that highlight key insights, trends, and recommendations.

## 8.3.2 Implementing LLMs in Enterprise Decision Support Systems

To integrate LLMs effectively into an enterprise decision support system, several components need to be considered:

1. **Data Integration:** The first step is to ensure that the LLM has access to the relevant data sources within the enterprise. This might involve integrating with databases, data warehouses, and external data

sources. Data preprocessing is also crucial to ensure that the information fed into the LLM is clean, accurate, and relevant.

2. **Model Customization:** While general-purpose LLMs are powerful, they may need customization to align with specific business needs. Fine-tuning the LLM on industry-specific data, historical decision-making patterns, and internal documentation can enhance its ability to provide relevant and actionable insights.

3. **User Interface:** The LLM's outputs need to be presented in a user-friendly manner. This could involve creating a dashboard that decision-makers can use to input queries and view results. The UI should be intuitive, allowing users to interact with the system without requiring deep technical expertise.

4. **Security and Compliance:** Given the sensitivity of business data, ensuring that the LLM operates within a secure environment is paramount. This includes implementing access controls, encryption, and compliance with regulations such as GDPR or HIPAA, depending on the industry.

5. **Continuous Learning and Adaptation:** The business environment is constantly evolving, and so should the LLM. Implementing a feedback loop where the LLM's recommendations are reviewed, and its performance is continually assessed, can help the system adapt to new information and changing business conditions.

Here are some systems in different domains:

1. **Executive Information Systems (EIS)**

   - **Example:** A dashboard used by C-suite executives to monitor key performance indicators (KPIs) across different departments. The system provides real-time data, trend analysis, and predictive analytics to help executives make strategic decisions quickly.

   - **Industry:** Any large enterprise (e.g., finance, retail, manufacturing).

2. **Clinical Decision Support Systems (CDSS)**

   - **Example:** A system that assists healthcare providers in diagnosing and treating patients. It might provide recommendations for drug prescriptions, highlight potential drug interactions, and suggest possible diagnoses based on patient symptoms and history.

   - **Industry:** Healthcare.

3. **Supply Chain Management Systems**

   - **Example:** A system that helps companies optimize their supply chain by analyzing data from suppliers, logistics, and inventory levels. The system can suggest the best suppliers, predict stock shortages, and recommend adjustments to procurement and distribution strategies.

   - **Industry:** Manufacturing, retail, logistics.

4.  **Financial Planning and Analysis (FP&A) Systems**

    - **Example:** A system used by financial analysts to create budgets, forecast future financial performance, and assess investment opportunities. The system integrates financial data, economic indicators, and market trends to help guide investment decisions and financial planning.

    - **Industry:** Finance, banking, corporate enterprises.

5.  **Customer Relationship Management (CRM) Systems with Decision Support**

    - **Example:** A CRM system that helps sales teams identify potential leads, prioritize customer interactions, and predict customer lifetime value. The system can analyze customer behavior, past purchases, and market trends to suggest the most effective sales strategies.

    - **Industry:** Sales, marketing, customer service.

6.  **Environmental Impact Assessment Systems**

    - **Example:** A DSS used by governments or companies to evaluate the potential environmental impact of new projects, such as infrastructure developments or industrial plants. The system models scenarios based on environmental data, regulations, and scientific studies.

    - **Industry:** Environmental management, urban planning, energy.

7.  **Human Resources (HR) Decision Support Systems**

    - **Example:** A system that assists HR managers in workforce planning, talent acquisition, and performance management. It might provide insights on employee turnover, suggest training programs, and recommend actions to improve employee satisfaction.

    - **Industry:** Corporate HR, talent management.

8.  **Agricultural Decision Support Systems**

    - **Example:** A system that helps farmers make decisions about crop management, irrigation, and pest control. The system uses weather data, soil conditions, and crop performance metrics to recommend optimal planting times, watering schedules, and pest control measures.

    - **Industry:** Agriculture.

9.  **Energy Management Systems**

    - **Example:** A system that helps utilities and large organizations manage energy consumption and production. The system can forecast energy demand, suggest energy-saving measures, and optimize the use of renewable energy sources.

    - **Industry:** Energy, utilities, large corporations.

10. **Risk Management Systems**

    - **Example:** A system used by financial institutions to assess and manage risks in investment portfolios. It analyzes market data, economic indicators, and financial models to predict risks and suggest mitigation strategies.

- **Industry:** Finance, insurance.

11. **Marketing Decision Support Systems**

    - **Example:** A system that helps marketing teams design and evaluate campaigns by analyzing customer data, market trends, and competitive positioning. It can suggest target demographics, recommend pricing strategies, and predict the success of marketing efforts.

    - **Industry:** Marketing, advertising.

12. **Transportation and Logistics Decision Support Systems**

    - **Example:** A system that helps logistics companies plan routes, optimize deliveries, and manage fleet operations. It might suggest the most efficient routes, predict delivery times, and manage vehicle maintenance schedules.

    - **Industry:** Transportation, logistics.

All these systems can be integrated with the LLM with the following components:

- RAG on documents as discussed in Chapter 4

- Multimodal LLMs

- Integration to data sources such as Salesforce and SAP with function calling as discussed in Chapter 6

# 8.4 Content Generation and Personalization

Content generation and personalization are increasingly vital in modern enterprises, helping to tailor communications, marketing efforts, and customer experiences to individual preferences and needs. Here are some examples of how enterprises can leverage content generation and personalization:

1. **Automated Marketing Campaigns**

   - **Example:** A marketing team uses AI-driven content generation tools to create personalized email campaigns for different customer segments. The system analyzes customer data, including past purchases, browsing behavior, and demographic information, to generate personalized email content, such as product recommendations, special offers, and relevant articles. Each email is tailored to the recipient's preferences, increasing engagement and conversion rates.

   - **Industry:** Ecommerce, retail, B2C marketing

2. **Dynamic Website Content**

   - **Example:** A company's website dynamically adjusts its content based on the visitor's profile and behavior. For instance, a returning visitor who previously viewed a specific product category might see personalized product recommendations or targeted promotions on the homepage. The content generation system uses cookies, browsing history, and customer data to create a unique and personalized website experience for each visitor.

   - **Industry:** Ecommerce, media, travel.

3. **Personalized Learning and Development Programs**

   - **Example:** An enterprise uses AI to generate personalized learning paths for employees. Based on an employee's role, past training, skills, and career goals, the system recommends and generates customized training modules, articles, and videos. The content is tailored to the employee's learning style and professional aspirations, ensuring more effective and engaging learning experiences.

   - **Industry:** Corporate training, education, human resources.

4. **Targeted Content for Sales Teams**

   - **Example:** A sales team leverages AI-generated content to create personalized pitches and proposals for potential clients. The system generates content by analyzing the client's industry, company size, challenges, and past interactions with the sales team. The result is a tailored proposal that directly addresses the client's specific needs, increasing the likelihood of closing the deal.

   - **Industry:** B2B sales, professional services.

5. **Customer Support Responses**

   - **Example:** An AI-driven customer support system generates personalized responses to customer inquiries. By analyzing the customer's history, previous interactions, and the nature of the query, the system creates a customized response that addresses the customer's specific issues and offers relevant solutions. This personalized approach improves customer satisfaction and efficiency in resolving issues.

- **Industry:** Customer service, telecommunications, ecommerce.

6. **Product Descriptions and Recommendations**

   - **Example:** An online retailer uses AI to generate personalized product descriptions and recommendations for each customer. The system analyzes a customer's past purchases, browsing behavior, and preferences to create tailored product descriptions that highlight features most likely to appeal to that customer. Additionally, personalized product recommendations are generated and displayed, increasing the chances of cross-selling and upselling.

   - **Industry:** Retail, ecommerce.

7. **Social Media Content Personalization**

   - **Example:** A company's social media marketing team uses AI to create personalized content for different audience segments. The system generates posts, images, and videos that resonate with specific groups based on their interests, demographics, and engagement history. Each piece of content is optimized for the target audience, leading to higher engagement rates on platforms like Facebook, Instagram, and LinkedIn.

   - **Industry:** Media, entertainment, digital marketing.

8. **Personalized Newsletters**

- **Example:** A news organization uses AI to generate personalized newsletters for its subscribers. Based on each subscriber's reading habits, favorite topics, and past interactions, the system curates and generates a unique newsletter that includes articles, news stories, and editorials most relevant to the subscriber's interests. This approach increases reader engagement and loyalty.

- **Industry:** Media, publishing.

9. **Personalized Video Content**

- **Example:** A streaming service generates personalized video recommendations and even custom previews based on a user's viewing history and preferences. The AI system analyzes what types of shows and movies the user enjoys and generates tailored content suggestions, including personalized trailers or sneak peeks of new releases that align with the user's tastes.

- **Industry:** Media, entertainment, streaming services.

10. **Custom Reports and Dashboards**

- **Example:** A financial services firm uses AI to generate personalized reports and dashboards for its clients. Each report is tailored to the client's investment portfolio, financial goals, and market trends. The AI system generates content that highlights the most relevant data, insights, and recommendations, helping clients make informed decisions about their investments.

- **Industry:** Finance, investment management, consulting.

11. **Employee Communication and Engagement**

- **Example:** An internal communication platform uses AI to generate personalized content for employees. This could include personalized news updates, company announcements, and recognition messages. The system tailors the content based on the employee's role, department, and previous interactions, ensuring that communications are relevant and engaging.

- **Industry:** Human resources, corporate communications.

12. **AI-Powered Blogging and Content Creation**

- **Example:** A company's content marketing team uses AI to generate personalized blog posts and articles. The AI system analyzes trending topics, audience interests, and SEO keywords to create content that is both relevant and optimized for search engines. Additionally, the content can be personalized for different audience segments, ensuring maximum engagement.

- **Industry:** Content marketing, digital media, blogging.

# 8.5 AI-Driven Anomaly Detection

AI-driven anomaly detection using Generative AI (GenAI) is a powerful tool for identifying unusual patterns, outliers, or deviations from the norm in various types of data. This capability is critical in a wide range of applications, from fraud detection to predictive maintenance. Here are some examples of how AI-driven anomaly detection with GenAI can be applied in different industries:

1. **Financial Fraud Detection**

   - **Example:** A bank uses GenAI models to monitor transactions across millions of accounts in real time. The AI analyzes transaction patterns to detect anomalies, such as unusual spending behavior, multiple small transactions designed to avoid detection, or unauthorized access to accounts. When an anomaly is detected, the system flags the transaction for further investigation, potentially preventing fraud before it occurs.

   - **Industry:** Banking, financial services.

2. **Network Security Monitoring**

   - **Example:** An IT security firm deploys GenAI to monitor network traffic and detect anomalies that might indicate a cybersecurity threat, such as a DDoS attack or a data breach. The AI can identify unusual patterns in data flow, such as spikes in traffic, unexpected data transfers, or unauthorized access attempts, allowing the security team to respond quickly to potential threats.

   - **Industry:** Cybersecurity, IT infrastructure.

3. **Manufacturing and Predictive Maintenance**

- **Example:** A manufacturing plant uses GenAI to monitor the performance of its machinery. The AI model is trained on normal operational data and can detect deviations from this norm, such as unusual vibrations, temperature fluctuations, or irregular noise levels, which might indicate equipment failure. Early detection allows the maintenance team to address issues before they result in costly downtime or equipment damage.

- **Industry:** Manufacturing, industrial automation.

4. **Healthcare and Patient Monitoring**

- **Example:** A healthcare provider uses GenAI to monitor patient data from wearable devices and electronic health records (EHR). The AI system detects anomalies in vital signs, such as sudden changes in heart rate, blood pressure, or glucose levels, which could indicate the onset of a medical condition or a need for immediate intervention. This enables healthcare professionals to provide timely care, potentially saving lives.

- **Industry:** Healthcare, medical devices.

5. **Supply Chain Management**

- **Example:** A global logistics company uses GenAI to monitor its supply chain for anomalies, such as delays, shortages, or unexpected changes in demand. The AI system can detect patterns that deviate from expected supply chain behaviors, such as a sudden drop in inventory levels or a spike in transportation costs. Early detection of these anomalies helps the company mitigate risks and maintain smooth operations.

- **Industry:** Logistics, supply chain management.

6. **Energy Consumption Monitoring**

- **Example:** An energy provider uses GenAI to monitor energy consumption across a smart grid. The AI model detects anomalies in energy usage, such as sudden spikes or drops that might indicate equipment malfunction, energy theft, or inefficiencies in the system. By identifying these anomalies early, the provider can take corrective action, ensuring reliable service and optimizing energy distribution.

- **Industry:** Energy, utilities.

7. **Retail and Inventory Management**

- **Example:** A large retail chain uses GenAI to monitor inventory levels and sales patterns across its stores. The AI system detects anomalies in sales data, such as sudden drops in sales for a particular product or unexpected inventory shortages. These anomalies might indicate issues like stock misplacement, theft, or changing consumer preferences. Early detection allows the retailer to adjust its inventory and sales strategies accordingly.

- **Industry:** Retail, ecommerce.

8. **Insurance Claim Processing**

   - **Example:** An insurance company employs GenAI to analyze claims data and detect anomalies that might indicate fraudulent activity. The AI system examines patterns in claims submissions, such as unusually high claim amounts, repeated claims from the same customer, or inconsistencies in the reported damages. By identifying these anomalies, the insurer can investigate potential fraud before processing the claims.

   - **Industry:** Insurance, financial services.

9. **Transportation and Fleet Management**

   - **Example:** A transportation company uses GenAI to monitor its fleet of vehicles for anomalies in performance data. The AI system detects unusual patterns in fuel consumption, vehicle speed, or maintenance needs, which could indicate issues such as mechanical failure, inefficient driving practices, or even potential tampering. Early detection helps the company optimize fleet performance and reduce operational costs.

   - **Industry:** Transportation, logistics.

10. **Quality Control in Manufacturing**

    - **Example:** A manufacturing company uses GenAI to monitor the quality of products on the production line. The AI system detects anomalies in product dimensions, weight, or other quality metrics, which might indicate defects or process deviations. By identifying these issues early, the company can address them before defective products reach the market, ensuring high quality and reducing waste.

- **Industry:** Manufacturing, quality assurance.

11. **Customer Behavior Analytics**

- **Example:** An ecommerce platform uses GenAI to analyze customer behavior and detect anomalies in purchasing patterns, such as sudden changes in shopping habits, unusual product combinations, or spikes in returns. These anomalies might indicate fraudulent activity, shifting consumer preferences, or issues with the user experience, allowing the company to respond proactively.

- **Industry:** Ecommerce, retail.

12. **Financial Market Analysis**

- **Example:** A financial institution uses GenAI to monitor stock market data and detect anomalies in trading patterns. The AI system identifies unusual trading volumes, sudden price movements, or unexpected correlations between assets, which could indicate market manipulation, insider trading, or emerging trends. Early detection allows traders and analysts to make informed decisions and mitigate risks.

- **Industry:** Finance, investment management.

13. **Anomaly Detection in Social Media and Content Platforms**

- **Example:** A social media platform uses GenAI to monitor user-generated content and detect anomalies, such as sudden spikes in inappropriate or harmful content, bot activity, or coordinated misinformation campaigns. The AI system flags these anomalies for moderation, helping to maintain a safe and trustworthy environment for users.

- **Industry:** Social media, content platforms.

14. **Telecommunications Network Monitoring**

- **Example:** A telecommunications company uses GenAI to monitor its network for anomalies in call patterns, data usage, or signal quality. The AI system detects issues such as unexpected drops in call quality, data breaches, or service outages, allowing the company to address problems before they affect customers on a large scale.

- **Industry:** Telecommunications.

# 8.6  Intelligent Document Processing

Intelligent Document Processing (IDP) involves the use of advanced AI technologies to automatically capture, extract, classify, and manage information from various types of documents. With the integration of Generative AI (GenAI), IDP systems can be significantly enhanced, offering more accurate, context-aware, and efficient processing capabilities. Here's how GenAI can be applied to intelligent document processing, along with examples of its usage in enterprises:

# 8.6.1 Key Capabilities of Intelligent Document Processing with GenAI

1. **Automated Document Classification**

   - **Description:** GenAI can automatically classify documents into predefined categories based on their content, such as invoices, contracts, purchase orders, or legal agreements. Unlike traditional rule-based systems, GenAI can understand the context of the document, making it more accurate even when dealing with complex or unstructured data.

   - **Example:** A legal firm uses GenAI to automatically sort incoming documents into categories such as contracts, legal notices, or client communications. This helps streamline document management, ensuring that files are routed to the appropriate departments without manual intervention.

2. **Data Extraction and Structuring**

   - **Description:** GenAI can extract relevant data from documents, even when it is embedded in unstructured formats such as paragraphs, tables, or handwritten notes. The AI can then structure this data for use in downstream processes, such as populating databases, generating reports, or triggering workflows.

   - **Example:** A financial services company uses GenAI to extract key information from loan applications, such as applicant names, income details, and loan amounts. The system automatically inputs this data into their CRM and loan processing systems, reducing manual data entry and minimizing errors.

3. **Intelligent Optical Character Recognition (OCR)**

- **Description:** While traditional OCR technology can convert scanned images of text into machine-readable text, GenAI-enhanced OCR goes a step further by interpreting the context of the text. This enables more accurate recognition of text in noisy, distorted, or complex documents.

- **Example:** A healthcare provider uses GenAI-powered OCR to digitize and process handwritten medical records, prescriptions, and patient notes. The system not only converts the handwriting into digital text but also understands the medical terminology and context, ensuring accurate data capture.

4. **Context-Aware Document Summarization**

- **Description:** GenAI can automatically generate concise summaries of long documents, focusing on the most relevant information based on the context and intended use. This is particularly useful for legal, financial, and academic documents where quick comprehension of content is essential.

- **Example:** A legal department uses GenAI to summarize lengthy contracts and legal briefs, highlighting key clauses, obligations, and risks. Lawyers can quickly review these summaries to make informed decisions without reading through the entire document.

5. **Language Translation and Localization**

- **Description:** GenAI can translate documents into multiple languages while preserving the original meaning and context. It can also adapt the content to suit cultural nuances, making the translated documents more relevant to the target audience.

- **Example:** A multinational corporation uses GenAI to translate policy documents, training materials, and marketing content into various languages for its global workforce. The AI ensures that the translations are contextually accurate and culturally appropriate.

6. **Intelligent Workflow Automation**

- **Description:** GenAI can trigger automated workflows based on the content of a document. For example, upon recognizing a specific type of document or key phrase, the system can initiate approval processes, send notifications, or update records in related systems.

- **Example:** In an insurance company, GenAI detects when a claim form is received, extracts the necessary information, and automatically routes the document to the appropriate claims adjuster. The AI can also flag potential issues, such as missing information or inconsistencies, for further review.

7. **Advanced Document Search and Retrieval**

- **Description:** GenAI enhances search capabilities by allowing users to search for documents based on natural language queries or specific content. The AI can understand complex queries, interpret context, and return the most relevant documents, even if the exact keywords are not present.

- **Example:** A research institution uses GenAI to enable advanced document searches within its vast database of academic papers. Researchers can ask complex questions, and the AI retrieves relevant papers, highlights key sections, and provides summaries, significantly speeding up the research process.

8. **Sentiment and Intent Analysis**

- **Description:** GenAI can analyze the tone, sentiment, and intent behind the content of documents, providing insights into the author's perspective or the document's purpose. This is particularly useful in customer communications, legal disputes, or any scenario where understanding the underlying sentiment is important.

- **Example:** A customer service team uses GenAI to analyze incoming customer emails and messages, identifying the sentiment (positive, negative, neutral) and intent (inquiry, complaint, feedback). The system routes the messages to the appropriate teams with suggested responses, improving customer satisfaction.

9. **Compliance and Risk Management**

   - **Description:** GenAI can analyze documents
     for compliance with regulatory requirements
     or internal policies, flagging any deviations or
     potential risks. This helps enterprises manage
     regulatory compliance and avoid legal issues.

   - **Example:** A financial institution uses GenAI to review
     contracts and other legal documents to ensure they
     comply with industry regulations, such as GDPR or
     SOX. The AI flags any clauses or terms that might pose
     a compliance risk, allowing for timely corrections.

# 8.6.2 Benefits of Integrating GenAI with Intelligent Document Processing

1. **Increased Efficiency:** Automating document
   processing tasks with GenAI reduces the need
   for manual intervention, allowing employees to
   focus on higher-value activities. This leads to faster
   processing times and improved productivity.

2. **Improved Accuracy:** GenAI's ability to understand
   context and extract relevant information from
   unstructured data results in fewer errors and higher
   accuracy compared to traditional rule-based systems.

3. **Scalability:** GenAI can process large volumes
   of documents quickly, making it suitable for
   enterprises dealing with massive amounts
   of paperwork, such as legal firms, financial
   institutions, and healthcare providers.

4. **Cost Savings:** By automating routine document processing tasks, enterprises can reduce labor costs and minimize the risk of costly errors or compliance breaches.

5. **Enhanced Decision-Making:** With faster and more accurate document processing, decision-makers have timely access to the information they need, leading to better and more informed decisions.

# 8.7 Customer Journey Optimization with GenAI Such As ChatGPT or Llama

Customer journey optimization involves enhancing every touchpoint that a customer experiences with a brand, from the first interaction to postpurchase follow-ups. By leveraging Generative AI (GenAI) models like ChatGPT or Llama, enterprises can gain deeper insights into customer behavior, predict customer needs, and deliver personalized experiences that drive engagement, satisfaction, and loyalty. Here's how GenAI can be used to optimize the customer journey, along with practical examples.

## 8.7.1 Key Capabilities of Customer Journey Optimization with GenAI

1. **Personalized Customer Engagement**

   - **Description:** GenAI can deliver personalized interactions at various touchpoints in the customer journey by analyzing customer data, including past behaviors, preferences, and real-time interactions. It tailors messages, recommendations, and offers to individual customers, enhancing their overall experience.

- **Example:** An ecommerce platform uses ChatGPT to provide personalized product recommendations based on a customer's browsing history and past purchases. When a customer visits the website, the AI chatbot engages them in a conversation, understanding their current needs and suggesting relevant products or promotions, leading to higher conversion rates.

2. **Predictive Customer Insights**

- **Description:** GenAI can analyze historical and real-time data to predict customer behaviors and needs. This allows companies to anticipate what customers are likely to do next and proactively offer solutions or products that meet those needs.

- **Example:** A telecom company uses Llama to predict when customers are likely to upgrade their devices or change their service plans. The AI analyzes usage patterns, contract expiration dates, and customer inquiries to offer timely suggestions, such as new phone models or more suitable data plans, before the customer even asks.

3. **Enhanced Customer Support and Interaction**

- **Description:** GenAI can power intelligent chatbots and virtual assistants that provide instant, 24/7 support to customers across multiple channels. These AI-driven assistants can handle complex queries, guide customers through processes, and resolve issues quickly, all while maintaining a personalized touch.

- **Example:** A banking institution uses ChatGPT to support customers with queries related to account balances, recent transactions, or loan applications. The AI chatbot can understand the context of each conversation, retrieve the necessary information, and provide accurate responses. If needed, it can also escalate issues to human agents seamlessly, improving overall customer satisfaction.

4. **Real-Time Sentiment Analysis and Response**

- **Description:** GenAI can analyze customer interactions in real time to gauge sentiment and adjust responses accordingly. This is particularly useful for customer service scenarios, where understanding a customer's emotional state can lead to more empathetic and effective responses.

- **Example:** An online retailer uses Llama to monitor live chat interactions between customers and support agents. The AI detects signs of frustration or dissatisfaction in a customer's tone and suggests appropriate responses to the agent, such as offering a discount or expedited shipping, to resolve the issue positively.

5. **Dynamic Content and Experience Personalization**

- **Description:** GenAI can dynamically generate and customize content based on individual customer journeys. Whether it's personalized landing pages, emails, or app experiences, the AI tailors the content to each customer's unique preferences and behaviors.

- **Example:** A travel company uses ChatGPT to create personalized trip recommendations and itineraries based on a customer's travel history, preferences, and budget. When a customer logs into the app, they are presented with a customized travel package that includes destinations, hotels, and activities that match their interests, enhancing their engagement and likelihood of booking.

6. **Customer Journey Mapping and Optimization**

   - **Description:** GenAI can help map out the entire customer journey by analyzing interaction data across multiple channels and touchpoints. It identifies pain points, drop-off points, and opportunities for improvement, allowing companies to optimize the journey for better outcomes.

   - **Example:** A software-as-a-service (SaaS) company uses Llama to analyze user interactions with its platform, from onboarding to ongoing usage. The AI identifies where users struggle or drop off, such as during the setup process or when navigating complex features. The company then uses these insights to refine the user interface, provide targeted tutorials, or offer in-app support, leading to smoother user experiences and higher retention rates.

7. **Proactive Customer Retention Strategies**

   - **Description:** GenAI can predict when customers are at risk of churning and suggest proactive measures to retain them. By analyzing patterns such as reduced engagement, negative feedback, or declining purchase frequency, the AI can trigger targeted retention strategies.

- **Example:** A subscription-based streaming service uses ChatGPT to predict when subscribers are likely to cancel their service based on viewing habits, payment history, and support interactions. The AI then generates personalized retention offers, such as a discounted subscription rate or exclusive content access, to re-engage the customer and reduce churn.

8. **Omnichannel Customer Experience Management**

   - **Description:** GenAI can seamlessly integrate customer interactions across multiple channels— such as social media, email, in-store, and online— providing a unified and consistent experience. It ensures that customer data and preferences are carried over across platforms, creating a cohesive journey.

   - **Example:** A retail brand uses Llama to manage customer interactions across its website, mobile app, and physical stores. If a customer browses products online and then visits a store, the AI can alert store associates to the customer's preferences, enabling personalized in-store assistance. The same AI-driven personalization continues in follow-up emails or app notifications, ensuring a consistent experience.

9. **Automated Customer Feedback and Improvement**

- **Description:** GenAI can automatically gather, analyze, and respond to customer feedback, closing the loop on customer satisfaction. It can generate surveys, analyze responses, and provide actionable insights to improve the customer journey.

- **Example:** A hotel chain uses ChatGPT to send out poststay surveys to guests. The AI analyzes the feedback in real time, identifies recurring issues or areas for improvement, and generates reports for the management team. It can also send personalized follow-up messages to guests, thanking them for their feedback and informing them of the improvements made based on their input.

10. **Sales and Marketing Funnel Optimization**

- **Description:** GenAI can optimize the sales and marketing funnel by providing personalized content, offers, and guidance at each stage of the customer journey. It ensures that customers receive the right message at the right time, moving them closer to conversion.

- **Example:** An automotive company uses Llama to optimize its sales funnel, from initial online research to in-person dealership visits. The AI tracks each customer's progress through the funnel, delivering personalized content such as car comparisons, financing options, and dealership promotions. This targeted approach increases the likelihood of converting leads into sales.

## 8.7.2 Benefits of Using GenAI for Customer Journey Optimization

1. **Increased Customer Engagement:** By delivering personalized and context-aware interactions, GenAI keeps customers engaged throughout their journey, leading to higher satisfaction and loyalty.

2. **Improved Conversion Rates:** GenAI helps identify and remove friction points in the customer journey, guiding customers smoothly from awareness to purchase, thereby improving conversion rates.

3. **Proactive Customer Service:** With predictive insights, GenAI enables companies to address customer needs and concerns before they escalate, enhancing customer service and reducing churn.

4. **Scalability:** GenAI can handle large volumes of customer interactions across multiple channels simultaneously, making it ideal for businesses with a broad customer base.

5. **Cost Efficiency:** Automating customer interactions with GenAI reduces the need for extensive human intervention, lowering operational costs while maintaining high service quality.

# Appendix

## A.1 References

1. **Scaling Laws for Neural Language Models**

   a. **Authors**: Jared Kaplan, Sam McCandlish, et al.

   b. **Summary**: This paper explores the scaling behavior of neural language models, discussing how model performance improves with increased model size, dataset size, and computation. It provides foundational insights into how scaling affects the overall capabilities and limitations of generative AI models.

   c. **Link**: https://arxiv.org/abs/2001.08361

2. **Efficient Large-Scale Language Model Training on GPU Clusters Using Megatron-LM**

   a. **Authors**: Mohammad Shoeybi, Mostofa Patwary, et al.

   b. **Summary**: This paper describes techniques to efficiently train large-scale language models on GPU clusters, focusing on performance optimization. It introduces Megatron-LM, a framework that helps scale models efficiently.

   c. **Link**: https://arxiv.org/abs/2104.04473

3. **Privacy and Security Concerns in Generative AI: A Comprehensive Survey**

   a. **Authors**: Kidus Mekonen, Amit Pandey, Anushka Singh, et al.

   b. **Summary**: This paper provides an overview of differential privacy techniques in AI. It discusses how these methods can be applied to generative AI to enhance security, ensuring that models do not inadvertently expose sensitive information.

   c. **Link**: https://ieeexplore.ieee.org/abstract/document/10478883

4. **Secure MLaaS with Temper: Trusted and Efficient Model Partitioning and Enclave Reuse**

   a. **Authors**: Fabing Li, Xiang Li, et al.

   b. **Summary**: This paper examines the security challenges in Machine Learning as a Service (MLaaS), particularly focusing on secure model serving. The techniques discussed are crucial for maintaining the security of generative AI models in production environments.

   c. **Link**: https://people.iiis.tsinghua.edu.cn/~gaomy/pubs/temper.acsac23.pdf

5. **Octopus v2: On-Device Language Model for Function Calling of Software APIs**

   a. **Authors**: Wei Chen, Zhiyuan Li, et al.

   b. **Summary**: This paper presents a methodology for leveraging on-device language models to invoke software APIs. It includes a comprehensive dataset compilation process and discusses the benefits of on-device deployment for privacy and performance.

   c. **Link**: https://ar5iv.org/abs/2404.01549

6. **APIGen: Automated Pipeline for Generating Verifiable and Diverse Function-Calling Datasets**

   a. **Authors**: Zuxin Liu, Thai Hoang, Jianguo Zhang, et al.

   b. **Summary**: This paper outlines an automated data generation pipeline designed to create high-quality datasets for function calling applications. The dataset includes thousands of executable APIs across various categories, enhancing decision-making in AI models.

   c. **Link**: https://arxiv.org/abs/2406.18518

7. **NexusRaven: a Commercially-Permissive Language Model for Function Calling**

   a. **Authors**: Venkat Krishna Srinivasan, Zhen Dong, et al.

   b. **Summary**: NexusRaven is an open source language model designed for function calling, particularly in commercial applications. The paper discusses the challenges and solutions in creating a model that balances performance and legal restrictions associated with proprietary LLMs.

   c. **Link**: https://openreview.net/pdf?id=5lcPe6DqfI

8. **An LLM Compiler for Parallel Function Calling**

   a. **Authors**: Sehoon Kim, Suhong Moon, et al.

   b. **Summary**: LLMCompiler is a system that optimizes multifunction calling in Large Language Models (LLMs) by executing function calls in parallel, reducing latency, costs, and inaccuracies seen in sequential methods. It includes three components: an LLM Planner for strategy, a Task Fetching Unit for dispatching, and an Executor for parallel execution. Benchmarks show up to 3.7× faster performance, 6.7× cost savings, and ~9% accuracy improvement over traditional methods. It also outperforms OpenAI's parallel function calling with 1.35× latency gain. LLMCompiler is compatible with open source models like LLaMA-2.

c. **Link**: https://huggingface.co/papers/2312.04511

9. **Chain-of-Thought Prompting Elicits Reasoning in Large Language Models**

a. **Authors**: Jason Wei, Xuezhi Wang, et al.

b. **Summary**: This work explores how using a "chain of thought"—a series of intermediate reasoning steps— enhances Large Language Models' performance in complex reasoning tasks. The method, called *Chain of Thought prompting*, involves providing a few reasoning examples to guide the model. Experiments across three large models show improvements in arithmetic, commonsense, and symbolic reasoning tasks. Notably, prompting a 540B-parameter model with just eight reasoning examples achieves state-of-the-art accuracy on the GSM8K math word problem benchmark, outperforming even fine-tuned GPT-3 with a verifier.

c. **Link**: https://arxiv.org/abs/2201.11903

10. **Self-Consistency Improves Chain of Thought Reasoning in Language Models**

a. **Authors**: Jason Wei, Xuezhi Wang, et al.

b. **Summary**: This work demonstrates how "Chain of Thought" prompting—providing intermediate reasoning steps— significantly enhances Large Language Models' ability to handle complex reasoning tasks. By offering a few reasoning examples, these abilities emerge naturally in large models. Experiments show improvements across arithmetic, commonsense, and symbolic reasoning tasks. Notably, a

540B-parameter model with just eight reasoning exemplars achieves state-of-the-art results on the GSM8K math word problem benchmark, surpassing even fine-tuned GPT-3 with a verifier.

c. **Link**: https://arxiv.org/abs/2203.11171

11. **Language Models Are Few-Shot Learners**

a. **Authors**: Tom B. Brown, Benjamin Mann, et al.

b. **Summary**: This paper explores the performance of GPT-3, a 175-billion parameter language model, in task-agnostic few-shot learning. Unlike traditional NLP models that require fine-tuning on large, task-specific datasets, GPT-3 is evaluated purely through text interactions without gradient updates or fine-tuning. GPT-3 demonstrates strong performance across various NLP tasks, such as translation, question answering, and cloze tasks, as well as tasks requiring reasoning or domain adaptation. However, the model faces challenges on certain datasets, especially due to its reliance on large web corpora. GPT-3 can also generate human-like text, raising important discussions about its societal impacts.

c. **Link**: https://arxiv.org/abs/2005.14165

12. **Prompt Programming for Large Language Models: Beyond the Few-Shot Paradigm**

a. **Authors**: Laria Reynolds, Kyle McDonell, et al.

b. **Summary:** This paper examines how traditional methods for adapting large generative language models to supervised tasks may miss the opportunity to fully explore their novel capabilities. Using GPT-3 as an example, the authors show that zero-shot prompts often outperform few-shot prompts, suggesting that few-shot examples primarily help locate an already learned task, rather than facilitate meta-learning. The paper advocates for rethinking how prompts are used to control and evaluate language models, focusing on prompt programming through natural language. It explores the potential of narratives and problem deconstruction to guide model performance, introducing the concept of a "metaprompt"—a prompt that encourages the model to generate its own task-specific prompts. Finally, the authors propose integrating these methods into future benchmarks and applications.

c. **Link**: https://arxiv.org/abs/2102.07350

13. **Exploring the Limits of Transfer Learning with a Unified Text-to-Text Transformer**

a. **Authors**: Colin Raffel, Noam Shazeer, et al.

b. **Summary:** This paper explores transfer learning techniques in natural language processing (NLP), where models are pretrained on a data-rich task and then fine-tuned on downstream tasks. The authors introduce a unified framework that reformulates all language problems into a text-to-text format, allowing systematic comparisons of various transfer learning methods, including pretraining objectives, architectures, and datasets. Their study spans numerous language understanding tasks and utilizes the "Colossal Clean Crawled Corpus" to achieve state-of-the-art results in summarization, question answering, and text classification. The authors also release their dataset, pretrained models, and code to support further research in transfer learning for NLP.

c. **Link**: https://arxiv.org/abs/1910.10683

14. **Zero-shot Learning - A Comprehensive Evaluation of the Good, the Bad and the Ugly**

    a. **Authors**: Yongqin Xian, Christoph H. Lampert, et al.

    b. **Summary**: This paper addresses the growing interest in zero-shot learning (ZSL), where models classify images without labeled training data. The authors highlight the lack of standardized benchmarks, which leads to inconsistent and sometimes flawed comparisons across studies. To address this, they propose a new unified ZSL benchmark that standardizes evaluation protocols and data splits, ensuring more accurate comparisons. They also introduce a new dataset, **Animals with Attributes 2 (AWA2)**, made publicly available. The paper provides an in-depth analysis of state-of-the-art methods in both classic and generalized ZSL settings and discusses limitations in the current approaches, offering insights for future research in the field.

    c. **Link**: https://arxiv.org/abs/1707.00600

15. **What Makes Good In-Context Examples for GPT-3?**

    a. **Authors**: Jiachang Liu, Dinghan Shen, et al.

    b. **Summary**: This paper investigates the effectiveness of selecting in-context examples for GPT-3's few-shot learning, as its performance is highly influenced by the choice of examples. The authors propose a retrieval-based strategy, selecting semantically similar examples to the test sample, which serves as more informative input compared to random sampling. Evaluating this method on several natural language understanding and generation tasks, they find consistent performance improvements over the random baseline. Fine-tuning sentence encoders on task-specific datasets further enhances results, with significant gains in tasks like table-to-text generation (41.9% on ToTTo) and open-domain question answering (45.5% on NQ). This approach aims to better leverage GPT-3's few-shot capabilities and improve Large Language Models' general performance and analysis of state-of-the-art methods in both classic and generalized ZSL settings and discusses limitations in the current approaches, offering insights for future research in the field.

   c. **Link**: https://arxiv.org/abs/2101.06804

16. **Rethinking the Role of Demonstrations: What Makes In-Context Learning Work?**

   a. **Authors**: Sewon Min, Xinxi Lyu, Ari Holtzman, et al.

   b. **Summary**: This paper investigates the mechanics of in-context learning in Large Language Models (LMs), where models perform tasks by conditioning on a few input-label examples. Surprisingly, the study finds that accurate labels in demonstrations are not essential for success—randomly replacing labels has minimal impact on performance across a variety of classification and multichoice tasks, including GPT-3. Instead, the key contributors to performance are elements such as (1) exposure to the label space, (2) the input text distribution, and (3) the sequence format. This analysis sheds new light on how in-context learning works and raises questions about the extent of knowledge that can be gained through inference alone in large models.

   c. **Link**: https://arxiv.org/abs/2202.12837

17. **ReAct: Synergizing Reasoning and Acting in Language Models**

    a. **Authors**: Shunyu Yao, Jeffrey Zhao, et al.

    b. **Summary**: This paper introduces *ReAct*, a novel approach that interleaves reasoning and action generation in Large Language Models (LLMs), combining the strengths of both. Instead of treating reasoning (e.g., Chain of Thought prompting) and action (e.g., action plan generation) separately, ReAct allows LLMs to simultaneously generate reasoning traces and task-specific actions. This synergistic approach enables better action planning, exception handling, and interaction with external sources like knowledge bases. ReAct improves performance on question answering (HotpotQA) and fact verification (Fever) by reducing hallucinations and error propagation while also making task-solving trajectories more interpretable. In interactive decision-making benchmarks (ALFWorld and WebShop), ReAct outperforms imitation and reinforcement learning by 34% and 10% success rates, respectively, using minimal in-context examples. This approach enhances both effectiveness and human interpretability compared to state-of-the-art baselines.

    c. **Link**: https://arxiv.org/abs/2210.03629

18. **Recipes for Building an Open-Domain Chatbot**

    a. **Authors**: Stephen Roller et al.

    b. **Summary**: This paper addresses the challenges of building open-domain chatbots, emphasizing that scaling models by parameters and data size, while effective, is not sufficient for optimal performance. A successful chatbot must seamlessly integrate various skills, including engaging conversation, listening, demonstrating knowledge, empathy, and maintaining a consistent persona. The authors demonstrate that large-scale models can acquire these skills with the right training data and generation strategies. They develop models with 90M, 2.7B, and 9.4B parameters, releasing the models and code publicly. Human evaluations reveal that their best models outperform existing approaches in multiturn dialogue based on engagement and humanness. The paper also discusses limitations by analyzing failure cases of these models.

c. **Link**: https://arxiv.org/abs/2004.13637

19. **Towards a Human-like Open-Domain Chatbot**

a. **Authors**: Daniel Adiwardana et al.

b. **Summary**: This paper introduces **Meena**, a multiturn open-domain chatbot trained on 2.6 billion parameters using public domain social media conversations. Meena is trained end-to-end by minimizing the perplexity of predicting the next token in conversation. The authors also propose a new human evaluation metric, **Sensibleness and Specificity Average (SSA)**, which captures key qualities of human-like multiturn conversations. Experiments reveal a strong correlation between lower perplexity and higher SSA scores, with Meena achieving 72% SSA, suggesting that a human-level SSA of 86% could be possible with further optimization. The full version of Meena, incorporating a filtering mechanism and tuned decoding, scores 79% SSA, outperforming existing chatbots by 23% in absolute SSA.

c. **Link**: https://arxiv.org/abs/2001.09977

20. **Repairing the Cracked Foundation: A Survey of Obstacles in Evaluation Practices for Generated Text**

   a. **Authors**: Sebastian Gehrmann, Elizabeth Clark, Thibault Sellam, et al.

   b. **Summary**: This paper reviews the flaws in current evaluation practices for natural language generation (NLG) and highlights the urgency for better approaches, as neural NLG models have advanced beyond the capabilities of older, surface-level metrics. It surveys 20 years of critiques on both human and automatic evaluations, as well as commonly used datasets, categorizing the key issues and exploring how researchers have attempted to address them. The paper proposes a long-term vision for NLG evaluation, offering concrete steps to improve practices. Additionally, it analyzes 66 recent NLG papers to assess how well they follow these recommendations and identifies areas where significant improvements are needed.

   c. **Link**: https://arxiv.org/abs/2202.06935

21. **The Power of Scale for Parameter-Efficient Prompt Tuning**

   a. **Authors**: Brian Lester et al.

   b. **Summary**: This paper introduces "prompt tuning," a method for learning "soft prompts" to condition frozen language models for specific tasks. Unlike GPT-3's discrete text prompts, soft prompts are learned via backpropagation and can leverage any number of labeled examples. This approach significantly outperforms GPT-3's few-shot learning and becomes increasingly competitive as model size grows, matching the performance of full model tuning for models with billions of parameters. Prompt tuning offers a cost-effective way to reuse large frozen models for multiple tasks, reducing the burden of model sharing and serving. The paper compares prompt tuning with other techniques, such as prefix tuning, and demonstrates its advantages in domain transfer robustness over full model tuning.

   c. **Link**: https://arxiv.org/abs/2104.08691

22. **Eliciting Knowledge from Language Models Using Automatically Generated Prompts**

   a. **Authors**: Taylor Shin et al.

   b. **Summary**: This paper introduces **AutoPrompt**, an automated method for generating prompts to assess the knowledge learned by pretrained language models (LMs) during pretraining. Traditionally, fill-in-the-blank tasks like cloze tests have been used to gauge model knowledge, but writing suitable prompts is time-consuming and imprecise. AutoPrompt uses a gradient-guided search to automate prompt creation for various tasks. Experiments show that masked language models (MLMs) can perform tasks like sentiment analysis and natural language inference without additional parameters or fine-tuning, sometimes matching state-of-the-art supervised models. AutoPrompt also elicits more accurate factual knowledge from MLMs than manually crafted prompts and outperforms supervised models in relation extraction. These findings suggest that automatically generated prompts can serve as a parameter-free alternative to existing methods and potentially replace fine-tuning as LMs become more advanced.

   c. **Link**: https://arxiv.org/abs/2010.15980

# A.2 Code

The code for this book is available at the following links. These will also be listed in the respective chapters.

https://github.com/banup-kubeforce/ragwithevaluator
https://github.com/banup-kubeforce/functioncallinginspringai
https://github.com/banup-kubeforce/health-rag
https://github.com/banup-kubeforce/aibook-webflux
https://github.com/banup-kubeforce/aibook-webflux-streams
https://github.com/banup-kubeforce/SimpleAI
https://github.com/banup-kubeforce/ai-vectordb

# Index

## A

Access controls, 134, 135
Accountability, 299
Action plan, 300
    enterprise, 296
    gaps, 296
    governance structure, 297
    guidelines, 297
    policies, 297
    review processes, 298
    step-by-step approach, 296
Agricultural decision
        support systems
    farmers, 370
AI Chat UI, 283
    client.js file, 285
    conversation, 289
    index.html file, 283
    output, 289
AI-driven anomaly
        detection, 377
    ecommerce platform, 381
    energy consumption, 379
    financial fraud detection, 377
    financial institution, 381
    healthcare, 378
    insurance company, 380
    manufacturing and predictive
        maintenance, 378
    network security monitoring, 377
    quality of products, 380
    retail chain, 379
    social media, 382
    supply chain, 378
    telecommunications, 382
    transportation company, 380
AI-driven customer support
        system, 373
AI-driven security tools, 294
AI governance, 296
    accountability, 296
    AI decisions, 292
    characteristics, 295
    compliance and
        performance, 292
    customers, 295
    ethical principles, 291
    explainable, 295
    laws and regulations, 291
    mitigating risks, 292
    performance, 296
    security and privacy, 293
    sound principles, 295
AI-powered educational tools, 5

# M

GPSR Compliance
The European Union's (EU) General Product Safety Regulation (GPSR) is a set
of rules that requires consumer products to be safe and our obligations to
ensure this.

If you have any concerns about our products, you can contact us on

ProductSafety@springernature.com

In case Publisher is established outside the EU, the EU authorized
representative is:

Springer Nature Customer Service Center GmbH
Europaplatz 3
69115 Heidelberg, Germany

www.ingramcontent.com/pod-product-compliance
Lightning Source LLC
LaVergne TN
LVHW051636050326
832903LV00022B/770